Data Management

PRACTICAL GUIDES FOR LIBRARIANS

About the Series

This innovative series written and edited for librarians by librarians provides authoritative, practical information and guidance on a wide spectrum of library processes and operations.

Books in the series are focused, describing practical and innovative solutions to a problem facing today's librarian and delivering step-by-step guidance for planning, creating, implementing, managing, and evaluating a wide range of services and programs.

The books are aimed at beginning and intermediate librarians needing basic instruction/guidance in a specific subject and at experienced librarians who need to gain knowledge in a new area or guidance in implementing a new program/service.

About the Series Editor

The **Practical Guides for Librarians** series was conceived by and is edited by M. Sandra Wood, MLS, MBA, AHIP, FMLA, Librarian Emerita, Penn State University Libraries.

M. Sandra Wood was a librarian at the George T. Harrell Library, the Milton S. Hershey Medical Center, College of Medicine, Pennsylvania State University, Hershey, PA, for more than thirty-five years, specializing in reference, educational, and database services. Ms. Wood worked for several years as a development editor for Neal-Schuman Publishers.

Ms. Wood received an MLS from Indiana University and an MBA from the University of Maryland. She is a fellow of the Medical Library Association and served as a member of MLA's Board of Directors from 1991 to 1995. Ms. Wood is founding and current editor of *Medical Reference Services Quarterly*, now in its thirty-fifth volume. She also was founding editor of the *Journal of Consumer Health on the Internet* and the *Journal of Electronic Resources in Medical Libraries* and served as editor/coeditor of both journals through 2011.

Titles in the Series

1. *How to Teach: A Practical Guide for Librarians* by Beverley E. Crane

2. *Implementing an Inclusive Staffing Model for Today's Reference Services: A Practical Guide for Librarians* by Julia K. Nims, Paula Storm, and Robert Stevens

3. *Managing Digital Audiovisual Resources: A Practical Guide for Librarians* by Matthew C. Mariner

Data Management

A Practical Guide for Librarians

Margaret E. Henderson

PRACTICAL GUIDES FOR LIBRARIANS, NO. 28

ROWMAN & LITTLEFIELD
Lanham • Boulder • New York • London

Published by Rowman & Littlefield
A wholly owned subsidiary of The Rowman & Littlefield Publishing Group, Inc.
4501 Forbes Boulevard, Suite 200, Lanham, Maryland 20706
www.rowman.com

Unit A, Whitacre Mews, 26-34 Stannary Street, London SE11 4AB

British Library Cataloguing in Publication Information Available

Library of Congress Cataloging-in-Publication Data Available

ISBN 978-1-4422-6438-0 (pbk. : alk. paper)
ISBN 978-1-4422-6439-7 (ebook)

♾™ The paper used in this publication meets the minimum requirements of American National Standard for Information Sciences—Permanence of Paper for Printed Library Materials, ANSI/NISO Z39.48-1992.

Printed in the United States of America

In memory of Elizabeth Wallentiny, my grandmother,
expert cataloger, and the best mentor a young librarian could have.

Contents

List of Figures and Tables

⊚ Figures

⊚ Tables

Preface

Data has become a part of everyday life. Headlines proclaim that data is the new oil, or the new bacon, or the new black. There is a data deluge or a data tsunami. The data people create as they make purchases and interact with people and websites online becomes a digital footprint. There are so many different ways to try and explain the impact of data. All of the data being collected—about people, businesses, industry, education, medicine, technology, and even the environment—can be used to understand how things and people work, leading to better communities, products, and health, but it can also be used against people and communities. Libraries, as traditionally neutral institutions that value patron privacy and provide access to information for everyone, are the ideal place to provide data services for communities and institutions.

Data Management: A Practical Guide for Librarians has been written for people working in libraries at all career stages. Many librarians did not have the opportunity to take courses related to data curation or management in their library school programs, but have since discovered that data management is important to the communities they help. Others might have taken a course on data curation but don't have experience with how that fits into the data life cycle in research. There are also some people working in libraries with advanced subject degrees, but no library degree, who know about data management but don't have a full understanding of the discipline of library and information science. And of course, there are some people who are just interested in data management and want to learn more, and others who have been thrown into data management, whether they want to learn about it or not.

Organization

The first eight chapters give an overview of the background knowledge needed by data librarians. Chapter 1 provides some data definitions and terms and explains why libraries and librarians should be involved in data management. Chapter 2 focuses on researchers and how they see data in relation to their daily activities. Chapter 3 introduces a simplified data life cycle and basic best practices for working with data throughout that life cycle. Chapter 4 covers one of the most important skills of librarianship, the reference interview. Although it may not be apparent how important this skill is to data librarians, this chapter will cover the basics of how to interview and ask questions, and why these skills are essential for data librarians.

Chapters 5 to 8 cover various parts of the data life cycle. Chapter 5 looks at storing, curating, and preserving data, which involve knowledge of computing infrastructure, policies, and security. Chapter 6 covers documentation, including organizing and describing data, but also the formats and ontologies for metadata, an area where librarians already have expertise. Chapter 7 discusses the various ways researchers can publish and share their data, so issues of ownership and funder public access policies are also discussed. Chapter 8 pulls together all the information in chapters 3 to 7 to show how to create a data management plan that will comply with funder requirements, or will help researchers create ongoing plans to organize their research and preserve it for the future. Throughout this section there will be mention of how librarians can help with data, but the main purpose of these chapters is to make sure the reader has a basic understanding of research data management and the researchers.

As you read through the general chapters you will see references to other chapters and sections. Data management is interconnected at many points, which explains the cyclical structure of many models. There is more detail, subject specialization, and software specifics in data management than could possibly be covered in one book, let alone part of a book, so it will be necessary for librarians to educate themselves further. In some cases, librarians will concentrate on the subject, software, or hardware specifics of the data they will be managing. In other cases, they might delve into the policy and security of data by reading up on funding agency requirements and developing institutional policies. Whatever direction is followed, this book will provide a good basic overview of the field.

The last six chapters provide some ideas for setting up research data management services. Chapter 9 starts with some basics on establishing the need for data management services, and the need for an environmental analysis that includes a literature review, an examination of other institutional data management services, and an assessment of local services, resources, and needs. Once the need is established, there are suggestions for planning needed services and evaluation of those services. Chapter 10 explores the many institutional partnerships that can be helpful when setting up data management services. At some point, there will be enough demand for data management services that expansion must be considered, so chapter 11 looks at the directions data management services might grow. Chapter 12 covers teaching data management, including some basic teaching skills and a framework for teaching data literacy. Chapter 13 covers data reuse, which fits with funder goals for public access and reuse of research data, but is also an area that will allow librarians to enter into data services without a large investment in infrastructure or need for institutional data policies. Chapter 14 wraps up the book with a wide-ranging review of the many areas in which librarians are already involved with data and suggests some other areas where librarians could help with data management and analysis.

While every effort has been made to include the most up-to-date information possible on all topics, as with any book, some references may be out of date and some URLs may no longer link to the correct web page. Data management, open access, funder requirements, and data publishing are active fields and policies change regularly, so it is good practice to do a web search for updated information before giving a presentation or writing a paper or policy statement.

A Note on Terminology

Throughout the book I have used the term "librarian" when discussing a person with a master's degree in library and/or information science OR equivalent. A data librarian is a librarian who works all or part of the time with data. This book also assumes that most librarians will be working in some sort of institutional library, be it academic, school, public, business, or other special library. There are librarians working with data outside of libraries, for example, creating a corporate taxonomy or working with researchers outside of a library setting, and it is likely that there will be more jobs outside of libraries as employers realize how a well-trained librarian can help find, organize, and analyze information.

The glossary includes definitions for data management words and phrases, and the meaning for some more commonly used terms from a data management perspective. There are many terms that have a slightly different meaning, depending on discipline, so it is helpful to review the terms in the glossary.

Acknowledgments

Many thanks to my editor, Sandy Wood, for all her help and guidance, and for asking me to write this book for the series. We have both been through many ups and downs during the writing of this book, and her dedication has made the final product possible.

The community of data librarians I have met and worked with through Twitter and at meetings have been very important to my work. Many have been a sounding board for my thoughts, which has helped me clarify my understanding of data librarianship. I have referenced many of their excellent writings throughout this book.

I also had support at work, especially from Teresa Knott, who was understanding when I needed to work from home as I was trying to finish up a chapter.

Finally, I must thank my family for all their support during the writing of this book. My husband, Scott, has been my biggest cheerleader as I worried that I might not be able to get the manuscript done. My daughter Elizabeth helped with figures, and my daughter Emily made sure I had lots of coffee and baked goods for energy.

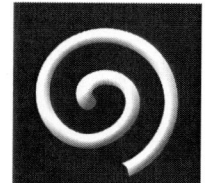

CHAPTER 1

What Is Data and Why Should Librarians Be Involved?

WHEN YOU MENTION DATA TO PEOPLE, it is important to be clear what you are talking about. Data can be used as a singular and plural noun. Researchers might think of diaries, photographs, survey results, digital results from lab equipment, lab notebooks, field notes, or spreadsheets. Administrators probably think of the enrollment data or graduation rates they need to send to accrediting organizations. Students might use data collected by a government agency when writing a report. Some people might think of the data that is part of their phone plan. And some think of "big data" used by businesses to track consumer behavior.

Data generally means individual facts, statistics, or items of information (Dictionary. com, 2015), but the *Oxford English Dictionary* definition includes mention of how data is created: "Related items of (chiefly numerical) information considered collectively, typically obtained by scientific work and used for reference, analysis, or calculation" (*OED Online*, 2015). The mention of scientific work makes this definition too specific. It does not encompass all the types of research that use data. A broader definition is needed when working with academic research: "Data is the output from any systematic investigation involving a process of observation, experiment or the testing of a hypothesis, which when assembled in context and interpreted expertly will produce new knowledge" (Pryor, 2012: 3).

⊚ The Diversity of Data

Data also has more specific meanings in different subjects, such as computer science, so the term "research data" can be helpful to convey further what is actually meant when talking with researchers about their work. Research data is data that is collected, observed, recorded, or created, for purposes of analysis to produce original research results for a study. Many libraries use the name "research data management (RDM)" for their data management department to distinguish their services from the administrative data management that goes on in other parts of an organization. Many of the same steps are involved in both areas of data management, but administrative data management is a form of records management. The actual data that is considered research data for the purposes of institutional policy, intellectual property applications, or grant compliance can also differ. Depending on the subject or the definitions used at your organization, research data can include:

- Documents (text, Word), memoranda, notes, evaluations, case records, study protocols
- Spreadsheets
- Laboratory notebooks, field notebooks, diaries
- Questionnaires, transcripts, codebooks
- Audiotapes, videotapes, MP3 files
- Photographs, films, TIF files
- Protein or genetic sequences, cloned DNA
- Spectra, crystallographic coordinates
- Test responses
- Slides, artifacts, specimens, samples, cell lines, organisms
- Collection of digital objects acquired and generated during the process of research
- Database contents (video, audio, text, images)
- Models, algorithms, scripts
- Contents of an application (input, output, logfiles for analysis software, simulation software, schemas)
- Methodologies and workflows
- Technical information
- Standard operating procedures and protocols

Some institutions will have explicit policies that spell out exactly what constitutes data. The definition could be dictated by state laws, funder mandates, or intellectual property issues. Funding from companies will carry other definitions and restrictions on intellectual output. There are some smaller institutions or organizations that have no mention of research data in any policy, in which case it may be useful to review the contracts employees sign or check the employee handbook. Most places will have some sort of policy dealing with intellectual property developed or created by employees that may provide some guidance on what is considered data.

Government Interest in Research Data

Complicating local policies and legal issues related to research data and intellectual property are official rules or mandates from funders. Although the following examples all come from U.S. federal funders, the definition of data changes. The National Institutes of Health (NIH) data sharing requirements for grants more than $500,000 requires sharing of final research data, which they define as "recorded factual material commonly accepted in the scientific community as necessary to document, support, and validate research findings" (NIH, 2003). Specifically, funded researchers need to be willing to share the data on which summary statistics and tables are based. As of August 2014, NIH also has a Genomic Data Sharing (GDS) Policy that covers human or nonhuman large-scale data including genome-wide association studies (GWAS), single nucleotide polymorphisms (SNP) arrays, and genome sequence, transcriptomic, metagenomic, epigenomic, and gene expression data (NIH, 2014). The National Science Foundation (NSF) requires data management plans for all grants. "What constitutes such data will be determined by the community of interest through the process of peer review and program management. This may include, but is not limited to: data, publications, samples, physical collections, software and models" (NSF, 2010). The plan should include information such as data types, how and where it will be stored, and how it will be shared, but each NSF directorate has slightly different requirements.

The Office of Digital Humanities in the National Endowment for the Humanities also sees data as something that is generated or collected during research. "Examples of humanities data could include citations, software code, algorithms, digital tools, documentation, databases, geospatial coordinates (for example, from archaeological digs), reports, and articles" (Office of Digital Humanities, 2015). The most recent government initiative that impacts research data is the February 2013 memo from the Office of Science and Technology Policy (OSTP) on the subject "Increasing Access to the Results of Federally Funded Scientific Research." This memo specifies that "digital data" from federally funded scientific research must be stored and publicly accessible to search, retrieve, and analyze (more on grant requirements in chapters on sharing, storage, and data management plans).

Even if a researcher doesn't have funder requirements, he or she will find that many journals now require that the data behind tables, figures, and conclusions in an article are made available, as an appendix or in a repository. Some policies also require that materials and protocols be made available to readers (PNAS, http://www.pnas.org/site/authors/journal.xhtml). Sharing data, software, materials, and so forth, is recommended in a 2003 publication from the National Research Council that is referenced by many scientific journals, *Sharing Publication-Related Data and Materials: Responsibilities of Authorship in the Life Sciences.*

Managing Data

It is also important to be clear about what you mean when you start talking with faculty, researchers, administrators, and students about data management (DM). Data management is the organization, storage, access, and preservation of data. It could be making sure notebook pages are scanned and saved by date, or it could be creating a complex database of normalized tables on a computer that can be queried using special commands. Later chapters in this book will cover various aspects of data management, such as:

- File naming
- Data access
- Data documentation
- Metadata creation and controlled vocabularies
- Data storage
- Data archiving and preservation
- Data sharing and reuse
- Data privacy
- Data rights
- Data publishing

It is important for you to be clear what the library will offer. In fact, Jake R. Carlson (2014) suggests that there are two types of data services in libraries. Data management services help researchers as they are working with their data—developing data management plans, training assistants to document and organize data, and finding and securing storage for the data. Data curation services securely store and preserve the data for long-term storage once active research is finished, and make the data available for sharing and reuse.

CONTENT VERSUS THE CONTAINER

Librarians have always been interested in format, in the container of information and knowledge. We are fascinated by the clay tablet or the parchment scroll, by the illuminated manuscripts of earlier times. . . . [My purpose] is to consider the value of content vs. the container. Has the container become more important than the content? Are we learning better? Are students doing better? Is the material better, more accurate? I believe that knowledge rather than the format or container should drive our work.—Lucretia McClure, 1997

Data and Research

It is useful for librarians who must learn about data, and those who want to learn about data, to forget about size and complexity and computerization, and think instead of Thomas Jefferson's Garden Book, a notebook with daily weather and garden observations that he kept for many years, and now available online at Massachusetts Historical Society (http://www.masshist.org/thomasjeffersonpapers/garden/). How would you describe the notebook? You would start by describing the outside. Take measurements to identify dimensions and materials. Record who wrote the observations, the dates covered, and maybe how often entries were written. To make your description even more useful, you'd want to describe things that were noted in most entries—weather, seeds planted, flowers in bloom, vegetables harvested, and so forth. If you described the notebook properly, somebody who was interested in the weather in the Charlottesville area of Virginia for a date covered by the notebook should be able to find the book and possibly get the information needed. While the original book is data for a historian, the weather and growing dates could become data for an ecologist or climate scientist. And, if the pages have been digitized, it would be fairly easy to download the data for use in a database.

So, when thinking about the storage, sharing, and management of data, think about the data set as just another container, like the article, book, album, blog post, and so forth. Scholarly output that needs to be described and saved in such a way as to allow others to find it, use it, and cite it. If you remember this when dealing with research data, it will be much easier to understand what needs to be done and how you can help researchers.

Data as an Asset

There is another view of research data that is starting to become popular and important—that of data as an asset. Businesses see customer data as a way to learn more and sell more. Google and Facebook commodify your data to be sold (Fuchs, 2012). The World Economic Forum report on personal data (2011) acknowledged the importance of using customer data for business purposes, and suggested that governments could use the data to provide better, more directed services. But they also acknowledged that individuals are becoming more concerned with the personal data they are generating, and those who collect the data will need to be sensitive to this in the future. Open Government Data advocates for making as much government-collected data as possible available freely on the web in a form that can be reused. The group hopes that having open government data available will increase transparency, access, sharing, and participation, but also that the data will help with the creation of new business and services with economic and social value (http://opengovernmentdata.org/).

Gradually, institutions have begun to see research data as a commodity, part of the intellectual property that a university owns. And that has led governments and other granting agencies to realize that what they are funding is an asset to be shared. The OSTP memo only requires digital data to be shared, but NSF and NIH require sharing of all types of data and some specimens as well. The U.S. government recognizes these things as assets that must be shared to promote health, research, and technology.

Because governments, universities, and businesses have begun to see data as an asset, researchers are starting to think about getting credit for their data. While the journal article and book are still the most accepted forms of scholarly communication, there is a push to recognize data, software, and other research outputs. In order to keep track of who is reusing data, descriptive standards need to be created to identify these formats and allow for easy data citation (Data Citation Synthesis Group, 2014). Alternative metrics to complement article citation counts are being developed, for example, Data Citation Index on Web of Science produced/published by Thomson Reuters.

Why should anyone be so worried about data? As Leslie Bradshaw (2014) points out, "If we collect the right data; filter, analyze, and contextualize them intelligently; and narrate and visualize them based on the right set of logic, then data . . . can be transformative in so many aspects of society."

◎ A Role for Librarians

Some people might think that because most data now is digital, be it photographs from digital cameras, interviews as MP3 or WAV files, specialized data files from expensive equipment, or even electronic laboratory notebooks, computer science is the natural field to help with data management. Or maybe mathematics because of the statistical analysis and visualization of data once it has been collected. But the field of library and information science (LIS) includes a broad range of skills, which are all needed to help with data management. The framework of LIS fits with the role of data management (Bates, 1999). What are the features of the information? How is information found and used by people? How can people access information easily? With all the changes in the types of resources and materials and services that libraries provide it is important to remember that "the fundamental role of helping users access the information that they require will continue" (Stuart, 2011: 141). The commitment to helping people find what they need is especially useful when dealing with data. "Librarianship is a people profession; a librarian's job is to connect people with the information they are seeking, whatever format that may take" (Cragg and Birkwood, 2011).

There is already some historical precedence for librarians and libraries working with data. Even before government mandates required data sharing and management plans, there were libraries working to help with large data sets created by the new computerized equipment that was dominating the sciences: "social science data, geo-referenced data (GIS), and bioinformatics" (Gold, 2007). A small number of libraries and data centers began to extend beyond traditional digital assets (i.e., print materials in digital form) and started to look at managing scientific and scholarly research data (Walters, 2009). While some programs started in response to large amounts of data that needed curation, other programs grew from institutional repository initiatives, such as the program at Georgia Tech. As Walters (2009) notes, librarians and archivists affiliated with early institutional repositories saw digital data sets as just another format of digital information that could be managed.

Transferring Skills

Marcia J. Bates (2015) classes the field of librarianship as one of the information disciplines, a metadiscipline that deals with all types of subject matter from a particular perspective. The information disciplines all deal with the collection, storage, organization, retrieval, and presentation/dissemination of information in whatever subject they relate to. Like other information disciplines, data management cuts across all subject areas. The aspects of data management discussed earlier in the chapter fit into these areas:

Collection
- Data documentation

Storage
- Data storage
- Data archiving and preservation

Organization
- Metadata creation and controlled vocabularies
- File naming

Retrieval
- Data sharing and reuse
- Data access

Presentation/Dissemination
- Data privacy
- Data rights
- Data publishing

All the same services and tasks that librarians have been providing their users with for books, articles, audiovisual materials, and so forth, are applicable to data. Data and data sets need to be collected, acquired, described, and organized. Users need to find data pertinent to their questions, gain access, and have a way to cite that data. Researchers need to organize and find their own data by learning the same skills librarians already know. Students need to learn how to find and organize data in a similar way to current information literacy instruction that teaches finding and organizing resources for essays, research papers, lab reports, and dissertations. Libraries don't collect and organize traditional materials in a vacuum. Librarians work with stakeholders to make sure collections and instruction serve the needs of their target population and support the goals of their organization, so working with other groups to collect, organize, sort, and preserve data is just an extension of current practice.

Technical Services and Data

It is not a big jump from collecting, cataloging, and providing access to electronic resources such as journals, books, and digitized special collections to doing the same steps for data. In fact, some libraries already provide access to government or commercially available data sets. For example, many libraries are responsible for their institutions' membership in the Inter-university Consortium for Political and Social Research (ICPSR), and subject librarians help researchers use the data. Acquisitions departments are familiar with licensing issues. Cataloging departments deal with electronic materials and many are now called metadata departments or have individual metadata librarians. Computer or technology departments have experience dealing with varying types of restricted access to electronic materials and providing secure links. Various departments usually work together to provide digitization services for special collections. And libraries are often responsible for electronic theses and dissertations. And as mentioned, experience setting up and running institutional repositories has given many libraries the experience needed to move into storing and providing access to data that is collected at that institution.

Public Services and Data

A core part of librarianship that is essential to data management is the reference interview. The reference interview is a chance to find out what an information seeker really wants to know. But the skills of clarifying needs, translating those needs into possible solutions, and working to find the best solution can apply equally to a researcher who needs to find the best way to organize or store data and to a student who needs to find and analyze a data set. Just like a reference interview can save time that might be spent looking for the wrong thing (Ross, 2003), good interviewing skills when helping with data organization can ensure future access and understanding of data sets.

During the reference interview, teaching often takes place as questions are answered. This is especially important when conducting data reference interviews. Kristin Partlo (2009) has found that it is important to help undergraduates learn data terminology and consider how to clean and process the data that is found during the reference transaction. Purdue University Libraries developed Data Curation Profiles (http://datacurationprofiles.org/) to learn more about researcher data curation and sharing needs, and knowledge of the reference interview process has been helpful in conducting these profile interviews (Carlson, 2011). The relationships reference librarians had developed with their constituencies, including individual faculty, administrators, students, and others, was also helpful in finding researchers to work with for the interviews and allow for further refinement of services.

Teaching is another area where librarians have traditionally participated. Bibliographic instruction has long been a role for librarians interested in teaching patrons how to find the information they need (Hopkins, 1982). Librarians have expanded their teaching role as digital information sources become more complex and specialized. Health sciences librarians teach specialized searching for evidence-based medicine and integrate their teaching into the curriculum using team-based learning (Knapp, 2014). Information literacy instruction has become an essential service of most academic libraries, with librarians customizing the examples and resources of their classes to fit with the courses they support (Grassian, 2009). And research has found that librarians embedded in courses have a positive impact on student success (Kumar, Wu, and Reynolds, 2014). Data librarians have already started developing instruction around the idea of data information literacy (Wright et al., 2015), and several groups have developed whole curricula for data management instruction, for example, the New England Collaborative Data Management Curriculum (NECDMC, http://library.umassmed.edu/necdmc/index) (see chapter 12 on teaching).

Data Management in Libraries

Whether a library is just starting to think about providing services related to data, or already has started to offer help with data management, the institutional issues that need to be considered will be the same. Stephen Pinfield, Andrew M. Cox, and Jen Smith (2014) identified seven "drivers" in interviews with library practitioners:

1. Storage—immediate storage for a wide variety of data sets
2. Security—appropriate to sensitivity or confidentiality of the data
3. Preservation—medium- and long-term archiving, including selection protocols and support
4. Compliance—requirements and policies of funders, legal obligations
5. Quality—enhancing research quality in general as well as data quality
6. Sharing—with targeted users and open/public access when required
7. Jurisdiction—who the institutional stakeholders are and what role they have in RDM

Throughout this book, these issues will be discussed further and potential ways to deal with these aspects of RDM will be explored.

Many people will suggest that the low-hanging fruit should be the first target in any endeavor. In the area of data management, compliance is the low-hanging fruit because it impacts funding and most institutions do not want to be involved in legal cases. In the United States, Canada, UK, and many European countries, there are funding mandates from government and other funders for public access to articles and data. Storage, security, preservation, and sharing are all impacted by the need for compliance. By starting with the basics of data management necessary to comply with these mandates, data librarians can build relationships with researchers and staff in grants and research offices. Working on storage and security will usually involve building relationships with computer or technology services. In these interactions with other groups around the institution, libraries and librarians can act as facilitators, translators, and intermediaries, respecting the jurisdiction of each group, but helping researchers get to the help they need for all aspects of data management.

Whatever role a library decides to take in the range of tasks and drivers needed to provide data management services in an institution, the main thing is to find something and start testing the waters. As Bates (2015) says, "It is important to be proactive, lest others, with far less understanding of the requirements of information collection, organization, storage, and retrieval, set an agenda . . . that is founded on ignorance of the actual requirements of information management."

🌀 Key Points

There are many types of data, and how data is defined and used depends on the field of research. No matter what the field, data needs to be organized and stored, and librarians are usually well positioned to help with these tasks.

- Read policies, regulations, and grant descriptions to clarify what is included in "data."
- Data is scholarly output that needs to be preserved for future use.
- Many of the skills needed for work in library and information science are easily transferred to working with data.
- Libraries and librarians already work with many other groups at their institutions, making them natural collaborators on institutional data management strategies.

Working with data involves understanding the research processes and workflows of researchers, as well as knowing how to organize data, so the next chapter will provide an overview of the researcher work cycle.

🌀 References

Bates, Marcia J. 1999. "The Invisible Substrate of Information Science." *Journal of the American Society for Information Science* 50, no. 12: 1043–50.
———. 2015. "The Information Professions: Knowledge, Memory, Heritage." *Information Research* 20, no. 1 (March): paper 655. http://InformationR.net/ir/20-1/paper655.html.
Bradshaw, Leslie. 2014. "Beyond Data Science: Advancing Data Literacy." Medium.com. https://medium.com/thelist/moving-from-data-science-to-data-literacy-a2f181ba4167.
Carlson, Jake R. 2011. "Demystifying the Data Interview: Developing a Foundation for Reference Librarians to Talk with Researchers about Their Data." *Reference Services Review* 40, no. 1: 7–23.
———. 2014. "The Use of Life Cycle Models in Developing and Supporting Data Services." In *Research Data Management: Practical Strategies for Information Professionals*, edited by Joyce M. Ray, 63–86. West Lafayette, Ind.: Purdue University Press.

Cragg, Emma, and Katie Birkwood. 2011. "Beyond Books: What It Takes to Be a 21st Century Librarian." *Guardian*, Monday, January 31. Accessed June 10, 2015. http://www.theguardian.com/careers/job-of-21st-century-librarian.

Data Citation Synthesis Group. 2014. *Joint Declaration of Data Citation Principles*. Edited by M. Martone. San Diego, Calif.: FORCE11. https://www.force11.org/group/joint-declaration-data-citation-principles-final.

Dictionary.com. 2015. "Data." Accessed June 8, 2015. http://dictionary.reference.com/browse/data.

Fuchs, Christian. 2012. "The Political Economy of Privacy on Facebook." *Television & New Media* 13, no. 2: 139–59. doi:10.1177/1527476411415699.

Gold, Anna. 2007. "Cyberinfrastructure, Data, and Libraries, Part 2. Libraries and the Data Challenge: Roles and Activities for Libraries." *D-Lib Magazine* 13, no. 9/10 (September/October). doi:10.1045/july20september-gold-pt2.

Grassian, Esther S. 2009. *Information Literacy Instruction: Theory and Practice*. 2nd ed. New York: Neal-Schuman.

Hopkins, Frances L. 1982. "A Century of Bibliographic Instruction: The Historical Claim to Professional and Academic Legitimacy." *College and Research Libraries* 43, no. 3: 192–98.

Knapp, Maureen "Molly." 2014. "Instruction in Health Sciences Libraries." In *Health Sciences Librarianship*, edited by M. Sandra Wood, 275–302. Lanham, Md.: Rowman & Littlefield.

Kumar, Sajeesh, Lin Wu, and Rebecca Reynolds. 2014. "Embedded Librarian within an Online Health Informatics Graduate Research Course: A Case Study." *Medical Reference Services Quarterly* 33, no. 1 (January–March): 51–59. doi:10.1080/02763869.2014.866485.

McClure, Lucretia W. 1997. "Knowledge and the Container." In *Health Information Management. What Strategies? Proceedings of the 5th European Conference of Medical and Health Libraries, Coimbra, Portugal, September 18–21, 1996*, edited by Suzanne Bakker, 258–60: Springer Netherlands. doi:10.1007/978-94-015-8786-0_86.

National Research Council. 2003. *Sharing Publication-Related Data and Materials: Responsibilities of Authorship in the Life Sciences*. Washington, D.C.: National Academies Press. http://www.nap.edu/catalog/10613/sharing-publication-related-data-and-materials-responsibilities-of-authorship-in.

NIH (National Institutes of Health). 2003. "NIH Data Sharing Policy and Implementation Guidance." March 5. http://grants.nih.gov/grants/policy/data_sharing/data_sharing_guidance.htm.

———. 2014. "NIH Genomic Data Sharing Policy NOT-OD-14-124." August 27. http://grants.nih.gov/grants/guide/notice-files/NOT-OD-14-124.html.

NSF (National Science Foundation). 2010. "Data Management & Sharing Frequently Asked Questions (FAQs)." November 30. http://www.nsf.gov/bfa/dias/policy/dmpfaqs.jsp#1.

OED Online. 2015. "datum, n." Oxford University Press. Accessed June 15, 2015. http://www.oed.com/view/Entry/47434.

Office of Digital Humanities. 2015. "Data Management Plans for NEH Office of Digital Humanities Proposals and Awards." National Endowment for the Arts. Accessed June 14, 2015. http://www.neh.gov/files/grants/data_management_plans_2014.pdf.

OSTP (Office of Science and Technology Policy). 2013. "Memorandum for the Heads of Executive Departments and Agencies." Executive Office of the President. Accessed June 9, 2015. https://www.whitehouse.gov/sites/default/files/microsites/ostp/ostp_public_access_memo_2013.pdf.

Partlo, Kristin. 2009. "The Pedagogical Data Reference Interview." *IASSIST Quarterly* 33/34, no. 4: 6–10.

Pinfield, Stephen, Andrew M. Cox, and Jen Smith. 2014. "Research Data Management and Libraries: Relationships, Activities, Drivers and Influences." *PloS One* 9, no. 12: e114734. doi:10.1371/journal.pone.0114734.

Pryor, Graham. 2012. "Why Manage Research Data?" In *Managing Research Data*, edited by Graham Pryor, 1–16. London: Facet.

Ross, Catherine S. 2003. "The Reference Interview: Why It Needs to Be Used in Every (Well, Almost Every) Reference Transaction." *Reference & User Services Quarterly*. 43, no. 1: 38–43.

Stuart, David. 2011. *Facilitating Access to the Web of Data: A Guide for Librarians*. London: Facet.

Walters, Tyler O. 2009. "Data Curation Program Development in U.S. Universities: The Georgia Institute of Technology Example." *International Journal of Digital Curation* 3, no. 4. doi:10.2218/ijdc.v4i3.116.

World Economic Forum. 2011. *Personal Data: The Emergence of a New Asset Class*. Geneva, Switzerland: World Economic Forum. http://www3.weforum.org/docs/WEF_ITTC_Personal-DataNewAsset_Report_2011.pdf.

Wright, Sarah J., Jake R. Carlson, Jon Jeffryes, et al. 2015. "Developing Data Information Literacy Programs: A Guide for Academic Librarians." In *Data Information Literacy: Librarians, Data, and the Education of a New Generation of Researchers*, edited by Jake R. Carlson and Lisa R. Johnston, 205–30. West Lafayette, Ind.: Purdue University Press.

Understanding Research and the Role of Data

▷ Learning about research in different disciplines

▷ Considering the many responsibilities of researchers

▷ Comparing the research cycle and the data life cycle

▷ Changing research methodology due to data and technology advances

IT IS IMPORTANT TO UNDERSTAND the research communities you will be working with when you start helping with data management, the same way embedded or liaison librarians need to understand the research program, subject, or curriculum they will be supporting. You will need to be aware of different disciplinary research practices, publishing norms, and vocabularies. Despite these differences, there are many similarities in the process of research and how data is managed.

The Research Process

Research starts with a hypothesis, and data is collected to test that hypothesis. Researchers need to think ahead, as much as possible, to decide on the data to be collected. It may be that initial data collection shows the need for a change in how data should be collected or a new value needs to be added to the data collected, and the researchers will need to adapt or rethink their work in some way. But any of these factors can cause delays and increase costs, so thinking about data ahead of time is helpful. Observational studies can be the hardest to redo, if that is even feasible, so it is also important to collect as much as possible from the beginning.

Jane Goodall's research on the Gombe chimpanzees changed many long-held assumptions about chimpanzee behavior. While Goodall herself made most of the early observations, over time, students, research assistants, field assistants, and collaborating scientists have collected data. Standard training methods and a *Gombe Glossary* (Goodall, 1986: 605) of terms were used to ensure that there was consistency in data collection over time. Various methods, including check sheets, written and recorded observations, association charts, and maps, combine to provide a rich archive of data that researchers are still using today. The JG Archive at Duke University (http://today.duke.edu/showcase/janegoodall/) is being used by researchers who are mining fifty years of data, reusing and repurposing data that was presented in other papers and books, to give new insight into chimpanzee behavior. Data used to support articles on sexually coercive males (Feldblum et al., 2014a; Feldblum et al., 2014b) and female competition (Pusey and Schroepfer-Walker, 2013a; Pusey and Schroepfer-Walker, 2013b) was made openly available in Dryad, a digital repository. And a stand-alone data set of chimpanzee vocalizations was published in *Scientific Data* and deposited in Dryad (Plooij et al., 2014a; Plooij et al., 2014b).

Most types of academic research follow a similar process that is based on the iterative scientific method: hypothesis—test the hypothesis—evaluate the results. A problem or idea is defined (hypothesis). An experiment is designed or the necessary information determined. The experiment is conducted or information is collected (test the hypothesis). Results or information are analyzed (evaluate the results). A paper or presentation is written and the research is shared. This process is often described as a series of steps or shown as a cyclical figure, since the results usually lead to more questions and ideas for study. But this simple process is not really how an academic researcher works.

Researcher Work Cycle

In reality, the process is more complex and involves a lot more than research. Figure 2.1, "Researcher Work Cycle," is a combination of research and scholarly communication life cycles that are often used to describe research.

When researchers start on a project, they do a literature search, or work with a librarian to do a search (to check if others are doing something similar), or discuss the idea with colleagues. Then they need money to carry out the project, so they develop a proposal. In order to even apply for grants they must complete multiple mandatory courses on grant administration, financial administration, protection of research subjects (human and/or animal), and ethics training. Humanities or arts researchers might need to secure permissions to travel to archives or historic sites and make use of special collections or rare materials. They must comply with all regulations related to their research. Then they must write the grant to the specifications of the funder's announcement. Often, preliminary data will need to be collected to support a grant application.

But sending in a proposal and receiving an award or grant is just the start of the process. Now they must hire and train research assistants, which means further training from human resources and more mandatory paperwork related to supervising employees at their institution. There will be further paperwork related to the human or animal testing they are doing, or related to any chemicals they are using. If any part of the research is technical data related to defense articles or services (Department of Defense or NASA research, for instance), International Traffic in Arms Regulations (ITAR) (https://www.pmddtc.state.gov/regulations_laws/itar.html) will need to be followed or exemptions will need to be explained. As researchers collect data, they need to make sure it is all saved in case there are any questions about its accuracy. They need to save the data for the length

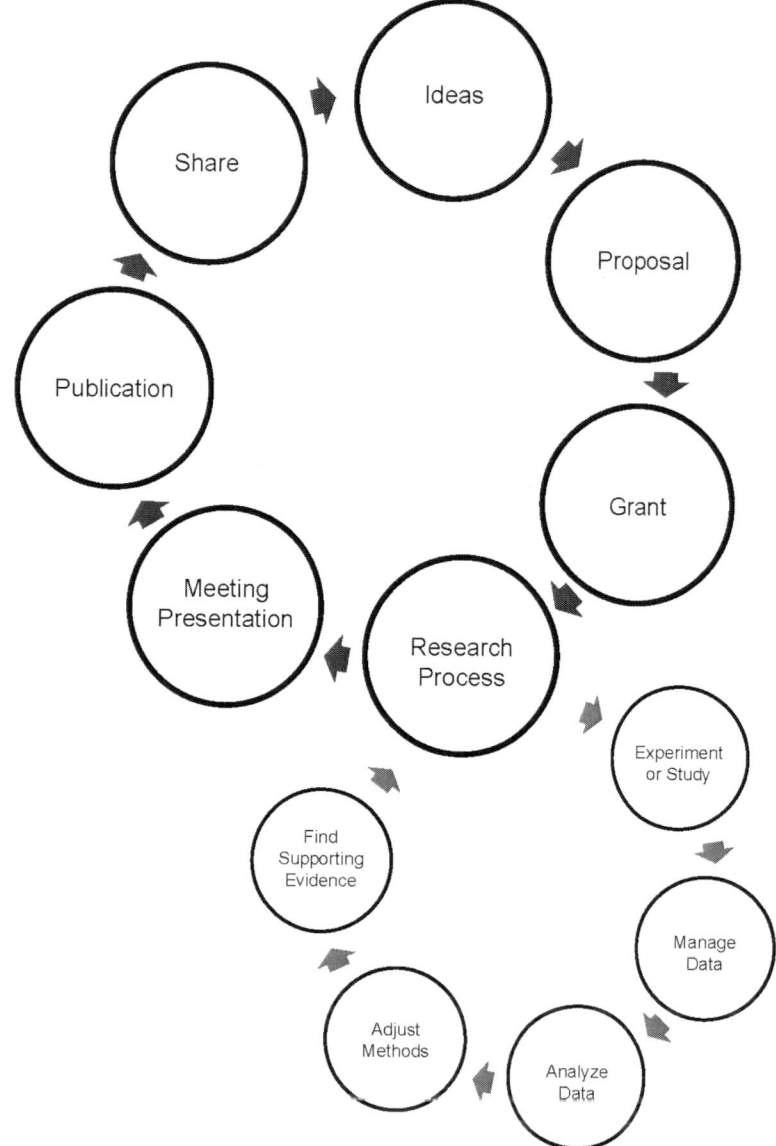

Figure 2.1. Researcher Work Cycle. *Credit:* Margaret Henderson

of time required by the grant (and maybe their institution or state), so they need to find a place to save it, whether it is physical or digital data.

Analysis of the data may require collaborations with colleagues who understand advanced statistics. Even before the analysis is complete, researchers will be thinking about where to present their research. Should it be a meeting poster or presentation? Should it just be a paper? Which journal or meeting? Should the paper be open access? Who will pay for publication? Who will pay for the meeting? And it is always possible that comments at a meeting will require more research to fix the project.

Once the work is finalized, researchers must decide where to publish their papers (usually based on subject and journal impact factor), format their papers correctly, and submit them to a journal. After peer review, there will either be a few changes and some rewriting or the paper will be rejected, in which case the manuscript will be sent to another journal, after possibly incorporating some of the peer reviewer's comments.

Nonresearch Responsibilities

In the past, publishing the paper was the end of the process, but now there are public relations offices that take care of spreading the word about exciting results, and social media can be used to share research ideas, or at least direct people to a new paper. The sharing of ideas leads to new ideas, either by the researchers or somebody who reads about their work. Of course there are variations. Sometimes, the analysis of data will show errors in data collection, so a researcher has to try an experiment again. Or a grant can lead to a long-term project that produces interim reports. National Science Foundation grants often need to show broader impact, so educational materials for the public must be created. All the while, at most academic institutions, teaching courses and participating in committees or other institutional groups is mandatory for faculty. This means time to prepare curricula and lectures, writing and grading tests, marking essays or reports, meetings with students, and meetings with committees.

And over the years, mandatory training for things like terrorism and security, information security, or human subjects' compliance will need to be updated multiple times. Literature will need to be checked regularly to make sure the competition has not published their similar research first, and new articles will need to be read to keep up with the researcher's field of study. Reports will need to be written for funders. And usually, researchers need at least a couple of grants to support their research, so grant writing is an ongoing process. While there might be some lucky researchers who don't need to worry about writing grants to carry out the work they wish to do, other mandatory training and teaching requirements will still be there.

Overlaying all the myriad steps of the researcher work cycle are the ethical considerations that must be part of all the work being done. Most institutions have responsible conduct of research policies that require good record keeping as part of the work being done, and these policies usually indicate that faculty are responsible for the training of their students in ethics and proper record keeping. Some grants, for instance, those from the National Science Foundation, require that students and postdoctoral fellows receive responsible conduct of research training. Concerns about reproducibility (Collins and Tabak, 2014) and transparency voiced by funders and journals has increased the pressure to ensure that research data is properly collected, used, saved, and preserved. So the researcher work cycle actually ends up looking rather more complex when all the responsibilities of an academic position are considered (see figure 2.2).

Researchers working in industry or business will have different responsibilities outside of their actual research, and even patrons of a public library doing genealogy research or looking for information for other personal projects will have more to focus on outside of their research project. As librarians become involved with the collection, organization, storage, access, and analysis of data in all types of libraries, it is helpful to remember that data is not the sole focus of the person being helped. Usually it is a means to an end, and librarians must keep that end in mind.

Data Life Cycle

Academic researchers know that they must publish as many papers as they can in the best possible journals in order to get promoted and gain tenure. When you view the researcher work cycle and see the many things a researcher must do, it becomes obvious why it is so hard for junior researchers to get started and gain tenure. They must work constantly

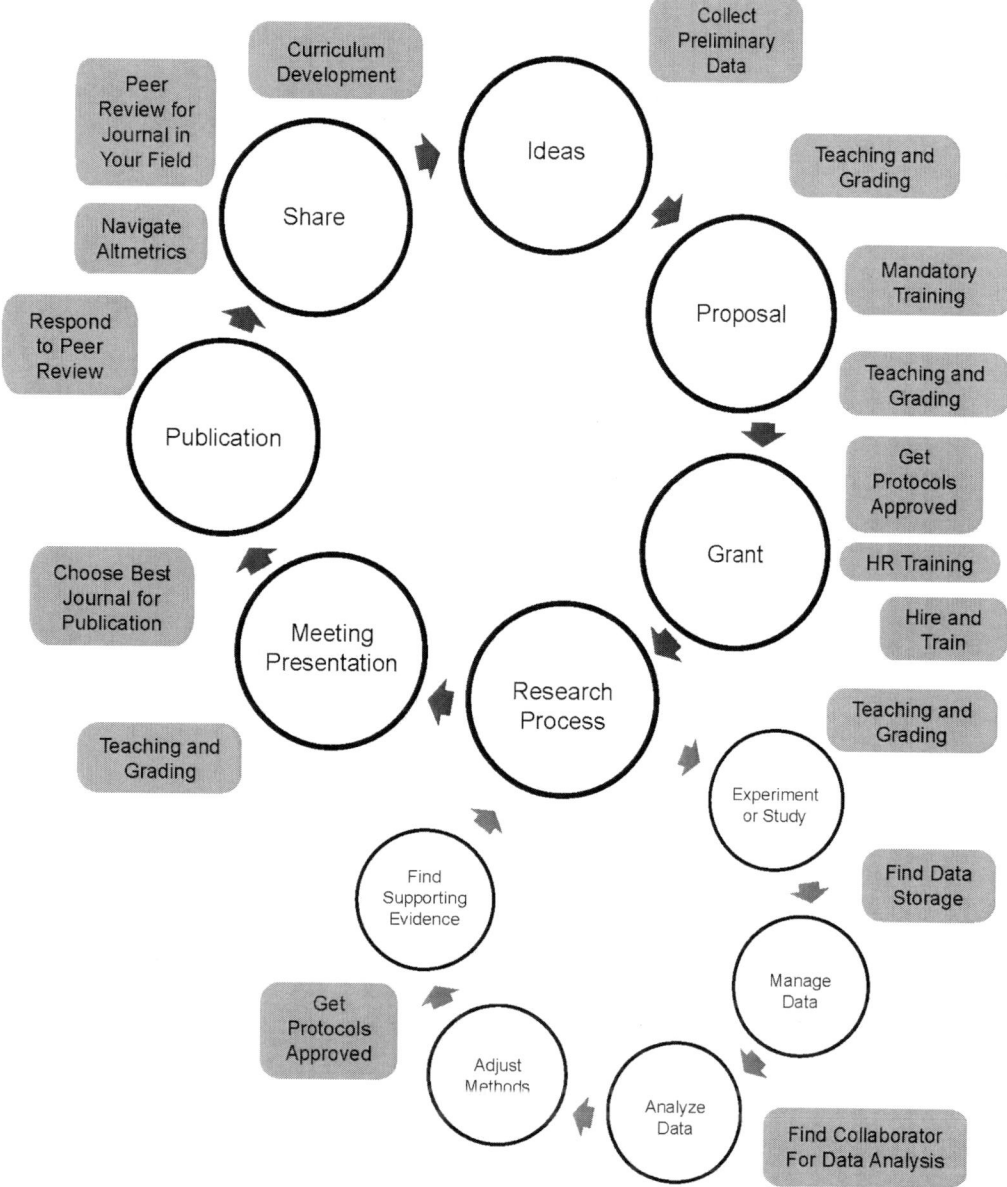

Figure 2.2. Researcher Work Cycle with Additional Tasks Necessary for Completing Job. *Credit:* Margaret Henderson

to get grants, conduct research, teach, and so forth. Imagine how they feel when, in the middle of writing a grant, they come across a new requirement for a data management plan (DMP). They do a quick search and find a data life cycle diagram like the data life cycle from the Inter-university Consortium for Political and Social Research (ICPSR) (see figure 2.3) or a checklist, such as those developed by the Digital Curation Centre (DCC) (http://www.dcc.ac.uk/resources/data-management-plans/checklist) and DMP-Tool (https://dmptool.org/dm_guidance), that appears overwhelming, with so many steps and things to consider and questions to answer. How on earth can most researchers deal with all those requirements just for a couple of pages in their grant? They may feel that this has nothing to do with the subject they want to research, but they still must comply.

So, most researchers will ask a colleague with a grant for a copy of their data management plan to use as a template, or as is. Maybe they will ask their grants office for

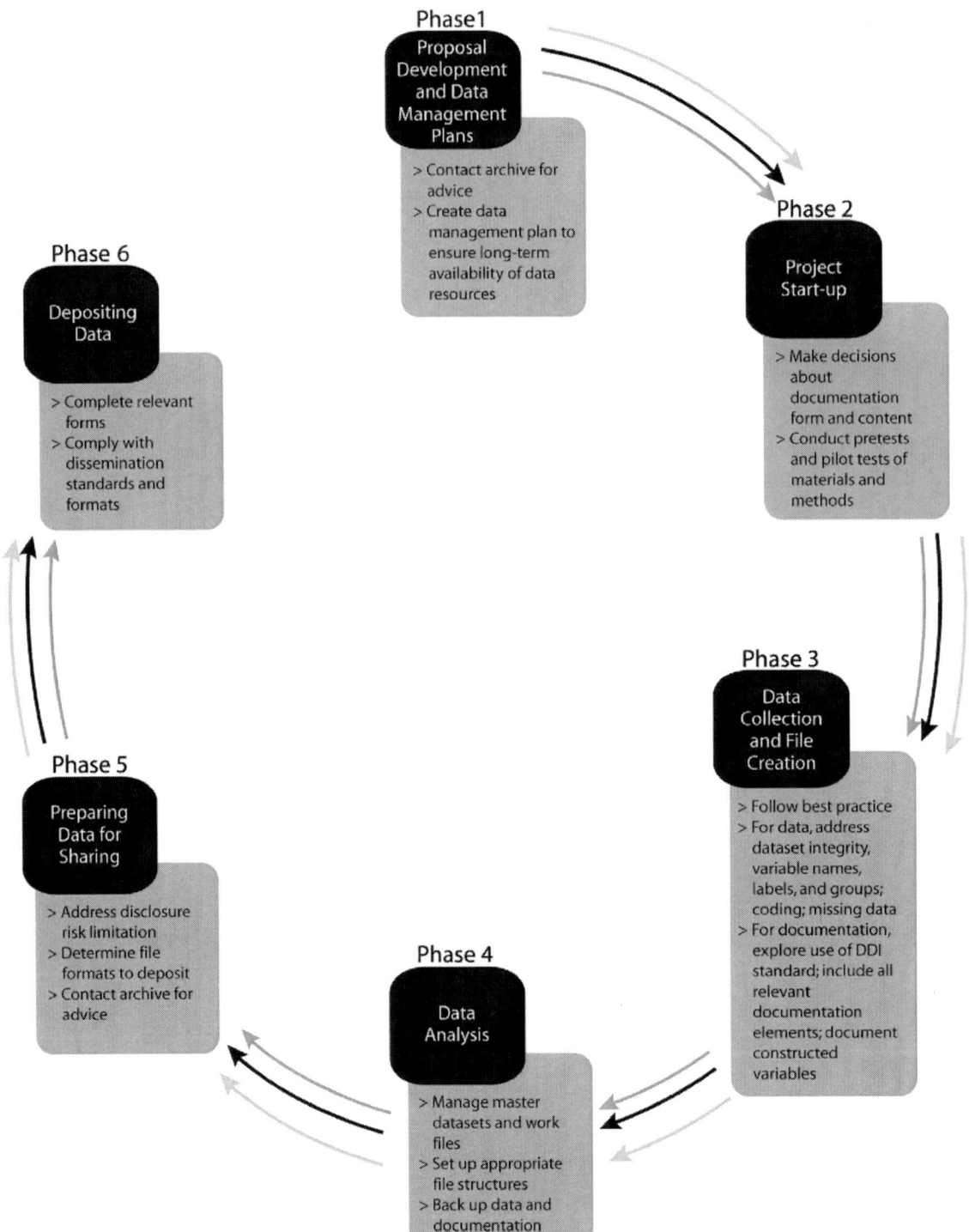

Figure 2.3. ICPSR Data Life Cycle. *Credit:* Inter-university Consortium for Political and Social Research (ICPSR). 2012. Guide to Social Science Data Preparation and Archiving: Best Practice throughout the Data Life Cycle. 5th ed. Ann Arbor, Mich. ISBN: 978-0-89138-800-5

help (see chapter 10, "Leveraging Partnerships"). They will do the minimum required to create a DMP, and it will usually be done at the last minute. Unless data management and storage is an integral part of the work being done, such as the Worldwide LHC Computing Grid (http://wlcg.web.cern.ch/) for data from the Large Hadron Collider, most researchers will not worry about data management at this point in the process.

As librarians trying to help researchers, it should be obvious that your efforts to get researchers to include perfect data management plans in their proposals will be difficult. And it will be equally difficult for researchers to follow through with extensive plans for secure storage, long-term preservation, and metadata in XML. Following every step in the data life cycle is such a small part of the entire process of research, and with all the extra things they need to do, it can be hard to convince researchers they need to worry about every step. Researchers are most concerned with their need to find all the data required for their current project. The time and effort needed to document and clean data for sharing or publication is more than most researchers are willing to expend.

Jonathan Petters started out doing atmospheric science research and then became an AAAS (American Association for the Advancement of Science) Science and Technology Policy fellow in the Department of Energy's (DOE) Office of Science. He is now a data management consultant in Johns Hopkins Sheridan Libraries Data Management Services, so he understands the researcher point of view on DMPs: "As a former researcher I often repeat to myself, 'Researchers want to do research!' When talking about data curation/management at DOE, we often talked about the need for a 'clear science driver.' When researchers see benefits to their own research in data sharing and management, that's when we can expect a quick push for change" (Petters, 2015).

◎ Twenty-First-Century Research

The researcher work cycle only consists of one person and that person's research associates of various levels, but quite a bit of research is done by teams and there is a trend in many fields toward collaborative research, either with multiple researchers in the same field doing a large project, like the 1000 Genomes Project with different groups around the world sequencing the genome of one-thousand-plus individuals (http://www.1000genomes. org/); or an interdisciplinary group doing a project that needs many areas of expertise, such as the NIH Blueprint for Neuroscience Research that brings together human and animal studies, imaging work, informatics, gene and protein expression, and includes the Human Connectome Project that is mapping neural pathways (http://www.neuroscienceblueprint.nih.gov/resources_tools.htm). Either way, group research involves trying to merge multiple researcher work cycles, with regulations from different institutions, states, and countries, various time zones, and different languages, in order to complete a project.

Caroline S. Wagner (2008) categorized team research as centralized or distributed and came up with four types of research. Megascience projects, such as the Large Hadron Collider (http://home.cern/topics/large-hadron-collider), are expensive and highly centralized, and usually have government funding. Geotic activities need access to a certain place, such as the South Pole or rain forests, making them partly centralized, as researchers who wish to study in the area need to coordinate their work. Participatory projects are highly organized, often by a government agency, a centralized function, but individuals and small teams working on the project are spread out, such as the completed Human Genome Project (http://www.genome.gov/10001772) and now the Human Microbiome

Project (http://www.hmpdacc.org/). Coordinated projects are initiated by scientists and organized by scientists working toward a common goal, such as the Global Biodiversity Information Facility (GBIF) (http://www.gbif.org/), and tend to be distributed.

Data and Advances in Technology

The availability of computerized networks and high-powered computers has changed the way research is conducted in all subject areas. Not only are people able to connect with each other through the Internet, with communication tools such e-mail, chat, phone, or video, but information resources, documents, and data can be connected and shared, as can software to analyze and visualize information (Borgman, 2007: 11). Technology has also changed the equipment that researchers deal with. Super-resolution microscopy is a poster child for interdisciplinary research. Advances in mathematical algorithms and computer programming have advanced image processing and analysis. Advances in physics have contributed hardware improvements in the optics, lasers, illumination, and detectors used in microscopes. These math, computer, and physics advances have combined with chemistry and biology discoveries of new, smaller probes, making possible very high-resolution images of individual molecules. Three scientists, Eric Betzig, Stefan W. Hell, and William E. Moerner, won the 2014 Nobel Prize in Chemistry for this new research technique. As well as information that needed to be collected and shared to develop the technique, the images and data produced by super-resolution microscopes are extensive—hundreds of images per second, plus the processed results.

Technology has also had an impact in the humanities. While many people use the term "digital humanities" to describe work done with extensive networking and computerization, some feel it is already the norm and see no need to add "digital" (Borgman, 2015). Digitization projects have scanned in primary source materials around the world, and the addition of metadata, combined with online search tools, has made things easier to locate than old archival collection print finding aids that were often only available on-site with the collection they described. Artifacts can be scanned in 3D to be studied anywhere, and some can even be printed in 3D for close examination or educational use. Photographs, videos, and sound can be made available digitally, but new programs allow researchers to search for a specific person in a photo, or word in a recording. Mapping technologies combined with geographic information systems (GIS) allow new views of archaeological sites. Text mining of digitized texts has been used to study the evolution of languages (Petersen et al., 2012) and the authorship of texts, including the works of Shakespeare (Visa et al., 2001).

In the social sciences, the data that has been made available from governments and social media has been a boon to researchers. Online tools have made sending out surveys and the analysis of answers much faster and easier, and tools that allow researchers to overlay census and other government data onto maps has made geographic studies easier. Businesses can use data to decide where to locate plants (Kutzbach, 2010), and crime patterns can be studied (Phillips and Sandler, 2015). Trends in search topics by consumers have been used to predict everything from award show winners (Tolentino, 2014) to financial market trading behavior (Preis, Moat, and Stanley, 2013). And in one infamous experiment, Facebook posts were faked to study emotional contagion (Kramer, Guillory, and Hancock, 2014).

Technology, specifically the ability of networks to facilitate collaboration, has also led to many crowdsourced projects that have given citizen volunteers a chance to help with research projects. Originally called citizen science projects, the projects have gone on to include other subject areas. One of the earliest projects to show that crowdsourcing was feasible was Galaxy Zoo (http://www.galaxyzoo.org/), which started asking volunteers to categorize galaxies in 2007 using data from the Sloan Digital Sky Survey. The work of more than two hundred thousand volunteers has led to more than fifty papers about the discoveries and huge amounts of data being made available on the website. Now, Galaxy Zoo is part of Zooniverse (https://www.zooniverse.org/), a collection of projects that include moon, sun, and planet studies, climate research, nature (e.g., classifying giant kelp), biology (e.g., classifying cancer cells), and even humanities projects that involve transcribing materials from ancient Greece or World War I. Other groups have started similar projects, for example, the Smithsonian has set up a website, Smithsonian Digital Volunteers Transcription Center (https://transcription.si.edu/), where people can go and choose from many projects that present digital data for transcription or classification. In all these projects, not only does the original data and its classification or transcription need to be managed, but the information about all the volunteers and the verification of their work needs to be managed.

How Can Librarians Help?

Librarians need to remember that researchers don't think about their work the way librarians do. Librarians think in terms of making sure a literature search is thorough so no important work is missed, and the citations are clear and consistent so cited materials can be found again. Data librarians think of proper data organization, making sure the data is stored properly, and making sure the best metadata is used when data sets are deposited in a repository. But for a researcher, "the goal is knowledge discovery, not data collection" (Mons, 2013: slide 15). If librarians want to be able to work with researchers and actually be a part of the research cycle, they need to make sure that adherence to a good data cycle is not onerous.

Libraries and librarians are in a time of transition. As more resources become digital and reference question numbers go down in many libraries, it is important to look ahead to new resources and new areas where libraries and librarians can help. As noted in chapter 1, librarian skills are ideal for working with data. Librarians, as academics in their own right, also have an understanding of how research is conducted, making them ideal collaborators in the research life cycle. Librarians just need to reach out to researchers to discover how they can support ongoing projects.

Connecting with Researchers

To help make things easier for researchers, librarians need to be familiar with funder requirements and disciplinary standards, and combine that knowledge with specifics about local resources and policies. Do a database search on any researcher you will be meeting so you have some understanding of what he or she is studying. Attend seminars, grand rounds, open lectures, and any other special event that will help you learn about research, and specifically the research going on with the groups you work with. Search grants at government agencies to see which funder is most common at your institution. Check with your grants office to find out what nongovernment awards have been received, since some philanthropic groups (e.g., Gates Foundation) require DMPs. Talk with people in the grants office to learn when the prime grant times are for different agencies and subjects, so you know when to promote services. Attend grant writing workshops if possible so you understand what the process entails. Librarians working in research data management need to add value, not work, to a researcher's project.

Librarians can also help with research ethics education at their institutions. Responsible data management is essential to research integrity and transparency, and librarians should "leverage our instructional skills to improve the data management practices of researchers and take a more active role in preventing misconduct throughout the research process" (Coates, 2014: 600).

Key Points

Researchers are responsible for many things outside of data management. Librarians with an understanding of the researcher work cycle will have a more realistic view of the data management needs of researchers.

- All researchers should have training in ethical and responsible research practices.
- Researchers will usually want easy-to-use data management and storage solutions.
- Advances in technology have changed the way research is done in all fields, and the amount of data collected has increased for most researchers.

Data librarians can help researchers by encouraging data management steps that will gradually lead to researchers following best practices for data management, which is the topic of chapter 3.

References

Borgman, Christine L. 2007. *Scholarship in the Digital Age: Information, Infrastructure, and the Internet.* Cambridge, Mass.: MIT Press.

———. 2015. *Big Data, Little Data, No Data: Scholarship in the Networked World.* Cambridge, Mass.: MIT Press.

Coates, Heather. 2014. "Ensuring Research Integrity." *College & Research Libraries News* 75, no. 11: 598–601.

Collins, Francis S., and Laurence A. Tabak. 2014. "Policy: NIH Plans to Enhance Reproducibility." *Nature* 505, no. 7485: 612–13.

Feldblum, Joseph T., Emily E. Wroblewski, Rebecca. S. Rudicell, et al. 2014a. "Sexually Coercive Male Chimpanzees Sire More Offspring." *Current Biology* 24, no. 23 (December): 2855–60. http://dx.doi.org/10.5061/dryad.v4h76.

———. 2014b. Data from "Sexually Coercive Male Chimpanzees Sire More Offspring." Dryad Digital Repository. http://dx.doi.org/10.5061/dryad.v4h76.

Goodall, Jane. 1986. *The Chimpanzees of Gombe: Patterns of Behavior.* Cambridge, Mass.: Harvard University Press.

Kramer, Adam D. I., Jamie E. Guillory, and Jeffrey T. Hancock. 2014. "Experimental Evidence of Massive-Scale Emotional Contagion through Social Networks." *Proceedings of the National Academy of Sciences of the United States of America* 111, no. 24: 8788–90. doi:10.1073/pnas.1320040111.

Kutzbach, Mark J. 2010. *Access to Workers or Employers? An Intra-Urban Analysis of Plant Location Decisions.* Center for Economic Studies, U.S. Census Bureau. http://ideas.repec.org/p/cen/wpaper/10-21r.html.

Mons, Barend. 2013. "ELIXIR and Open Data: View from an ELIXIR Node." ELIXIR Launch, December 18, 2013. http://www.elixir-europe.org/sites/default/files/documents/3_barend-1. pdf.

Petersen, Alexander M., Joel. N. Tenenbaum, Shlomo Havlin, et al. 2012. "Languages Cool as They Expand: Allometric Scaling and the Decreasing Need for New Words." *Scientific Reports* 2: article number 943. doi:10.1038/srep00943.

Petters, Jonathan. 2015. E-mail message to author. April 3.

Phillips, David C., and Danielle Sandler. 2015. "Does Public Transit Spread Crime? Evidence from Temporary Rail Station Closures." *Regional Science and Urban Economics* 52: 13–26. http://dx.doi.org/10.1016/j.regsciurbeco.2015.02.001.

Plooij, Frans X., Hetty van de Rijt-Plooij, Martha Fischer, and Anne Pusey. 2014a. "Longitudinal Recordings of the Vocalizations of Immature Gombe Chimpanzees for Developmental Studies." *Scientific Data*. 1: 140025doi:10.1038/sdata.2014.25.

———. 2014b. Data from "Longitudinal Recordings of the Vocalizations of Immature Gombe Chimpanzees for Developmental Studies." Dryad Digital Repository. http://dx.doi. org/10.5061/dryad.5tq80.2.

Preis, Tobias, Helen Susannah Moat, and H. E. Stanley. 2013. "Quantifying Trading Behavior in Financial Markets Using Google Trends." *Scientific Reports* 2, article number 752. http:// dx.doi.org/10.1038/srep01684.

Pusey Anne E., and Kara Schroepfer-Walker. 2013a. "Female Competition in Chimpanzees." *Philosophical Transactions of the Royal Society B* 368, no. 1631. doi:10.1098/rstb.2013.0077.

———. 2013b. Data from "Female Competition in Chimpanzees." Dryad Digital Repository. http://dx.doi.org/10.5061/dryad.jg05d.

Tolentino, Mellisa. 2014. "Big Data Correctly Predicts Some GRAMMY Winners: Spotify the Best Indicator." *siliconAngle* (blog). http://siliconangle.com/blog/2014/01/27/big-data-correctly-predicts-some-grammy-winners-spotify-the-best-indicator/.

Visa, Ari J. E., Jarmo Toivonen, Sami Autio, et al. 2001. "Data Mining of Text as a Tool in Authorship Attribution." *Proc. SPIE 4384, Data Mining and Knowledge Discovery: Theory, Tools, and Technology III* 149 (March 27). doi:10.1117/12.421068.

Wagner, Caroline S. 2008. *The New Invisible College: Science for Development*. Washington, D.C.: Brookings Institution Press.

CHAPTER 3

Best Practices for Working with Research Data

IN ART, MUSIC, WRITING, EVEN IN LIFE, THERE IS A SAYING, "You have to know the rules before you can break them." This applies to data management as well. It is important to be aware of best practices for data management, and the discipline-specific variations, before trying to adjust a data management plan to fit with a particular workflow or reflect the time constraints of the researcher work cycle discussed in chapter 2. It is also a good idea to consider the reasons for data management when deciding on best practices. Researchers who want to find and understand the data collected by their students will have different needs from researchers who must contribute their data to a government repository. Researchers who must share their data to comply with a funding agency requirement will want to be sure it can be found and cited properly, and will want good documentation so the data is not misinterpreted.

Reasons for Best Practices

Most researchers probably consider best practices, especially guidelines from a subject repository they must use, to be just another set of hoops they must jump through to conduct their research. But adhering to best practices can help ensure consistent data that is easier for researchers to process and use for analysis and visualization, and later sharing. Best practices for long-term storage mean that data can be found and used by the researcher or anyone who wishes to conduct a meta-analysis or reanalyze the data. There are many reasons to adhere to some best practices while collecting and using data.

Individual Reasons

Good data documentation practices make it easier for researchers and everyone they work with to collect, find, understand, and analyze the data needed for their work. Standard practices also make a researcher less dependent on "lab members who may have graduated or moved on to other endeavors" (White et al., 2013: 13). Well-documented data saves time by being easier to locate and easier to clean up for analysis. It is also easier to share data with collaborators if it is properly documented. Time and money are spared when experiments do not need to be repeated due to lost or messy data. Having well-documented data makes it easy to prove results if there are questions about findings in publications. Also, data sharing increases reputation and reuse increases impact (see chapter 7), and good documentation (chapter 6) is necessary for reuse.

Following best practices can also avoid problems that might result in misconduct investigations. Several problems related to data have been noted in responsible conduct of research training offered through the Office of Research Integrity (ORI), of the U.S. Department of Health & Human Services (HHS):

- technical data not recorded properly;
- technical data management not supervised by the primary investigator (PI);
- data not maintained at the institution;
- financial or administrative data not maintained properly;
- data not stored properly;
- data not held in accordance with retention requirements; and
- data not retained by the institution (Boston College, 2015).

Institutional

In the United States, most data generated by research that is funded by the federal government belongs to the institution where the funded researcher works (Blum, 2012). Some institutions have developed data policies that require the researcher to be a data steward or custodian, which means the researcher must know where data is stored and be able to present data if needed for potential intellectual property or misconduct questions, or freedom of information requests. Some institutional responsible conduct of research (RCR) policies or intellectual property (IP) policies also address data management issues, and state institutions might have added state policies covering the retention of data and other products of research.

For example, Johns Hopkins University Data Management Services recommends that researchers check the Data Ownership and Retention, Institutional Review Board, Intellectual Property, and Responsible Conduct of Research Policies, and includes highlights of these policies to consider when writing a data management plan (https://dmp.data.jhu.edu/resources/jhu-policies/). The provost at the University of Pittsburgh provides research data management guidelines (http://www.provost.pitt.edu/documents/RDM_Guidelines.pdf). And Columbia University has a section on data acquisition and management in their Responsible Conduct of Research training (http://ccnmtl.columbia.edu/projects/rcr/rcr_data/introduction/index.html).

Funder

Funders around the world are realizing that requiring data sharing increases the value of the research they support. The U.S. OSTP memo (Stebbins, 2013) requires public access to data from the research supported by about twenty federal agencies, not only for reuse to produce new insights, but it also "allows companies to focus resources and efforts on understanding and exploiting discoveries."

Other federal governments have similar requirements, and private funders such as the Gates Foundation and Wellcome Trust now require data be shared publicly. Most of these funders are also asking for data management plans, and progress reports need to address adherence to the plan. Data sharing is expected by these funders, so data needs to be usable and clear to minimize misinterpretation.

REASONS FOR SHARING DATA

Data sharing achieves many important goals for the scientific community, such as

- reinforcing open scientific inquiry
- encouraging diversity of analysis and opinion
- promoting new research, testing of new or alternative hypotheses and methods of analysis
- supporting studies on data collection methods and measurement
- facilitating education of new researchers
- enabling the exploration of topics not envisioned by the initial investigators
- permitting the creation of new datasets by combining data from multiple sources.

(NIH, 2003)

Journal

Many publishers are supporting efforts of various groups, societies, and government agencies to promote transparency and reproducibility of research by requiring authors to make data available and register clinical trials, for example, *Nature* (http://www.nature.com/sdata/data-policies) and *PLOS* (https://www.plos.org/plos-data-policy-faq/). Recent papers that attempt to reproduce research results or reanalyze shared data have shown that conclusions from original data were wrong, confirming the need for data sharing requirements. For example, Ben Goldacre (2015) describes how the reassessment of deworming trials data found analysis problems that resulted in an outcome that suggests there should be different recommendations for the use of deworming medicines. Force11 (https://www.force11.org/) has developed Transparency and Openness Promotion (TOP) Guidelines (Alter et al., 2015) for use by publishers to help facilitate more widespread adoption of standards by journals. The TOP Guidelines cover eight standards at three levels, allowing adoption of standards based on the discipline covered by the journal, and data transparency is one of the standards.

Repository

Subject repositories are used to make data available for sharing and provide long-term preservation, so they require well-documented, clean, consistent data and have specific guidelines for data that will be deposited. ICPSR's Guide to Social Science Data Preparation and Archiving (https://www.icpsr.umich.edu/icpsrweb/content/deposit/guide/) has a section on preparing data for sharing and another on depositing data. GenBank (NCBI) has a couple of ways to deposit nucleotide sequences—BankIt (http://www.ncbi.nlm.nih.gov/WebSub/html/requirements.html) and Sequin (http://www.ncbi.nlm.nih.gov/Sequin/QuickGuide/sequin.htm#BeforeYouBegin)—and each has specific documentation requirements for any accepted sequence deposits.

Overview of Basic Best Practices

There are some basic suggestions that are common to most best practice lists. These are repository independent and work for most subject areas. The researcher work cycle (shown in chapter 2, figure 2.1) is complex, so it is easier to look at best practices focusing just on the data life cycle. It is helpful to look at data management through the whole data cycle before starting to identify when actions or interventions might need to be taken (Corti et al., 2014). The sections below list these basic best practices arranged in the order they appear in a simplified data life cycle (see figure 3.1) based on the ICPSR (shown in chapter 2, figure 2.3) and DataONE (https://www.dataone.org/best-practices) data life cycles.

Plan

Even if it is not required for a grant, a data management plan can ensure consistent practice throughout a project and among all people involved in the project. Chapter 8 has more complete information on writing data management plans. The plan should include:

- Data backup policy for all data, not just digital data
- Assignment of responsibilities for data collection and data management upkeep through the life cycle

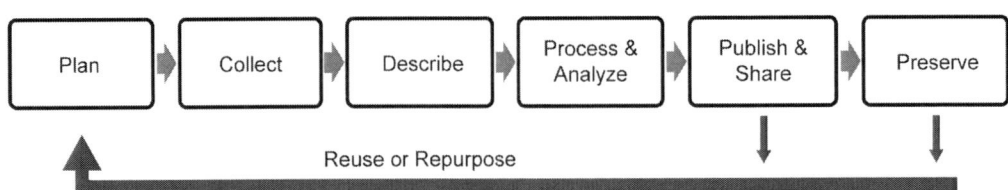

Figure 3.1. *Simplified Data Life Cycle. Credit:* Margaret E. Henderson

- Available storage, and the like, based on data sensitivity and local security classification
- Potential repositories or journals, so their policies can be considered
- Length of time the data must be stored after the project, based on funder requirements, institutional requirements, or applicable government requirements (e.g., state records management policy for state-funded institutions)
- Estimated budget for data collection, processing, storage, and so forth

Collect

Data collection needs to be easy and intuitive enough to fit the workflow of the research being done, but also thorough and accurate enough to be used for calculations, visualizations, and conclusions later.

- Define and list the types of data and file formats for the research, and use consistently.
- Choose a naming convention for files and folders, and ensure that the rules are followed systematically by always including the same information in the same order.
- Avoid using:
  - Generic data file names that may conflict when moved from one location to another
  - Special characters
  - Periods or spaces
- Use a standardized data format. Check with subject repository or find disciplinary standards if data will be shared or reused.
- Reserve the three-letter file extensions for the codes the system assigns to the file type (e.g., WRL, CSV, TIF).
- Don't rely on file names as your sole source of documentation.
- Ensure that raw data is preserved with no processing. Document steps used to clean data for analysis.

Describe

Good data descriptions make it easier for researchers to reuse their own data in the future, as well as allowing others to replicate or repurpose the data.

- Readme files
  - General project files describing overall organization and models, responsible parties, instruments, and so forth
  - Specific files for the contents of data files that define parameters, contents, date and time formats, measurements, and so forth; anything that will help facilitate the use of the data
  - For analyzed or processed data, include descriptions and references to software or code used
- Choose a meaningful directory hierarchy/naming convention.
- Create a data dictionary that explains terms used in files and folders (e.g., units of measurement and how they are collected, standards, calibrations).

Process and Analyze

Keeping track of all the steps needed to convert raw data to the figures and tables used in publication is important to ensure reproducibility and back up the results presented.

- Develop a quality assurance and quality control plan.
- Double-check data entry.
- Use consistent missing value coding.
- Document all analyses; include steps and complete software information where applicable.

Publish and Share

The need to deposit data in a recommended repository for journal publication, or make data publicly available in a repository to comply with a funder or institutional mandate, means that researchers will need to clean data up and add metadata as required by the repository they choose (see more in chapter 7 on sharing).

- Document all processing needed to ready data for sharing.
- Save data in formats that have lossless data compression and are supported by multiple software platforms (e.g., CSV, TXT).
- Add documentation that includes the basic information needed to make the data reusable. Formal metadata is not always necessary, as long as all the needed information is included in a readme file, data dictionary, or other open format documentation. Basic information fields include:
  - Title
  - Creator
  - Persistent identifier
  - Subject
  - Funders
  - Rights
  - Access information (restrictions, embargo)
  - Language
  - Dates
  - Location
  - Methods
  - Processing
  - File names
  - File format
  - Variables
  - Codes
  - Versions

Preserve

Data needs ongoing storage and backups while experiments are being conducted. And once the research project is finished, data needs to be stored according to funder and institutional policies (see more on long-term storage in chapter 5).

- Keep three copies of your data: original; another location on-site; an off-site/remote location.
- Back up data, and copies, at regular intervals. Hard-to-replicate data should be backed up daily.
- Try to keep data unencrypted unless necessary, and uncompressed.
- Use a reliable device for backups. Managed network drives or cloud storage will also be backed up, providing more insurance against loss.
- Ensure backup copies are identical to the original copy.
- Store final data using stable file formats.
- Refer to funder or publisher policies as well as institutional data and intellectual property policies and federal and state laws for duration of storage for data retention.
- Document policy for data destruction. This can be based on the institutional records management policy procedures and forms for disposal of materials.

Even these basic best practices are not set in stone. Researchers will need more, and sometimes less, than is listed here, depending on their project, their funder, and the institution. Librarians working with researchers can help by being aware of institutional, subject, and funder requirements pertaining to data documentation, and providing templates and guidelines to help researchers comply. The section that follows, "Available Best Practices," provides a listing of best practices suggested by some of the major repositories and data management groups.

Available Best Practices

Suggestions for best practices have come from many groups. Articles by groups of scientists encourage their peers to use some basic rules to make their data more usable. RDM services based in libraries offer lists of suggestions for documenting data. Usually repositories have more formal lists of requirements for deposit, be they subject or government repositories.

Libraries

More and more libraries are developing data management services, and providing best practices guidance is one of the RDM services, other than DMP support, that many libraries provide (Fearon et al., 2013). Some examples of best practices for data management services can be found at the following locations:

- Data Management Services at Stanford University Libraries http://library.stanford.edu/research/data-management-services/data-best-practices
- Research Data Management Services Group at Cornell University http://data.research.cornell.edu/content/best-practices
- Research Data Management Services at the University of Oregon https://library.uoregon.edu/datamanagement/guidelines.html

Repositories

Institutional repositories may or may not allow data deposit, and some, like Purdue University, have a separate data repository. Requirements vary, although in general, open formats are encouraged. Size limits may be in place for data sets.

- The Purdue University Research Repository (PURR) provides a collaborative working space as well as a data sharing platform. File formats for preservation are recommended: https://purr.purdue.edu/legal/file-format-recommendations.
- eCommons at Cornell University has size and format requirements in their Data Deposit Policy: https://ecommons.cornell.edu/policy.html#data.
- ResearchWorks at University Libraries, University of Washington, will take most digital formats but has a list of suggested formats that will retain functionality over time: http://digital.lib.washington.edu/preferred-formats.html.

Subject repositories encourage and advertise reuse, so there are usually more requirements for properly formatted and documented data. In some cases, the forms that must be filled out during the deposit process are converted into the required metadata. Chapter 7 will discuss sharing in depth and include a list of repositories, but a couple of examples of repository requirements include the following:

- The Inter-university Consortium for Political and Social Research (ICPSR) supports data deposit and reuse, and provides educational materials for instructors who wish to teach with the poll, census, or research data sets in the collection. ICPSR has recommended elements listed in their "Guide to Social Science Data Preparation and Archiving" (ICPSR, 2012).
- Crystallography Open Database provides information on the page "Advice to Potential CIF Donators: Fair Practices" (http://www.crystallography.net/cod/donators/advices.html).

General repositories usually have fewer requirements or guidelines for data deposit, but learning about any discipline-specific standards will help make the data more usable in the future. Dryad and Figshare are well-known repositories that accept data in all subject areas, and they are used by many journals as the repository for supporting data, or at least one of the accepted repositories.

- Dryad does not have file format restrictions but encourages submission in open formats such as ASCII and HTML so preservation and reuse are easier. There is, however, a list of suggestions to help optimize the data that is submitted (https://datadryad.org/pages/faq).
- Figshare does have a list of file types supported, but the list is extensive (https://figshare.zendesk.com/hc/en-us/articles/203993533-Supported-file-types), and when data is deposited, there is a form that guides the researcher to include categories, tags, and descriptions, to help findability.

Funders

Best practices can also be required by funding agencies when deposit into an agency repository is required. U.S. federal initiatives for open government data have mandated that agencies make their data available to the public, including both research data and data about their activities (The White House, 2009).

- The Oak Ridge National Laboratory Distributed Active Archive Center (ORNL DAAC) curates biogeochemical data collected with NASA-funded research and has prepared a best practices guide (https://daac.ornl.gov/PI/BestPractices-2010.pdf) for those who must deposit data.

- The National Centers for Environmental Information, part of the National Oceanic and Atmospheric Administration (NOAA), collects, processes, preserves, and shares oceanographic data from around the world. This data is very important for many agencies and researchers, so there are many guidelines that must be followed (http://www.ncddc.noaa.gov/activities/science-technology/data-management/). As well as a best practices guide (http://service.ncddc.noaa.gov/rdn/www/media/documents/activities/community-best-practices.pdf), there are lists of policies, plans, examples, and the Data Management Resources section has links to resources outside of NOAA that are also helpful for researchers depositing their data.

Health Data

The sensitive nature of health data that includes personal information requires another layer of best practices to ensure confidentiality. For example, there have been recent cases of DNA data that hackers have been able to use to identify the patients in a study (Hayden, 2013), so restrictions on data publication will need to be considered, or more secure protocols for anonymization need to be developed before sharing data. The Office for Civil Rights, in the Department of Health & Human Services (HHS), provides guidance on the deidentification of patient data (http://www.hhs.gov/ocr/privacy/hipaa/understanding/coveredentities/De-identification/guidance.html); further information on working with human subjects data can be found in chapter 7.

The Slow Creep of Best Practice Usage

A panel session at the 10th International Digital Curation Conference (IDCC15) on the topic of "Why is it taking so long?" echoed the question that comes up at many meetings of research data managers. The international panel debated about whether the RDM culture change really is taking a long time, or whether good progress actually is being made (Cope, 2015). The issues include the current practice of giving funds to individual projects for their data management needs, as opposed to contributing to institutions for the development of infrastructures that support the whole research community with short- and long-term data management and storage needs. Amy Hodge suggested that data managers and librarians should ask researchers what they need, rather than telling them what the institution has for them (Digital Curation Center, 2015).

In the end, it doesn't matter how well best practices for data management support necessary curation and long-term preservation if researchers find them too cumbersome to follow. Data managers should recognize, as records professionals were found to realize, that they may be part of the problem by having unrealistic or constraining demands (McLeod, Childs, and Hardiman, 2011). Better to create a series of steps that lead researchers to best practices gently, based on what they must do to get funded. As they recognize the benefits of having clean, organized, shared data, it will become easier to make those practices more robust.

◎ Key Points

Following a few guidelines will make it easier for researchers to find, share, and use the data they collect.

- Planning through the data life cycle before research starts makes the whole process easier.
- Check for specialized deposit requirements before starting data collection.
- Work with researchers to develop realistic plans for data documentation.

The next chapter will cover the interview process, based on the reference interview, that can be used to learn about research workflows and data management needs.

◎ References

Alter, George, George C. Banks, Denny Borsboom, et al. 2015. "Transparency and Openness Promotion (TOP) Guidelines." *Open Science Framework*. June 27. https://osf.io/9f6gx.

Blum, Carol. 2012. *Access to, Sharing and Retention of Research Data: Rights and Responsibilities*. Washington, D.C.: Council on Governmental Relations, Council on Governmental Relations. http://www.cogr.edu/COGR/files/ccLibraryFiles/Filename/000000000024/access_to_sharing_and_retention_of_research_data-_rights_&_responsibilities.pdf.

Boston College. 2015. "Examples of Problems." Administrators and the Responsible Conduct of Research. Office for Research Integrity and Compliance, via Office of Research Integrity, U.S. Department of Health & Human Services. Accessed August 1, 2015. https://ori.hhs.gov/education/products/rcradmin/topics/data/tutorial_12.shtml.

Cope, Jez. 2015. "International Digital Curation Conference 2015." *Open Access and Digital Scholarship Blog*. March 12. http://www.imperial.ac.uk/blog/openaccess/2015/03/12/international-digital-curation-conference-2015/.

Corti, Louise, Veerle Van den Eynden, Libby Bishop, and Matthew Wollard. 2014. *Managing and Sharing Research Data: A Guide to Good Practice*. London: Sage.

Digital Curation Center. 2015. "IDCC15: Why Is It Taking So Long?" YouTube video. 1:02:12. February 13. https://www.youtube.com/watch?v=2M6v7d2VdYo.

Fearon, David, Betsy Gunia, Sherry Lake, et al. 2013. *SPEC Kit 334: Research Data Management Services*. Washington, D.C.: Association of Research Libraries, Office of Management Services.

Goldacre, Ben. 2015. "Scientists Are Hoarding Data and It's Ruining Medical Research." BuzzFeed, August 3. http://www.buzzfeed.com/bengoldacre/deworming-trials.

Hayden, Erika C. 2013. "Privacy Protections: The Genome Hacker." *Nature* 497 (7448): 172–74. doi:10.1038/497172a.

ICPSR (Inter-university Consortium for Political and Social Research). 2012. *Guide to Social Science Data Preparation and Archiving: Best Practice throughout the Data Life Cycle*. 5th ed. Ann Arbor, Mich.: ICPSR. http://www.icpsr.umich.edu/files/ICPSR/access/dataprep.pdf.

McLeod, Julie, Sue Childs, and Rachel Hardiman. 2011. "Accelerating Positive Change in Electronic Records Management—Headline Findings from a Major Research Project." *Archives & Manuscripts* 39, no. 2: 66–94.

NIH (National Institutes of Health). 2003. "Grants and Funding. Frequently Asked Questions. Data Sharing." National Institutes of Health. http://grants1.nih.gov/grants/policy/data_sharing/data_sharing_faqs.htm.

Stebbins, Michael. 2013. "Expanding Public to the Results of Federally Funded Research." *Office of Science and Technology Policy Blog*. February 22. http://www.whitehouse.gov/blog/2013/02/22/expanding-public-access-results-federally-funded-research.

White, Ethan P., Elita Baldridge, Zachary T. Brym, et al. 2013. "Nine Simple Ways to Make It Easier to (Re)Use Your Data." *PeerJ PrePrints* 1: e7v2 https://dx.doi.org/10.7287/peerj.preprints.7v2.

The White House. 2009. "Transparency and Open Government Memorandum (Memorandum to the Heads of Executive Departments and Agencies)." 74 Fed. Reg. 4,685. January 21. http://www.gpo.gov/fdsys/pkg/FR-2009-01-26/pdf/E9-1777.pdf.

Data Interviews

THE QUESTION OF WHAT DEPARTMENT SHOULD run research data management services at an institution comes up regularly. Information technology (IT) departments deal with computer storage, networks, and security, all important parts of data management. The department that administers grants and awards, usually part of the Office of Research (OR), must deal with compliance issues for all funder requirements. Both of these groups have some interest in helping with research data management. And yet, it seems that libraries are the department that usually start developing RDM services (Tenopir et al., 2014). There is often collaboration with IT or OR, but libraries are the ones reaching out to researchers. Some cite the library's neutral position in an institution. IT and OR are always pushing to have things done a specific way, whereas libraries try to make research easier. It could also be that liaison librarians have found, during their reference interviews with researchers, there is a need for data services and have adapted to fill the void.

Reference Interview Skills

As mentioned in chapter 1, many of the skills and theories that underlie librarianship can be transferred to data management. Interviewing skills are integral to research and reference interviews, and those same skills can be used to learn about the data management needs of researchers. Finding out about the data management needs of researchers can be difficult. Like doctors who don't answer all their clinical questions because they don't have enough time or don't think the answer to their questions exists (Del Fiol, Workman, and Gorman, 2014), researchers in the middle of doing experiments may wonder if there is a better way to deal with their data but don't have the time to find out more, or they don't think there is any other way. Data problems might come up while researchers are seeking help with literature searching or citation management, and reference or liaison librarians can offer help if they have a dual role (Carlson, 2011). Or reference or liaison librarians can refer the researcher to a data librarian. Data librarians can also reach researchers in need by promoting services to help with requirements for data management plans or public access to data.

While data interviews may not start with a specific question like reference interviews, many of the same skills are needed to find out what researchers need. Sayeed Choudhury (2013), in an opening keynote talk, said that the reference interview was an important part of data management. He has had interviews where researchers start out thinking one thing about data, and end up in a totally different place at the end of the interview.

Data librarians, who may have concentrated on other skills in library school and continuing education, will find it helpful to learn a bit more about the theories behind reference interviews. Learning how to ask good questions and listening carefully will make it easier to understand what researchers are trying to do and what aspects of data management are needed to improve workflow. A good list of interview skills, with descriptions and examples, can be found in *Conducting the Reference Interview*, 2nd ed. (Ross, Nilsen, and Radford, 2009). The first few skills discussed here are useful for establishing an open and approachable manner. The later skills will help with the negotiation of the question, problem, or need. These skills will work with one-time encounters or long-term collaborations, and will help build relationships. The nonverbal skills will not be helpful when using e-mail or text to conduct an interview, but the rest of these skills can be applied to written correspondence.

Nonverbal Attending Skills

The first section in the RUSA (Reference and User Services Association) "Guidelines for Behavioral Performance of Reference and Information Service Providers" (2013) covers visibility and approachability. Making eye contact, facing the person when speaking or listening, establishing a comfortable physical distance, nodding, smiling, pausing, leaning toward a person, and waiting until a person has finished talking all signal interest and attention toward the person. These skills are especially important when visiting offices or laboratories or other workspaces. Researchers need to feel that they can trust the data librarian. When first learning about the data management practices of a group, body language and facial expressions should not give the impression of annoyance or ridicule of the current system. Nonjudgmental listening will create a relationship that allows the data librarian to learn as much as possible about how the research group works, and about the personalities involved and their resistance or acceptance of change.

Acknowledgment

Acknowledgment is the skill of restating what the other person has said to confirm or clarify what he or she is trying to tell you (Ross, Nilsen, and Radford, 2009). The varying definitions of data covered in chapter 1 show how easily the comments or questions of a researcher could be misunderstood, making acknowledgment an important skill. In a reference interview, the librarian is usually trying to clarify a question, but in a data interview, the librarian will be trying to clarify the data activities or needs of a researcher. It is not necessary to parrot back exactly what a person has said; just make a short statement to show that you are listening and confirm what the person is trying to say. A brief reply is fine, and it is important to be accepting, rather than judgmental. If there are any ambiguous terms, provide a paraphrasing of the comment to clarify the meaning.

Minimal Encouragers

Phrases that encourage a person to say more or continue are important to getting the whole picture of what is needed or what is going on. Examples of words and phrases that can help include:

- I see.
- Go on.
- Tell me more.
- Interesting.
- Anything else?
- Do you have an example?

Nonverbal cues that indicate you are interested and listening are important as well. Pausing before or after saying one of the above encouraging questions or words indicates that you are listening or want the person to go on talking.

Open, Closed, and Sense-Making Questions

Asking questions is a method for librarians to find out what people really want to know. Using different types of questions can complement the specific questions a data librarian uses for developing a data management plan (see chapter 8 textbox, "Topics and Questions for Developing Data Management Plans") or conducting a data curation interview (see below), as well as helping with data reference questions.

Open questions allow people to respond in their own terms. Open questions can be used to learn more about what people want and need, to find out more about their problem, to encourage them to elaborate on their topic, or to get clarification. The librarian should be careful not to assume anything about what the person wants or needs when asking open questions because that could limit the response.

Closed questions are generally yes/no questions or have a limited range of answers. They are best used later in an interview, after the librarian has learned more about the needs of the researcher. Closed questions can be used to refocus an interview that might be getting off topic, to verify what the researcher needs, or to find out specifics about what is needed or wanted.

Sense-making questions, also called neutral questions, are a subset of open questions that are used to find out the underlying situation, the gaps faced, and the uses the person will make of the information found (Dervin and Dewdney, 1986). Sense-making questions are important because open questions can bring up irrelevant conversation, and closed questions limit answers to what is available in a system. Sense-making questions have a little more structure than open questions and are focused on the person being interviewed. The three elements, situation, gap, and use, come from Brenda Dervin's Sense-Making model (1998). Dervin's work on sense-making theory is relevant to data librarianship because not only does it strive to learn about what people need and what will help their situation, but it also takes into account the emotional nature of people's problems and focuses on having knowledge management systems change to be responsive to users. In the long run, there will be no one-size-fits-all answer to data management, so librarians must be flexible when working with researchers. (See textbox for examples of open, closed, and sense-making questions).

EXAMPLES OF OPEN, CLOSED, AND SENSE-MAKING (NEUTRAL) QUESTIONS

Open

- What requirements do you have for your project?
- What else can you tell me about your data?
- If you could have the perfect data management system, what would it include?
- Why do you want a data management plan?

Closed

- Are there metadata requirements in your field?
- Do you need to retain your data for a specific length of time?
- What file types do you collect?
- Where do you save your original data files?

Sense-Making (Neutral)

- What are you doing now to record your data?
- What seems to be missing in your data management plan?
- What is your final goal for the data collected in this project?

Using questions appropriately while trying to answer a reference questions, learning about the work somebody is doing to devise a data management plan, or helping to streamline data collection will make the work of a data librarian much easier. "Why" questions are one of the hardest types of questions to use because they are often perceived as being intrusive or rude, when really the librarian is just trying to get a better understanding of the question or need (Dewdney and Michell, 1997). By framing why questions with an explanation of how the information will help with the answer, there is less likelihood of the person getting upset. Sense-making questions that ask the user to explain the situation, gap, and use for the information are also helpful. For example, "If you could tell my why you need to collect this value, we might be able to come up with an easier input method."

Avoid Premature Diagnosis

Data librarians should be careful not to jump to conclusions, especially when first working with a researcher or group. Making assumptions can lead to inappropriate questions, and then useful or relevant information might not be revealed. It is tempting to jump in with information about what is available at your institution, especially when a researcher seems to indicate something is not available and you know that it is. There will be time later to suggest use of institutional resources the researcher may not be aware of. It is better to listen to the whole story or problem, and be sure you are getting the complete story and offering the best solution.

Reflecting Content

While acknowledgment (see above) is used to clarify meaning or confirm what has just been said, reflecting content is an attempt to pull together what the person has said after he or she has answered multiple questions, and it can be used to confirm what that person needs. Paraphrasing uses a preface, such as "You mean," or "As I understand you," followed by a short restatement of what was meant. Summarizing uses a few sentences to pull together the gist of a larger conversation, to confirm that the problem or situation is understood. Both methods of reflecting content should end with a question that allows for correction or further explanation if needed, such as: "Was that it?" or "Have I got that right?"

Listening

Good listening is not just not talking. It is tempting to be thinking of an answer or the next question while listening to somebody, but that can lead to miscommunication. Instead, active listening, listening using attending skills, should be employed to get the most out of an interview. Active listening has been recommended for emotional reference interviews as a way of defusing tensions (Smith and Fitt, 1982), but it is also helpful when discussing data management. Many researchers are passionate about their research and possessive of their data, so this technique is applicable (see textbox, "Active Listening Skill Set"). Although active listening did not start as a reference interview technique, the skills have many similarities to those reviewed above. Amanda K. Rinehart (2015) found that active listening techniques were applicable to an e-mail consultation about a data management plan, and she was able to gain the trust and thanks of the researcher she was working with.

ACTIVE LISTENING SKILL SET

Pay Attention: Be present, focused on the moment. Use non-verbal skills that show interest. Observe the other person's behavior.

Hold Judgment: Have an open mind. Demonstrate empathy. Be patient.

Reflect: Paraphrase what was said but also what you think the person is feeling.

Clarify: Use open-ended questions to draw people out.

Summarize: Briefly summarize what you have understood.

Share: When you have a clear understanding of the other person's perspective, introduce your ideas, feeling, suggestions, or concerns.

(Hoppe, 2006)

Follow-Up

In a reference transaction, making sure the person has the answer he or she needs is the last RUSA guideline (2013). The same skills used to ask questions to elicit more information about a problem can be used to ask if the person has found what that person needs. In a data interview, it is just as likely that the data librarian will have further questions, so a follow-up e-mail to thank the researcher for his or her time can be used to either ask for clarification or leave the door open for another question or two. Follow-up could also be a data management plan or interview transcripts, and a final comment, such as "Let me know if there is anything I've missed" or "Don't hesitate to contact me if you need anything further," will leave the door open for continued interaction.

Types of Data Interviews

Data interviews combine the interview skills covered above with knowledge of data covered in chapters 3, 5–7, and available data resources (found during an environmental scan, covered in chapter 9). Data interviews can be long and formal, such as data curation interviews that collect in-depth information about all the data a researcher produces and how it is stored and shared and preserved. They can be short data reference questions; a student needs a data set for a project, a researcher needs a repository. Other researchers may have a little more time, but they only want to discuss certain aspects of the data cycle, such as how to share their data or how to add basic metadata, so the data librarian would conduct a data consultation. And then there are times when a researcher needs a data management plan interview for a DMP or data sharing plan. Although, for a grant due the next day, there might only time for some basic, general questions, which can be used to customize boilerplate language available for storage and sharing options. A workflow analysis can be used to help a research group optimize data collection, organization, and description. The same techniques can be used to conduct stakeholder interviews when working to learn more about the resources and services available at an institution.

Data Reference Questions

Data questions are not new for most reference librarians. Census data, manufacturing data, the *Statistical Abstract of the United States* (http://www.census.gov/compendia/statab/), public opinion polls, and more are requested in all types of libraries. The requester may be hoping for statistics and receive raw data instead, without understanding the difference or knowing how to analyze the raw data. Kristin Partlo (2009) makes the point that most undergraduates with data reference questions need help discovering the data and instruction in using the data, so she recommends using a data reference worksheet to conduct a teaching reference interview. For any question, follow-up, in person or via e-mail, is essential. If there is no analysis or statistics help available in your library, it is helpful to know where that help can be obtained at your institution. An example of an e-mail reference question is in the textbox.

E-MAIL DATA REFERENCE QUESTION TRANSACTION

Student: For my project I am looking at food consumption and income in the United States. I think I need to find raw data that I can use with SPSS [software].

Data librarian: I am happy to help you. There are various sources that cover food consumption and income in the U.S. Is there something specific you are interested in studying?

Student: I think more specifically, I would like to look at BMI or body fat and see what the relationship is to income. My hypothesis tentatively is—Income is not related to obesity, high BMI, or fatty food consumption.

Data librarian: You may have to combine data from a couple of sources to get what you need.

The CDC has quite a bit of information, for example, this NCHS data brief on obesity and socioeconomic status in adults: http://www.cdc.gov/nchs/data/databriefs/db50.htm. The article links you to the original source of the data, which is the National Health and Nutrition Examination Survey, http://www.cdc.gov/nchs/nhanes/nhanes_questionnaires.htm. You might find additional data in the Food Environment Atlas from the USDA, http://www.ers.usda.gov/data-products/food-environment-atlas.aspx.

If these sources don't have the information you need, we can meet next week to discuss your topic further.

Student: You are awesome! I found that site after I e-mailed you today, but had a hard time finding the actual data. After receiving your e-mail, I was able to access the data. It is very impressive to me. It looks like I can match variables to counties throughout the data set, and so I am testing combinations for analysis I want. I would like to reserve your time on Wednesday anyway if that is still OK with you, just in case I can't seem to match this up and instead need further counseling. But I am going to keep working with it throughout the weekend and consult my professor as well.

A few days later:

Data librarian: Do you still need to meet with me tomorrow? If you still need to mull over what you have, we can meet next week sometime.

Student: Again, you are awesome! I was just sitting down to write you. I received feedback from my professor today and he told me I was on the right track. I am going to see him tomorrow at class and will ask him some more questions in person. I might request a meeting for next week but I do not need to meet tomorrow.

Data Consultation

A data consultation is really just an extended data reference question. It can be thought of as a basic or introductory data interview, made up of a short series of questions to get an overall view of the research and data management practices of the group, with specific questions to learn more about the problem that prompted the researcher to contact a data librarian. Michael Witt and Jake R. Carlson (2007) compiled a list of questions used by librarians to learn about data sets that might be useful to include in their institutional repository. These questions are a good start for learning some basic information about the data a researcher is collecting:

1. What is the story of the data?
2. What form and format are the data in?
3. What is the expected lifespan of the data set?
4. How could the data be used, reused, and repurposed?
5. How large is the data set, and what is its rate of growth?
6. Who are the potential audiences for the data?
7. Who owns the data?
8. Does the data set include any sensitive information?
9. What publications or discoveries have resulted from the data?
10. How should the data be made accessible?

After getting a good overall picture of the research, the data librarian can then ask specific questions based on concerns that spurred the researcher to ask for help. This list of questions is not set in stone. Each data librarian will find his or her own wording and series of questions that elicits the desired information during an interview.

Data Management Plan Interview

In a perfect world, researchers would create data management plans with the help of librarians at the start of their research, so everyone would know what data is being collected, how it will be stored and saved and organized and shared, and who is supposed to take care of the process. In reality, very few researchers do this, and most usually don't think about writing a data management plan until they need one for a grant. With more and more federal agencies and funders adding a data management plan requirement to their grants, data librarians should expect to see more DMP help requests. The Simplified Data Management Plan outline from the New England Collaborative Data Management Curriculum (NECDMC, http://library.umassmed.edu/necdmc/necdmc_simplified_dmp.docx) gives some helpful questions to ask when working on a DMP:

1. Types of Data
   a. What types of data will you be creating or capturing? (experimental measures, observational or qualitative, model simulation, existing)
   b. How will you capture, create, and/or process the data? (Identify instruments, software, imaging, etc. used)
2. Contextual Details (Metadata) Needed to Make Data Meaningful to Others
   a. What file formats and naming conventions will you be using?

3. Storage, Backup and Security
    a. Where and on what media will you store the data?
    b. What is your backup plan for the data?
    c. How will you manage data security?
4. Provisions for Protection/Privacy
    a. How are you addressing any ethical or privacy issues? (IRB, anonymization of data)
    b. Who will own the copyright or intellectual property rights to the data?
5. Policies for Re-use
    a. What restrictions need to be placed on re-use of your data?
6. Policies for Access and Sharing
    a. What is the process for gaining access to your data?
7. Plan for Archiving and Preservation of Access
    a. What is your long-term plan for preservation and maintenance of the data?

Data librarians should be prepared to provide some standardized or boilerplate language for the answers to some of these questions. Some libraries will have an institutional repository that can take data, so the data can be open access through the repository once the grant has finished. An institutional scan will ensure that the data librarian is aware of other resources needed to support the data management plan. The Office of Sponsored Programs or grants office might also have some boilerplate language for institutional resources. Further information on using the information collected about a project to write a data management plan can be found in chapter 8.

Workflow Analysis

A workflow analysis is helpful to see how data is collected, where it is stored, and how it is organized. "Workflow" refers to the interaction of processes, made up of tasks or steps, through which various research projects are carried out. Workflow analysis is often thought of in relation to business practices or manufacturing, but the process is also being used extensively to help with the implementation of electronic health record (EHR) systems in health care settings (AHRQ, 2016).

In a sense, workflow is a recipe or protocol, and studying the steps and why they are done can help improve the process. In the case of research, the analysis should help show where there are problems in data collection and documentation, and what improvements could be made. In order to give context to the workflow analysis, a consultation interview should be conducted first. Active listening is important in a workflow analysis to avoid having people get defensive about how they are doing their work. The best way to collect information about the workflow is to watch somebody working, but that may not always be possible, so some questions are necessary:

1. What is the process/experiment/procedure?
2. What tasks or steps make up the process?
3. What variations might come up? Why?
4. When is the process complete?
5. How long does it take?
6. Where and how is data collected along the way?
7. What are the problem points, if any, in this process?
8. Can you think of a better way to do any of the steps?

An outside person with minimal knowledge of the research project can actually point out problem areas that do not seem obvious to the participants because they have been doing the work for so long. For example, one of the first things to confirm are details about time and measurements. A standard date format should be chosen, especially for international projects, and the units of measurement should be agreed upon and noted, and any measurement that must be collected should note specifics about units and collection methods. While the ideal is to have the entire picture of the data, the reality is, there isn't always time. Only some researchers will be willing to take the time to fully catalog all their data sets and all the types of data collection in their labs. And most researchers will not want to sit down for a one- to two-hour interview to discuss all their data management needs. As discussed in chapter 2, there are many demands on researchers, so often they will only request a consultation and allow a workflow analysis if there is a problem, and they will only take enough time to deal with that specific problem. The key is to use reference interview skills to learn more each time a question comes, and eventually a complete picture of what that researcher needs will come together.

Data Curation Interview

A data curation interview is designed to allow data librarians and researchers to do an in-depth assessment of the data collection and output of a research group and also, to assess the plans for storing and sharing that data in the future. Some of the information is collected via forms or spreadsheets the research group fills out, and this information is combined with thorough interviews with key personnel. In some cases, the interview will be used to identify problems or find areas of improvement, but in other cases, the interview is used to learn more about the data management and curation needs of researchers in a particular subject area or institution. The best known of this type of interview is the Data Curation Profile (DCP) from Purdue University Libraries, which was developed to collect information on data sets that might be curated by the library (Witt et al., 2009). Librarians can download a Data Curation Profiles Toolkit (http://datacurationprofiles. org/) to get instructions and templates for interviews and forms for the entry of data set information. Once a profile is completed, the librarian and researcher can upload it to the Data Curation Profiles Directory (http://docs.lib.purdue.edu/dcp/), where others can learn from it.

A complete Data Curation Profile interview can take up to fifteen or more hours, so many librarians and researchers are reluctant to use it unless they are interested in contributing to the directory. Even if there is no intention to add the interview to the DCP Directory, the information collected can help a data librarian plan for the collection, organization, storage, documentation, sharing, and long-term preservation of the data sets generated by a researcher. It can also be helpful to use selected parts of the DCP Toolkit that relate to the problems a researcher could be experiencing.

Other groups have found that it is easier to adapt parts of the DCP Toolkit and add questions and techniques from other sources to create their own protocols. Data librarians from the University of British Columbia Library worked with the Centre for Hip Health Mobility and the university IT department to develop a shorter visual and interactive approach for the discovery of research data needs (Barsky, 2014). The resulting Research Data Discovery Manual (University of British Columbia Library, 2014) is available for those looking for an alternative to the DCP Toolkit.

Another option is to use some of the extensive checklists or questions developed to create data management plans as a starting point for the questions used for an in-depth interview. Data management plans will be covered in chapter 8, but using the DMP guidance from the following organizations is a good basis for a data curation interview:

- Inter-university Consortium for Political and Social Research (ICPSR): Framework for Creating a Data Management Plan http://www.icpsr.umich.edu/icpsr-web/content/datamanagement/dmp/framework.html
- DataONE: Primer on Data Management https://www.dataone.org/sites/all/documents/DataONE_BP_Primer_020212.pdf
- ANDS: Data Management Planning, What Does a Data Management Plan Need to Cover? http://ands.org.au/guides/data-management-planning-awareness.html

Stakeholder Interviews

Don't limit your interviewing to researchers, that is, those faculty who have grants or supervise labs. Postdoctoral fellows, graduate or undergraduate students, lab technicians, and research administrators are usually the ones taking care of the day-to-day data management. It is helpful to interview them with and without the researcher you are working with. There may be a disconnect between what the researcher thinks is going on and what is actually happening. A workflow analysis is a good way of finding out what is going on with experimental data collected by a specific person. A research administrator, who in some cases might also be a postdoc, is best interviewed with the research consultation questions, followed by specific questions to learn about problems or processes that work.

Administrators in information technology or technology services, research and grants offices, and the provost's office should be interviewed to gain an institutional perspective on data. This should be during the environmental scan that is part of setting up a data management service (see chapter 9). At a more granular level, departmental grant administrators or compliance officers, research deans for schools or programs (depending on the structure of the organization), and even department heads will probably have some thoughts on data management. People who run specialized facilities or programs, such as a high-performance computing center or a digital humanities program, can often provide a wealth of information on problems and available resources.

Throughout all the interviews, especially when talking with those who provide data services, it is important to use active listening skills to gauge how the persons being interviewed feel about libraries getting into data management services. It is important to reassure them that the library does not want to take over their service, unless that is actually what they want and the library can do it. There is so much data, of so many types, being collected at all institutions, there is more than enough work for everyone. For example, the groups that deal with high-performance computing or clinical trials may not have the time to deal with small data sets or writing data management plans. Chapter 9 will cover some of the different services libraries can offer their institution.

⌾ Key Points

Having good reference interview skills can help data librarians in a variety of situations. Using good interview skills to draw out complete information about what a researcher expects and needs is especially important when it comes to learning about their short- and long-term storage and computing needs, an area prone to misunderstanding.

- Sense-making questions and active listening are important when trying to understand the data management needs of researchers.
- Data librarians need to be flexible with interview formats. Fit the format and questions to the desired outcome of the interview.
- Be prepared for consultations and interviews by reviewing available interview and DMP outline resources to develop a customized list of questions for researchers.
- Helpful information for data management can be collected from many people around the organization.

An understanding of the whole data life cycle, including how data is stored, organized, described, shared, and preserved, is useful even when a data librarian is only working on certain aspects of the data life cycle, so the next few chapters will cover these areas, starting with storage and preservation.

References

AHRQ (Agency for Healthcare Research & Quality). 2016. "Workflow Assessment for Healthcare IT Toolkit." Accessed June 7, 2016. https://healthit.ahrq.gov/health-it-tools-and-resources/workflow-assessment-health-it-toolkit.

Barsky, Eugene. 2014. "Assessing Researchers' Data Needs—Research Data Discovery Manual." *Canadian Community of Practice for Research Data Management in Libraries* (blog). July 28. http://data-carl-abrc.ca/2014/07/28/assessing-researchers-data-needs-research-data-discovery-manual/.

Carlson, Jake R. 2011. "Demystifying the Data Interview: Developing a Foundation for Reference Librarians to Talk with Researchers about Their Data." *Reference Services Review* 40, no. 1: 7–23.

Choudhury, Sayeed. 2013. "Open Access & Data Management Are Do-Able through Partnerships." Talk presented at ASERL Summertime Summit, Atlanta, August 6. https://smartech.gatech.edu/handle/1853/48696.

Del Fiol, Guilherme, T. Elizabeth Workman, and Paul N. Gorman. 2014. "Clinical Questions Raised by Clinicians at the Point of Care: A Systematic Review." *JAMA Internal Medicine* 174, no. 5: 710–18.

Dervin, Brenda. 1998. "Sense-Making Theory and Practice: An Overview of User Interests in Knowledge Seeking and Use." *Journal of Knowledge Management* 2, no. 2: 36–46.

Dervin, Brenda, and Patricia Dewdney. 1986. "Neutral Questioning: A New Approach to the Reference Interview." *RQ* 25, no. 4: 506–13.

Dewdney, Patricia, and Gillian Michell. 1997. "Asking 'Why' Questions in the Reference Interview: A Theoretical Justification." *Library Quarterly* 67, no. 1: 50.

Hoppe, Michael H. 2006. *Active Listening: Improve Your Ability to Listen and Lead.* Greensboro, N.C.: Center for Creative Leadership.

Partlo, Kristin. 2009. "The Pedagogical Data Reference Interview." *IASSIST Quarterly* 33, no. 4: 6–10. http://www.iassistdata.org/sites/default/files/iq/iqvol334_341partlo.pdf.

Rinehart, Amanda K. 2015. "Getting Emotional about Data: The Soft Side of Data Management Services." *C&RL News* 76, no. 8 (September): 437–40.

Ross, Catherine Sheldrick, Kirsti Nilsen, and Marie L. Radford. 2009. *Conducting the Reference Interview: A How-To-Do-It Manual for Librarians.* 2nd ed. New York: Neal-Schuman.

RUSA (Reference and User Services Association). 2013. "Guidelines for Behavioral Performance of Reference and Information Service Providers." http://www.ala.org/rusa/resources/guidelines/guidelinesbehavioral.

Smith, Nathan M., and Stephen D. Fitt. 1982. "Active Listening at the Reference Desk." *RQ* 21, no. 3: 247–49.

Tenopir, Carol, Robert J. Sandusky, Suzie Allard, and Ben Birch. 2014. "Research Data Management Services in Academic Research Libraries and Perceptions of Librarians." *Library & Information Science Research* 36, no. 2: 84–90.

University of British Columbia Library. 2014. "Research Data Discovery Manual." In partnership with the Centre for Hip Health and Mobility. http://library-escience-collab.sites.olt.ubc.ca/files/2014/07/UBCLibrary_CHHM_RDMP_Manual_DataFlowAndNeedsDiscoverySessionManual_20140425_v11.pdf.

Witt, Michael, and Jake R. Carlson. 2007. "Conducting a Data Interview." Contributed paper presented at the 3rd International Digital Curation Conference, Washington, D.C., December 12–13.

Witt, Michael, Jacob Carlson, D. Scott Brandt, and Melissa H. Cragin. 2009. "Constructing Data Curation Profiles." *International Journal of Digital Curation* 4, no. 3: 93–103.

Storing, Curating, and Preserving Data

WHEN RESEARCHERS AND LIBRARIANS START talking about storing, curating, and preserving data, there may be misconceptions about what is going on. Researchers need to store data as they are collecting it. Some data may be data in physical forms, lab notebooks, printouts, and so forth, and usually there is digital data, spreadsheets, images, and the like. They may also need access to high-performance computing for processing of their data. Once they have finished analyzing their data, researchers need to save the data, at least for the length of time required by their funders or institutions. With new regulations in some countries, researchers will need to provide public access to the data supporting their grant-funded publications. Some researchers will be interested in depositing their data into a subject repository or other repository for long-term storage. But researchers will usually call all of these activities data storage, while librarians usually see storing and preserving as different things—that is, final research data should be stored for the required time period, but only some of that data might be worth preserving.

Dealing with Data during Research

Faculty and researcher surveys have shown that access to data storage, the media to which data files and software is saved, is one of their top needs. Brian Westra (2010) found that data storage and backup is a top data management issue during interviews with twenty-five scientists at the University of Oregon. At the University of Minnesota, four surveys were compiled, and storage and repositories were important needs (Johnson, Butler, and Johnston, 2012). The top three issues at the University of Nottingham were data management plans, storage, and metadata (Parsons, 2013). A large survey of 1,329 scientists (Tenopir et al., 2011) found that 29.2 percent agree strongly that they are satisfied with storing their data during the life of their project, but 43.9 percent only somewhat agreed (see figure 5.1).

Data storage is often institution dependent, so an environmental scan of institutional resources is a good first step for librarians setting up RDM services (see chapter 9). It may take some digging to find out how much network storage is allocated to each faculty member, by their department and/or the institution, and who maintains and sets up permissions for that storage. Don't forget to include options from the institutional repository, and locations that could be used to store physical materials. External storage, be it cloud, devices such as USB flash drives, or DVDs, need to be researched as well. Knowledge of storage availability is integral to a good data management plan, so any librarian helping with data management needs to research the latest possibilities for immediate and long-term storage.

Some researchers will find having their group's computers hooked up to networked servers to deposit data in a shared drive adequate for their needs, but others will prefer to buy their own external storage and servers, or use cloud services, or use a combination of institutional, personal, and cloud. A survey by Amanda Lea Whitmire, Michael Boock, and Shan C. Sutton (2015) found that more than 50 percent of respondents from the Colleges of Earth, Ocean and Atmospheric Sciences, Engineering, Science, and Vet Med, at the Oregon State University, use their own research group servers, although Engineering and Vet Med also use college and departmental servers as well.

I am satisfied with the process for...	Agree Strongly	Agree Somewhat	Neither Agree Nor Disagree	Disagree Somewhat	Disagree Strongly
... collecting my research data.	410 (31.6%)	626(48.2%)	139 (10.7%)	112 (8.6%)	11 (0.8%)
... searching for my own data.	298 (23.2%)	600 (46.7%)	230 (17.9%)	141 (11%)	16 (1.2%)
... cataloging/describing my data.	226 (18%)	526 (41.8%)	273 (21.7%)	194 (15.4%)	40 (3.2%)
... storing my data during the life of the project (short-term).	376 (29.2%)	559 (43.5%)	189 (14.7%)	143 (11.1%)	19 (1.5%)
... storing my data beyond the life of the project (long-term).	206 (16%)	369 (28.6%)	271 (21%)	334 (25.9%)	111 (8.6%)
... analyzing my data.	383 (29.7%)	598 (46.4%)	177 (13.7%)	118 (9.1%)	14 (1.1%)

doi:10.1371/journal.pone.0021101.t005

Figure 5.1. Scientists' Satisfaction with Current Practices. *Source:* Tenopir et al., 2011

DATA STORAGE OPTIONS

- Personal computers and laptops—The internal hard drives on these devices are fine for storing data during collection or while working on it, but the data should be backed up in other locations. Need to make sure there is adequate security and carry out regular backups. Need to send data to collaborators, so version control can be an issue. Laptops, especially, can be lost.
- Network storage—Usually has backup and security protocols that are needed, and allows for collaboration among group members at the same institution. All group members have access to the most recently uploaded data. Can be limited in size, or expensive.
- External storage devices—An external hard drive can be used to store large amounts of data and most allow automatic backups of data on the computer. An external server can be set up to allow access for multiple people. If the device is in the same location as the computer(s) it is backing up, there can be similar security issues, for example, theft, fire, and so forth.
- Removable storage devices—USB flash drives, CDs, and DVDs can all be used to store and transfer data. There are some size limitations, though, and backups are not automatic. Encryption should be used to protect stored data. Labeling, both on the outside of the device and adding a name to the device so it shows up when inserted in a computer, will make it easier to find required data later or share the proper data. These devices are easy to store in another location, but loss and damage will always be a concern.
- Remote storage—There are many free and fee-based cloud storage and data sharing services. They are generally easy to use, allow for secure access, and provide backup services. But before using any remote storage, it is important to read the provider contracts and institutional policies and funder requirements. Some cloud services may not be secure enough for all types of data. Some may have storage limits and automatically delete past versions of a file. And there can be issues of data loss if the provider goes bankrupt. Institutionally provided cloud services usually have different contracts, making them similar to institutionally provided network storage, with the advantage of being off-site.
- Physical storage—Standard naming conventions used for computer files can be used to label containers for physical specimens, paper copies of surveys, or printouts, anything that must be secure and identified later. Having a digital file that documents the locations of specimens, tapes, and the like, will reduce the chance of losing things. Information about who owns the object will help with the return of lost objects. Scanning is a useful backup for lab notebooks, surveys, printouts, and so forth. Scanned files can then be dealt with the same way digital data is handled.

(Adapted from Canavan, McGinty, and Reznik-Zellen, 2016)

Knowing the potential storage needs of a researcher will help dictate the storage services that can be used. Estimating the amount of data a research project will collect should be part of the data interview (see chapter 4) with a researcher or research group. It may be that departmental servers can't handle the amount of storage needed, and so other options must be considered. Cost can also be a factor. Often, it is cheaper to purchase a few terabytes of external storage than to use institutional facilities that have maintenance fees. But, researchers should remember that institutional servers have regular backup schedules, so they already have a second copy of their data (see the next section, "Backing Up Data"), and they regularly upgrade the hardware and software to keep the server running efficiently. As discussed in chapter 3, institutions own the data from federal funded research, and many institutions are starting to provide unlimited cloud or institutional server storage for all faculty or researchers, in recognition of the institution's stake in the data collected.

Researchers should also consider who will be working with their data and where those people are located. Even if a researcher is working alone, data stuck on the hard drive of a computer the researcher can't access from home will be frustrating. Networked servers or cloud storage solutions will need to be explored, and these options should be part of the environmental scan conducted by librarians who will be providing data management services. Research groups need to schedule data uploads from equipment or personal computers to the group folders so everyone is working with the most recent version of the data.

Micro data centers are an emerging technology that can help with data collection, storage, and analysis (Gartner, 2015). With built-in power, fire and environmental protection, seismic resistance, built-in security systems, and in some cases electromagnetic suppression systems, these centers are useful if research is being done in physically remote or inhospitable locations with no Internet access. As with any type of remote or external storage, there should be plans for data backup when feasible.

Data librarians should also be prepared to recommend that a researcher add storage costs to grant application budgets. Many funders now recognize that data storage is a necessary cost of research and are willing to provide funds. While researchers might not want to use part of a limited budget for storage, when they could instead pay somebody to

OPEN SCIENCE FRAMEWORK
FROM THE CENTER FOR OPEN SCIENCE

The Center for Open Science (COS, http://centerforopenscience.org/) was founded in 2013 in Charlottesville, Virginia, to provide free, open source products and services for researchers, including Open Science Framework (OSF, https://osf.io/), a cloud-based open lab notebook that includes project management software. At this time, the service is free, with unlimited, permanent storage for those who set up accounts. The company was set up to encourage open science, so the projects can be open, but project owners have the ability to set variable permissions on all parts of their project. OSF also connects to other storage options such as Google Drive, repositories such as Figshare (http://figshare.com/), and citation managers Mendeley (https://www.mendeley.com/) and Zotero (https://www.zotero.org/).

conduct experiments for that money, it still remains an option when there are no low-cost institutional options available. There are some other no- or low-cost options available, such as the Open Science Framework (see textbox), but researchers should check with their institutional intellectual property offices and data security policies before using an outside service for data storage.

Backing Up Data

In addition to the storage needed for working data, data needs to be regularly backed up in case of data loss or corruption, disaster, and so forth. Kristin Briney (2013) recommends the "rule of three." According to this rule of thumb, there should be three copies of all data: two on-site copies and one off-site copy. The off-site copy is especially important in the case of disaster, as recent hurricanes in the United States have shown how easy it is to damage the infrastructure of an institution. But day-to-day laboratory or computer malfunctions, theft, and loss can have an impact as well. Physical storage is susceptible to similar types of data loss.

Researchers should consider all of the storage options available to them and choose a combination that fits their workflow. It may be that all data is on a primary workstation, for example, a computer hard drive, which is backed up to an external hard drive each day. The data could then be copied to a network server or cloud storage every couple of days. These backup locations need to have the same security levels as the original storage location (see "Data Security" section later in this chapter).

Once the locations for data backup are chosen, the schedule for backup must be considered. The process can be automated and scheduled through the native utilities on most computers, or through third-party or open source programs. If data is being collected daily, and the experiments are expensive or impossible to replicate, then daily backup to at least one location is prudent. If equipment is being used by multiple people, then backing up and removing data from that piece of equipment after each experiment will ensure that no data is lost if another user damages the equipment. Check with the managers of networked storage for their backup protocols.

Backup utilities allow for different backup procedures, depending on how much needs to be saved and how often backups are done.

Full backup:
- Replicates all the files on the computer
- Includes software and other customized scripts
- Takes a long time
- Requires large amounts of storage
- Is the most complete method
- Restores quickly

Differential incremental backup:
- Copies only files that have changed since last full or incremental backup
- Is generally fast
- Requires least amount of storage
- Is time consuming to restore
- Requires going through each incremental backup since last full backup to restore

Cumulative incremental backup:
- Copies only those files that have changes since last full backup
- Creates full backup if no previous backup was done
- Only requires last full and last incremental to restore

Notebooks should be scanned on the same schedule as you would back up a computer drive. The scans can be e-mailed or saved to a folder based on the organizing system used, making them an easy way for researchers to check on the progress of the staff and students in their research groups, as well as backing up the work. As with other digital data, the notebook scans should be backed up in another location.

Testing the backup system at least once can help ensure the procedure works and data remains accessible. Backup systems should also be reconsidered every few years in case there are new institutional resources or new technology that would make the process easier, faster, or less expensive.

Working with Data

After collecting and managing data, researchers need to analyze their data (see figure 2.1 in chapter 2). Data analysis takes on many forms. Survey data needs could be analyzed with software such as SPSS (http://www.spss.co.in/) or R (https://www.r-project.org/). Some researchers may create their own programs with Python (https://www.python.org/). Qualitative data could be run through NVivo (http://www.qsrinternational.com/products_nvivo.aspx) for analysis, or any of the other digital research tools listed in DiRT (http://dirtdirectory.org/). Not all libraries will offer these sorts of analysis services, and not every data librarian can help with these services, but librarians can play a role in this phase of the research life cycle by knowing where researchers can find the help they need.

The range of programs and expertise at any institution varies. In some cases, the demand for a specific type of analysis will be strong enough that there will be an institutional commitment to providing a computer program and training for everyone who needs it, including the server that does the processing. In other institutions, researchers might need to find the local expert, and learn from that person, or they may want to collaborate with the expert so they don't have to learn a new program or train a student to use it.

Larger computing projects, with massive storage needs, will also have greater processing needs. In many cases, these researchers will not involve the library. Usually they know what they need and will include the costs on a grant. Conducting data interviews (see chapter 4) with researchers who already have a good data analysis solution in place can help librarians learn more about what is available at their institution and the variation in data management practices. Whatever the situation, data analysis options should be a part of the environmental scan done when starting a data management service.

⦿ Data Security

Data security plans should consider who can have access to the data, the security of the storage medium, and mechanisms that ensure data is not manipulated. At all stages of storage and preservation, the security requirements of the storage solution need to fit the sensitivity level of the data.

Institutions usually have a security policy that will classify data by sensitivity level. The number of levels and the naming of the levels can differ from place to place, but generally the levels range from public information that can be shared to highly sensitive data that would harm individuals or the university if it was shared. For example, the Harvard University policy has five levels (http://vpr.harvard.edu/pages/harvard-research-data-security-policy), Boston University has four levels (http://www.bu.edu/tech/about/policies/info-security/1-2-a-data-classification-guide/), and Carnegie Mellon University has three levels (http://www.cmu.edu/iso/governance/guidelines/data-classification.html). The policy can then be used to label institutional servers that are adequate for each sensitivity level. Servers with restricted access, proper firewalls, antivirus software, encryption capabilities, and regular hardware upgrade plans are usually provided by information technology departments for data with higher sensitivity levels.

Human subjects research that could contain identifying data or personal health information must include data security plans in the institutional review board (IRB) project application. Institutions that provide patient care must have security provisions adequate for Health Insurance Portability and Accountability Act (HIPAA) rules. Katherine G. Akers and Jennifer Doty (2013) found that while researchers in arts and humanities, social sciences, medical sciences, and basic sciences had statistically significant differences in their research data management needs, the social sciences and medical sciences researchers had similar concerns about the confidentiality and privacy of their data. Even if there is no human subjects research being conducted at an institution, confidential data or sensitive data such as social security numbers, credit card numbers, and other types of personal data will need secure servers, so there should be some help available for sensitive data.

Data classification policies may also include requirements for physically stored data as well. Removable computer storage devices need encryption if they contain sensitive data. Notebooks and removable computer storage devices should be in locked rooms or cabinets with limited access.

Keeping research data secure requires researchers to know the activities of those who collect, process, analyze, and share their data. The best way to do this is to have a unique sign-on for each person who is part of the team. If possible, people should only be given access to the folders they need for their work, and they should only be able to view or add to files, but not delete anything. Access to computers should also be based on the work each person is doing. Not all people who collect data need administrative privileges on each computer. Requiring unique ID log-ins and/or security passwords for access to computers and other devices will help data security.

Institutions have more than just research data to keep secure; financial and personnel records, e-mail and other business documents, student records and course information at academic institutions, and departmental records all need some level of security. This makes data security an institutional issue, so there will be other stakeholders who can help with research data security. As mentioned above, information technology and IRBs should have some helpful data security guidelines. The Office of Research, or similar department, and the intellectual property office will also have their own expectations surrounding the security of research data. Official institutional archives or records management offices should have experience with paper and digital records. Some of the data and reports generated by grant-funded research will be covered by state or federal regulations, and archivists and records managers should be able to help with this aspect of security. It is most helpful for researchers if a data management service can point them to the necessary storage and security resources for their work. If possible, take the human subjects research training at your institution. Not only will this help you learn about sensitive data, but it will also help your understanding of the security requirements when working with this type of data.

◎ Data Curation

Data curation is the active and ongoing management of data with the object of adding value to data to make it more usable in the future. It is useful to think about data collected in a physical form first, something like the observations and notes from Jane Goodall's work on chimpanzees mentioned in chapter 2. Knowing the current reputation of Jane Goodall and the importance of her work, it is an easy decision to save all her raw data, and even convert the notebooks and audio and video materials into digital formats so people don't have to travel to the Duke archives to use the data. But, most archives have limited space in their physical archives, so choosing the materials that should be saved has always been necessary. Archivists, curators, and librarians who work with these materials must decide on what is worth saving based on the subject matter, the condition of the materials, and the potential future use. With the decreasing cost of computer storage, and some cloud services offering unlimited storage, it is tempting to save all the digital data. But just saving the digital data files isn't enough.

If the files aren't described, they can't be found, so there must be some attempt to add descriptions to the file. And if there are no explanations about how the data was collected and what each data point means, the data won't be usable. If there are errors or ambiguous numbers, the data will need to be cleaned. And if the format of the files is proprietary, somebody needs to convert the data to an open format (and check the data integrity afterward) or save the software version needed to access the data or constantly upgrade the data for new versions of the software (and check the data integrity afterward).

Then, when the files are useful and readable, there must be regular backups (remember the rule of three). Somebody needs to manage the backups. And all the servers involved will need regular upgrades in order to have secure long-term preservation. With all that needs to be done with digital data, the costs of maintaining physical storage are comparable to those of maintaining digital storage, so it is impossible for all the data to be preserved past the institutional or funder retention requirements. Working with existing institutional archives or records management staff is a good way to start developing data curation policies that will help with the choices that must be made for long-term preservation.

Researchers will need to be aware of data curation criteria when they attempt to deposit their data into a repository. Subject repositories are generally very careful about the data they accept, especially if funding is limited, and require data to be appraised before acceptance. Researchers should be aware of this possibility when they list a repository on their data management plan and should have a second repository option in mind. Following repository requirements for documentation, size and format, licensing, copyright, permissions, and so forth, ahead of time will make acceptance more likely.

CRITERIA FOR DATA APPRAISAL

- Relevance to mission: Does the subject of the data fit with the goals and priorities of the institution? Is there a legal requirement to keep the data?
- Scientific or historical value: Is the data scientifically, socially, or culturally significant? For example, is it part of a larger project or important historical event?
- Uniqueness: Is the data set the only available copy? This might apply more to notebooks, or other physical data.
- Potential for redistribution: Is the data in a format that is reliable and usable, with reasonable criteria for future use if there are restrictions due to intellectual property or confidentiality issues?
- Nonreplicability: Is the data costly to replicate or was it derived from unrepeatable observations?
- Economic case: Are there future benefits to the data that justify the costs of curating and preserving it?
- Full documentation: Is all the metadata and documentation in order? Can the data be easily found with the descriptors provided? Is the provenance complete?

(Adapted from Whyte and Wilson, 2010)

Data Preservation

Many researchers will only worry about preserving their data for as long as their grant or other regulations require (see "Data Retention Requirements" section below), and they will only make their data available to others if they have a grant or journal that requires sharing or public access. But there are other reasons to preserve data that researchers should consider:

- Verification of published findings: Preserved data allows research to be reproduced or verified. This has been known to happen after the usual retention period required by grants. In 2015, a 2003 paper was called into question because of omitted data (Palus, 2015).
- Future use: The data could be used for further analysis when combined with other data or using new methods. This could be done by the researcher alone, or in collaboration with others, as well as a third-party (i.e., shared) analysis (see chapter 7).
- Promotion and tenure: If data is used and cited, it could increase the citation rate of published findings.
- Community resource development: The data could become part of a reference set, a methods collection, or a domain database, for example, National Center for Biotechnology Information (NCBI) databases (http://www.ncbi.nlm.nih.gov/).
- Learning and teaching: Using data in a teaching resource or public engagement activity can help others understand the research being done and contribute to broader impact. This can be very helpful for NSF grants.

- Personal use: Researchers will be able to find their data and use it more easily in the future if they have properly preserved it.

Like data curation, data preservation benefits from collaboration with archivists. Most archives already have some digital content, so there will be policies and preservation options that can be adopted for digital data. And archivists will be able to discuss the environmental conditions necessary for preservation of physical materials. In some situations, the institutional archives may be the best location for the preservation of data, so data librarians should have a good working relationship with archivists.

Data Retention Requirements

As well as funder requirements for data sharing and data management plans, some funders specify how long data should be kept after a particular award has been completed. Some tie the retention period to the data of the grant, others to the last paper produced by the grant. On top of funder requirements, there are often institutional records management requirements. Many institutions expect records related to grants and awards to be kept for a minimum amount of time, but they may not require every bit of data or documentation to be kept. Usually final reports that are sent to funders and some of the financial records are kept permanently. But different places have different policies about what must be kept and for how long. Depending on the institution, there may be local, state, or federal records management regulations that should also be consulted. Talking with the people in records management or institutional archives should also be included in the environmental scan. Not only will they be able to provide the regulations related to data retention, but they should have some knowledge of long-term data preservation policies, and access to forms needed for destruction of files and documents (if necessary).

Data retention requirements may also include the need to provide public access to the data. Most of the forthcoming policies for grants based on the Office of Science and Technology Policy memo (OSTP, 2013), specify that the digital data that supports a peer-reviewed paper must be made publicly available at the time of the paper or within twelve months. This may not be all the data affiliated with the grant, and it is possible that some data is never used in a publication, so different requirements can impact different data sets held by a researcher. Analog data does not fall under these policies, but samples, software, models, curriculum materials, and other products of research are part of NSF and NIH data sharing policies, so they should be included when thinking about data management and preservation.

Repositories

General, subject, and institutional repositories can all be good options for storing data long term and fulfilling sharing and, in some cases, public access, requirements of funders and journals. A repository also allows researchers to deposit their data when a project is done and not have to worry about giving access when requested, or taking care of maintenance and backups. Considerations when deciding upon a repository, whether it be to store data for the mandated period of time or for longer-term preservation, can be found in the textbox.

REPOSITORY CONSIDERATIONS

- Is the repository reliable and stable? Will it be around in five or ten years? What is the funding mechanism?
- Are other researchers in the discipline using the repository? NSF refers to this as the "community of practice."
- Are the security practices clear and appropriate for the types of data in the repository?
- What are the terms of use? What rights and licensing agreements must be signed in order to deposit data? Do these conflict with funder requirements of institutional intellectual property or data ownership policies?
- Are the policies for acceptable deposits clear? Are the deposit requirements clear?
- Does the repository allow the data set to be easily cited?
- Is there a persistent identifier, DOI, or the like?
- Is the repository indexed by major search engines? Does the repository use the Open Archives Initiative Protocol for Metadata Harvesting (OAI/PMH) or something similar?
- Is the repository considered "trusted," "appropriate," or "approved" by the funder or journal? For example, the journal *Scientific Data* publishes data articles but does not host data, so they provide a list of recommended data repositories (http://www.nature.com/sdata/data-policies/repositories).
- Does the repository allow for embargoes that might be required by publishers, funders, institutions, and so forth?
- Does the repository follow standards? Certification and standardization, such as the Trusted Repository Audit and Certification (TRAC) ISO Standard 16363, are in the early stages of development, but over time, more repositories will work toward certification.
- Does the repository provide any download metrics?
- What are the costs? Is there a one-time charge or a recurring payment?
- Are there appropriate deaccessioning/data removal procedures and clear policies about what can or should be removed?

(Based on White et al., 2013, and Lowe, White, and Gustainis, 2016)

General repositories permit deposit of data sets in any subject area, but there may be size or format limitations associated with free accounts, and long-term preservation may not be guaranteed. Paid accounts have more options, and more are reliable for preservation. Some general repositories, such as Figshare and Dryad, have affiliations with various journals to allow deposit of data connected with an article. The long-term preservation is then paid for by the journal.

Subject repositories often have better curation, although that usually means there needs to be more data documentation and metadata for a data set before it can be accepted into the repository. If researchers plan on depositing their data in a subject repository, they should review the policies for deposit early on in their research so they can take into account formatting requirements, documentation requirements, permissions, anonymization, and so forth, as well as any costs associated with the curation and preservation of the data.

Institutional repositories (IRs) can be either dedicated data repositories, or all-format repositories that could include preprints, articles, theses and dissertations, posters, reports, videos, data, and so forth. Some institutions have open access policies or other policies that require all peer-reviewed publications to be deposited in their IR. Data may or may not be included, so review any policies when looking into data deposit. Some funders and journals require a persistent identifier for data sets, to reduce the chance of bad links from agency data catalogs or articles. Again, check the appropriate policies or requirements before deciding on the IR for deposit.

Technology and resources related to data storage and preservation are constantly changing at an institutional level and with external data options. Funders, especially those complying with the OSTP memo, are refining their policies and developing data and article catalogs or repositories. Librarians working with data will need to keep up with the technology and policy changes that will impact the researchers at their intuitions.

Key Points

Researchers' understanding and needs for data storage and preservation vary wildly.

- Review all funder, journal, and institutional policies for data security, storage, and preservation requirements when working on any new grant or project.
- Understand that not all data needs full documentation and extended long-term preservation, and help researchers decide what works best for their data.
- Keep updated with repository and journal requirements to best advise researchers where and how to deposit their data.

Having things properly stored and preserved is only half of data management. Data also needs to be properly documented so others can find it and understand it, as will be discussed in chapter 6.

References

Akers, Katherine G., and Jennifer Doty. 2013. "Disciplinary Differences in Faculty Research Data Management Practices and Perspectives." *International Journal of Digital Curation* 8, no. 2: 5–26.

Briney, Kristin. 2013. "Rule of 3." *Data Ab Initio* (blog). November 20. http://dataabinitio.com/?p=320.

Canavan, M. J., Steve McGinty, and Rebecca C. Reznik-Zellen. 2016. "Module 4: Data Storage, Backup, and Security." New England Collaborative Data Management Curriculum, edited by Lamar Soutter Library, University of Massachusetts Medical School. Accessed June 6, 2016. http://library.umassmed.edu/necdmc/modules.

Gartner. 2015. "Gartner's 2015 Hype Cycle for Emerging Technologies Identifies the Computing Innovations That Organizations Should Monitor." Press release. August 18. http://www.gartner.com/newsroom/id/3114217.

Johnson, Layne M., John T. Butler, and Lisa R. Johnston. 2012. "Developing E-Science and Research Services and Support at the University of Minnesota Health Sciences Libraries." *Journal of Library Administration* 52, no. 8: 754–69. doi:10.1080/01930826.2012.751291.

Lowe, David B., Darla White, and Emily R. Novak Gustainis. 2016. "Module 7: Repositories, Archiving & Preservation." New England Collaborative Data Management Curriculum, edited by Lamar Soutter Library, University of Massachusetts Medical School. Accessed June 6, 2016. http://library.umassmed.edu/necdmc/modules.

OSTP (Office of Science and Technology Policy). 2013. "Memorandum for the Heads of Executive Departments and Agencies." Executive Office of the President. Accessed June 9, 2015. https://www.whitehouse.gov/sites/default/files/microsites/ostp/ostp_public_access_memo_2013.pdf.

Palus, Shannon. 2015. "Drugmaker Accused of Omitting Side Effects from 2003 Risperdal Paper." *Retraction Watch* (blog). August 12. http://retractionwatch.com/2015/08/12/drugmaker-accused-of-omitting-side-effect-data-from-2003-risperdal-paper/.

Parsons, Thomas. 2013. "Creating a Research Data Management Service." *International Journal of Digital Curation* 8, no. 2: 146–56. doi:10.2218/ijdc.v8i2.279.

Tenopir, Carol, Suzie Allard, Kimberly Douglass, Arsev Umar Aydinoglu, Lei Wu, Eleanor Read, Maribeth Manoff, and Mike Frame. 2011. "Data Sharing by Scientists: Practices and Perceptions." *PloS One* 6, no. 6: e21101. doi:10.1371/journal.pone.0021101.

Westra, Brian. 2010. "Data Services for the Sciences: A Needs Assessment." *Ariadne: A Web & Print Magazine of Internet Issues for Librarians & Information Specialists* 30, no. 64: 13–13. http://www.ariadne.ac.uk/issue64/westra.

White, Ethan P., Elita Baldridge, Zachary T. Brym, Kenneth J. Locey, Daniel J. McGlinn, and Sarah R. Supp. 2013. "Nine Simple Ways to Make It Easier to (Re)Use Your Data." *PeerJ PrePrints.* https://dx-doi-org.proxy.library.vcu.edu/10.7287/peerj.preprints.7v2.

Whitmire, Amanda Lea, Michael Boock, and Shan C. Sutton. 2015. "Variability in Academic Research Data Management Practices: Implications for Data Services Development from a Faculty Survey." *Program: Electronic Library and Information Systems* 49, no. 4. http://dx.doi.org/10.1108/PROG-02-2015-0017.

Whyte, Angus, and Andrew Wilson. 2010. "How to Appraise and Select Research Data for Curation." *DCC How-to Guides.* Edinburgh: Digital Curation Centre. http://www.dcc.ac.uk/resources/how-guides/appraise-select-data.

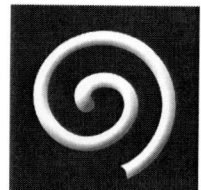

Documentation and Metadata

I T IS NOT ENOUGH TO SAVE DATA for the amount of time required by funders, institutions, or government agencies. Without adequate documentation, data can easily lose value, and the reasons for preserving that data are moot. Good documentation is essential for providing quality data for analysis, which leads to good publications. Good documentation can also help when there are transitions in the personnel of a project, or when a researcher needs to support intellectual property claims or protections. Good documentation can also back up a researcher if there are any allegations of misconduct. Metadata is a standardized and structured way to format documentation, which allows for enhanced usability and better searchability. Librarians' familiarity with ontologies and hierarchies, such as subject headings and call numbers, can support data organization. And librarians have knowledge of structured metadata, such as cataloging records, so they are well placed to provide support for researchers who need to use a specific metadata schema for their data before it can be deposited.

Documentation

Documenting research is nothing new. Alexander Graham Bell wrote about his experiments in laboratory notebooks, one of which has been scanned and can be viewed at the

Library of Congress (https://www.loc.gov/item/magbell.36500101/). Even though he wrote in the notebook between 1891 and 1893, most people viewing the pages can figure out what he was doing after a bit of time getting used to the nineteenth-century script writing. The figures and diagrams, with their accompanying notes, are all there together in the notebook. And as long as the notebook isn't lost, and there is no major damage to the book, the research notes will be usable in another hundred years.

Keeping good research notes is a little more complex now, with a mix of print and digital information being collected. Paper laboratory notebooks are used by some researchers, but taping printouts of results or images into a notebook isn't always the best way to manage data. Researchers need to be able to blend information and data coming from many sources and in many formats. Equipment might give data as digital files in various formats, for example, photos or scans of old documents and audio files from interviews, but the background information about the work is written in a notebook. Papers that are needed for research can be downloaded as PDFs and annotated in a bibliographic program such as Zotero (https://www.zotero.org/), but then notes for the research are in a different program or in a notebook. There are new electronic laboratory notebooks (ELNs) that are starting to be compatible with more and more sources of information. For example, Open Science Framework (OSF, https://osf.io), mentioned in chapter 5 as a platform with free storage for projects, is also an ELN, and integrates with Zotero for citations, as well as Figshare and GitHub, specific resources for sharing data and code, as well as many other resources. Whatever mix of resources is used, it is important for researchers to keep track of what they are doing.

Basics of Documentation

Properly documenting data starts with the best practices for documentation found in the "Collect" and "Describe" sections of chapter 3. When collecting data, it is important to consistently use naming conventions and standardized formats, and to itemize these for others in the research group and future members of the group. If one person starts a file name with his or her initials and another starts with the type of experiment, there will be confusion when looking at files. And there can be even more confusion if dates are not always in the same format.

Organization works best when researchers decide on a system for data and other resources that makes sense to them and works with their workflow. Maybe they want all their TIFF files together, so they organize by file type. Maybe the date makes sense if they are doing a longitudinal study. A researcher with multiple graduate students working on different projects may want data stored by person. A primary investigator (PI) needs to teach this organization to students and others in the lab. The PIs are the ones responsible for the data in the end, so they need to feel confident that the data is all there. A working group may want to work together to come up with a structure that works for the group. The main thing is to write out the structure and make sure everyone uses it.

File naming conventions should also be based on what makes sense for the work being done (see textbox). It is also helpful to look at the standardized values used in relevant subject repositories, if there are any. Preparing data to upload for saving and/ or sharing will be much easier if the data already adheres to the requirements of the repository. For instance, the Oak Ridge National Laboratory Distributed Active Archive Center (ORNL DAAC) is one of the NASA Earth Observing System Data and Information System (EOSDIS) data centers, which is responsible for providing scientific and other users access to data from NASA's Earth Science Missions. To facilitate data entry, guidance is provided in the Data Management for Data Providers (http://daac.ornl.gov/PI/pi_info.shtml) section of the website, which includes specifics on tabular and spatial data, and more.

POTENTIAL FILE NAME OR ORGANIZATIONAL SCHEME ELEMENTS

- File type
- Person
- Project/grant name and/or number
- Date and time of creation: useful for version control; use YYYYMMDD for easy sorting, hhmmssTZD for time (TZD = time zone)
- Name of creator/investigator: last name first followed by (initials of) first name
- Name of research team/department associated with the data
- Description of content/subject descriptor
- Data collection method (instrument, site, etc.)
- Version number
- Type of analysis

The basics of documentation are not specific to digital data; they are part of the necessary record keeping of research. Many good suggestions for how and what to document can be found in books on keeping laboratory notebooks (Kanare, 1985), chapters in books on research (Macrina, 2014; Pickard, 2013; Burroughs Wellcome Fund and Howard Hughes Medical Institute, 2006), or articles and reports on data management written by researchers (Borer et al., 2009; Hook et al., 2010; Goodman et al., 2014). Christine Borgman (2015) has excellent chapters on research methods and data practices for scholarship in the sciences, social sciences, and humanities. Librarians need to spend time learning about the norms and expectations for the areas they will be supporting, while recognizing that a broad knowledge of various types of organization can be helpful for all subjects, even art. When the Getty Research Institute received the archives of Frederick Hammersley, they discovered that the artist had kept meticulous records of how he created his paintings, with details about colors, materials, and timing (Zagorsky, 2013) that look somewhat like a laboratory notebook. These notes will help future conservation efforts of the artist's works, as well as other works of the time.

Ethics of Documentation

Documentation is a part of the responsible conduct of research. At the most basic level, proper documentation ensures that sources are credited. But keeping good notes and records also helps to show that the work appearing later in articles was actually done in the way described in the article. Good record keeping helps show that animal and human research subjects were treated properly. Grants require interim and final reports that document what was done and how money was spent. Without proper records, there is no way to support claims made in articles and reports, especially if there are negative results, which are usually harder to publish, or if there are intellectual property issues or misconduct allegations.

Good record keeping is also necessary for sharing data, which makes future analysis, publication, and collaboration possible. Clifford S. Duke and John H. Porter (2013) also suggest that a willingness to share data can increase the public trust in the results of science. Proper documentation also helps with transparency and reproducibility of research. When data is shared, those looking at it know how it was collected. Francis S. Collins and Lawrence A. Tabak (2014) mention that making data from grant-funded research available in a data discovery index (DDI) is an important part of the transparency initiatives at the National Institutes of Health.

Documenting Data Using a Data Dictionary

A data dictionary can be a very technical resource used by computer programmers when setting up and maintaining large databases. REDCap (http://projectredcap.org/), a software program used by many researchers to securely administer surveys, uses a data dictionary in this way. The REDCap data dictionary is a spreadsheet that defines the structure of a project. Each row on the spreadsheet defines the content and functions of a question or field on the data collection instrument. Technical details, such as numerical or text values, length of field, and so forth, are included in the spreadsheet.

A data dictionary can also be more like a regular dictionary or a glossary. It can be a listing of terms used in a research project with their definitions and any additional information that will help with data interpretation. For example, there might be a body weight measurement, and the data dictionary could give specifics about when the measurement is made and whether the weight is measured in grams or ounces. In some cases, it might be easier to use a separate tab in a spreadsheet if all data is tabular, so the column heading explanations stay with the spreadsheet. Figure 6.1 shows the data dictionary spreadsheet used in a collaborative project comparing the OSTP policies proposed by each U.S. govern-

4	Here is what the terms mean:		
5	Policy Coverage	Published outputs	A policy on published outputs e.g. journal articles and conference papers
6		Data	A datasets policy or statement on access to and maintenance of electronic resources
7	Policy Stipulations	Time limits	Set timeframes for making content accessible or preserving research outputs
8		Time frame	Details timeframes for making content accessible or preserving research outputs
9		DMP	Requirement to consider data creation, management or sharing in the grant application
10		Access/sharing	Promotion of OA journals, deposit in repositories, data sharing or reuse
11		Long-term curation	Stipulations on long-term maintenance and preservation of research outputs
12		Monitoring	Whether compliance is monitored or action taken such as withholding funds
13	Support Provided	Guidance	Provision of FAQs, best practice guides, toolkits, and support staff
14		Article repository	Provision of a repository to make published research articles accessible
15		Article location	Named repository where articles will be archived and made available
16		Data repository	Provision of a data repository to curate electronic resources or data
17		Dataset location	Named repository where datasets will be archived and made available
18		Costs	A willingness to meet publication fees and data management / sharing costs

+ ≡ **2** PublicAccessInfo ▾ **1** DataDictionary ▾ Contributors ▾

Figure 6.1. Data Dictionary from "A Table Summarizing the Federal Public Access Policies Resulting from the US Office of Science and Technology Policy Memorandum of February 2013." *Source:* Whitmire et al., 2015

ment agency. The main table of policy elements is the work of multiple data management community members, so it is important that everyone knows what the various terms mean.

Documenting Data Using Readme Files

Everyone knows the feeling of hearing a great piece of music or reading about a perfect book and thinking, "That is so good, I'll remember the name for later." But of course, it can't be remembered. This can also happen when researchers have to write out methods or explain their data. It is easy to think an experimental step or column label or citation will be remembered, because it seems so important at the time, but once the next experiment or project is started, things can be forgotten. One strategy is to ask researchers if they could use their own data in five years (Choudhury, 2013). Usually they realize they couldn't, so that is the time to recommend that they amend each data set with a readme file. Unlike metadata, covered in the next section, which requires specific formats, fields, and descriptors, readme files can be written in a way that makes sense to the researcher, include only the fields deemed necessary, and use natural language.

Readme files should include basics about who, what, where, when, why, and how (see textbox), but the main thing is to make sure others can understand what is in the file or folder, and that there is enough information for somebody to reuse the data. You may have seen readme files connected to software you are installing, serving the same purpose of giving you information to help with the use of the connected files. Readme files can also be used in project folders to document the reasoning of a project and list all the files

Readme files should contain:

- Who is creating the record (if there are multiple people, explain each person's role)
- Who owns the data
- What was done (by each person)
- When was the work done, clearly stating month, date, and year (use a standard format; see textbox on file naming earlier in chapter)
- Where it was done (use standard GIS formats if necessary)
- Why it was done
- What project the research is related to
- How you did it (including the methodology)
- What materials were used (e.g., reagents, surveys)
- Links to locations of any related data (e.g., if the file has processed data, where the raw data files are)

If appropriate the following could be added:

- Coding conventions used, for example, characters used for missing data or null sets, categories, classifications, acronyms, and annotations
- List of folders that relate to a project
- Interpretations
- What could be done next

that are part of that particular project. Whether they are at the project level or the folder level, readme files should be saved as TXT files, or whatever long-lived file format fits with the data, unless there are repository requirements for a different format.

The readme file layout can be set up as a template to be used throughout any project, and research or experiment folders a researcher maintains. Readme files can contain whatever a researcher feels is necessary to support the data collection, processing, and analysis methods, and the information needed for reuse of the data. Readme files complement metadata, which is machine-readable structured information based on general schema or fields specific to a subject. Figure 6.2 shows the main record for a data set in Dryad (http://datadryad.org/) that contains chimpanzee range data from the Gombe National Park. The top box, "Files in this package," contains a link to the readme file for the data, which can be seen in figure 6.3. The metadata link at the bottom of the main record goes to the structured metadata for the data (figure 6.4). The readme file includes specifics about how and where data was collected and explanations about terms. The metadata has basic citation information, the abstract (description), and subject headings, but also information specific to the paper the data supports and the unique identifier given by Dryad.

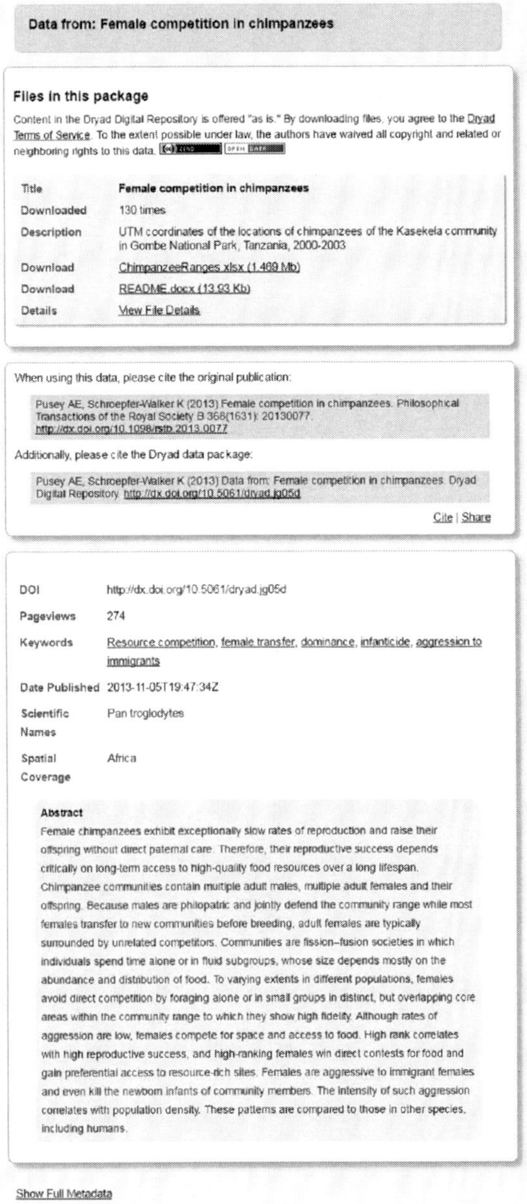

Figure 6.2. Data Record for "Female Competition in Chimpanzees" Data Set in Dryad. *Source:* Anne E. Pusey and Kara Schroepfer-Walker. 2013. Data from "Female Competition in Chimpanzees." Dryad Digital Repository. http://dx.doi.org/ 10.5061/dryad.jg05d

README

File: ChimpanzeeRanges

This file contains two sheets: AllPoints, AlonePoints

AllPoints

This sheet contains the XY UTM (zone 35M) coordinates of the locations of focal chimpanzees recorded every 15 minutes during day-long focal follows of adult chimpanzees of the Kasekela community at Gombe National Park, Tanzania in 2000-2003. It contains the following columns:

Follow Date: Date of the focal follow: Day-Month-Year

Sequence #: Consecutive 15 minute points for each follow, starting at #1 for the first observation of the day

X Coordinate: UTM coordinate, zone 35M

Y Coordinate: UTM coordinate, zone 35M

We used BIOTAS to calculate minimum convex polygons around these points.

AlonePoints

This sheet contains the XY UTM (zone 35M) coordinates of the first location on which a female was seen alone (including with her dependent offspring and adult daughters), during follows of any chimpanzee each day in 2000-2003. Females are classified as high (H), medium (M), or low (L) (see text of paper). Different females have different numbers (H1, H2, etc.). It contains the following columns:

ID: Identity of the female

Date: Date on which the female was seen alone: Day-Month-Year

X COORD: UTM coordinate, zone 35M

Y COORD: UTM coordinate, zone 35M

We used BIOTAS to calculate 50% minimum convex polygons around the points for each female.

Figure 6.3. Readme Data for "Female Competition in Chimpanzees" Data Set in Dryad. *Source:* Anne E. Pusey and Kara Schroepfer-Walker. 2013. Data from "Female Competition in Chimpanzees." Dryad Digital Repository. http://dx.doi.org/ 10.5061/dryad.jg05d

dc.contributor.author	Pusey, Anne E.
dc.contributor.author	Schroepfer-Walker, Kara
dc.coverage.spatial	Africa
dc.date.accessioned	2013-11-05T19:47:34Z
dc.date.available	2013-11-05T19:47:34Z
dc.date.issued	2013-10-28
dc.identifier	doi:10.5061/dryad.jg05d
dc.identifier	doi:10.5061/dryad.jg05d
dc.identifier.citation	Pusey AE, Schroepfer-Walker K (2013) Female competition in chimpanzees. Philosophical Transactions of the Royal Society B 368(1631): 20130077.
dc.identifier.uri	http://hdl.handle.net/10255/dryad.52993
dc.description	Female chimpanzees exhibit exceptionally slow rates of reproduction and raise their offspring without direct paternal care. Therefore, their reproductive success depends critically on long-term access to high-quality food resources over a long lifespan. Chimpanzee communities contain multiple adult males, multiple adult females and their offspring. Because males are philopatric and jointly defend the community range while most females transfer to new communities before breeding, adult females are typically surrounded by unrelated competitors. Communities are fission–fusion societies in which individuals spend time alone or in fluid subgroups, whose size depends mostly on the abundance and distribution of food. To varying extents in different populations, females avoid direct competition by foraging alone or in small groups in distinct, but overlapping core areas within the community range to which they show high fidelity. Although rates of aggression are low, females compete for space and access to food. High rank correlates with high reproductive success, and high-ranking females win direct contests for food and gain preferential access to resource-rich sites. Females are aggressive to immigrant females and even kill the newborn infants of community members. The intensity of such aggression correlates with population density. These patterns are compared to those in other species, including humans.
dc.relation.haspart	doi:10.5061/dryad.jg05d/1
dc.relation.isreferencedby	doi:10.1098/rstb.2013.0077
dc.relation.isreferencedby	PMID:24167307
dc.subject	Resource competition
dc.subject	female transfer
dc.subject	dominance
dc.subject	infanticide
dc.subject	aggression to immigrants
dc.title	Data from: Female competition in chimpanzees
dc.type	Article
dwc.ScientificName	Pan troglodytes
prism.publicationName	Philosophical Transactions of the Royal Society B

Figure 6.4. Metadata for "Female Competition in Chimpanzees" Data Set in Dryad. *Source:* Anne E. Pusey and Kara Schroepfer-Walker. 2013. Data from "Female Competition in Chimpanzees." Dryad Digital Repository. http://dx.doi.org/ 10.5061/dryad.jg05d

⌾ Metadata

As Jake R. Carlson notes, "Researchers have varying degrees of understanding about metadata, but often do not have a sense of what metadata should be applied to their data set to enable it to be discovered, understood, administered, or used by others" (2012: 17). Metadata is structured information about an item. Something like a MARC record with lots of labeled fields (see figure 6.4). Metadata is used to describe the object, give administrative information such as ownership and rights, and describe the structure of an item, which can be very important when there are multiple files. Marcus Banks points out that "librarianship gave the world the conceptual tools for classifying and organizing information" (2015), so helping researchers create and use metadata is well within the scope of libraries.

Why Add Metadata?

Metadata is necessary to assist with the discovery of data by humans and machines, and it is an important part of the guiding principles of Force11 Fair Data Principles to make data findable, accessible, interoperable, and reusable (https://www.force11.org/group/fairgroup/fairprinciples). Metadata is associated with all four principles, including metadata having a unique identifier; metadata can be accessible even if the data are no longer available; metadata use a shared, broadly applicable language; and metadata use community standards of the research domain. These principles should make it easy to find, reuse, and cite data in the future, by making all data interoperable.

Metadata helps make sure ownership of data is indicated. Not only are there elements for creator, author, publisher, and source, but the rights element or field can indicate the type of license attached to the data, and what sort of attribution is needed. And the description field can be used to indicate any special structures or features of the data, to ensure that the data are used properly. Metadata can also help researchers working with large sets of digital data. The controlled terms and structure of metadata can make searching and processing easier, and can facilitate collaboration because it will be easier to share with standardized formatting (Briney, 2015).

Finally, there are instances when researchers must add metadata, whether or not they see value in it for themselves. Metadata will be required for many of the new OSTP policies. The deposit of metadata in an agency database, even when the data is housed in a subject or institutional repository, is necessary for the agencies to have "an approach for optimizing search, archival, and dissemination features that encourages innovation in accessibility and interoperability, while ensuring long-term stewardship of the results of federally funded research," as listed in Section 2(c) in the Office of Science and Technology Policy memo (OSTP, 2013). Grants could require deposit to a specific repository, for example, the National Center for Biotechnology Information (NCBI) for genetic data, with their own metadata requirements, so it is important to read grants thoroughly and read over deposit requirements before starting to collect data (i.e., while writing the data management plan).

Basic Metadata

Data could be deposited as a single spreadsheet, it could be a series of spreadsheets representing different experiments needed to support a hypothesis, it could be a series of photographic studies for a final painting, or it could be a series of scans of a diary used for historical research. Each of these data sets can be considered a single resource when creating metadata. Laura Krier and Carly A. Strasser (2014) discuss three types of metadata, covering administrative, descriptive, and structural information about a resource (see textbox).

TYPES OF METADATA

- Administrative—creator, when and how a file is created, preservation details, IP rights
- Descriptive—describes the resource, whole data set and each element of the set, subject terms, resource type, abstract
- Structural—physical and logical structure of resource, relationship between files, ordering of files

One of the most widely adopted metadata schemas is Dublin Core. It is used for all types of resources and forms the basis for many other specialized schemas. The Dublin Core Metadata Element Set (http://dublincore.org/documents/dces/) includes the fifteen elements that have been found necessary to provide standard documentation for a resource. These elements can be found as the basis for other schemas that add elements specific to the resource type or subject (see section below). The textbox lists the core elements and gives some examples of how they relate to data. For large data sets, there could be metadata at the project level, describing the entire grouping of data, and at the data level, describing a specific data file, or set of related files.

DUBLIN CORE METADATA ELEMENT SET

- Contributor—person responsible for making contributions to the resource (e.g., primary investigator)
- Coverage—spatial or temporal topic of the resource. Applicable when the place or time of the data collection is pertinent to the research (e.g., the GIS coordinates of field locations for ecology studies)
- Creator—person responsible for data collection (e.g., graduate student)
- Date—when data was collected
- Description—could include abstract or other free-text account of the data, or other essential information necessary for reuse of the data
- Format—file formats, sizes, and so forth (e.g., TIFF images with resolution)
- Identifier—reference to the resource. The best would be the unique resources identifier (URI) for the deposited data, but could also be a file location if data has not been deposited
- Language—language of the resource
- Publisher—the person, organization, or service that makes the resource available (e.g., subject repository name)
- Relation—a related resource (e.g., the URI for an article that uses the data)
- Rights—property rights associated with the resource, including intellectual property rights (e.g., CC0 license)
- Source—used when the resource is derived from a related resource (e.g., the URI for a large government data set when only part of it is used for the research)
- Subject—keywords, phrases, or classification codes for the topic of the resource. Best practice is to use subject headings (see section below)
- Title—formal name of the resource
- Type—nature of the resource (e.g., data set, image, software, collection)

(Adapted from Dublin Core Metadata Element Set, Version 1.1, http://dublincore.org/documents/dces/)

When creating metadata in machine-readable formats that need to be shared electronically, syntax is needed to provide rules to structure the content. Various markup or programming languages can be used, for example, extensible markup language (XML) or resource description framework (RDF). XML and RDF have many applications outside of formatting metadata schema, so data librarians who have not learned these languages should seek out colleagues who might use these languages for cataloging or archiving resources for help.

One other basic schema is helpful when it comes to sharing. A basic schema has been developed by DataCite that includes the elements necessary for resource identification so data can be accurately identified and cited. A report by the Metadata Working Group (2015) includes the schema and instructions for use. It is especially worthwhile reviewing the elements in this schema when researchers are creating large data sets, with multiple files and types of data, which have the most potential for reuse. The report indicates that groups are working to include these elements in Dublin Core schemas, making these schemas interoperable.

Specialty Schemas

Metadata schemas have been created by many groups to support the features that are specific to certain fields of study. For example, ecology data needs to be able to support many species, locations, geographic features, climate data, and longitudinal sets, while archaeology may have some of the same needs related to location or geographic features, but there are specialized data collection and fieldwork needs that do not fit into other schemas. Even the U.S. government has created a special schema, Project Open Data Metadata Schema (https://project-open-data.cio.gov/v1.1/schema/), for the data sets that agencies send to Data.gov (https://www.data.gov/).

The choice of repository may impact the choice of a metadata schema, so it is important to check for requirements early in the research process. A specific schema might require information that can only be collected at a specific point in the research process, so it is best to find out all the details ahead of time, especially if data is observational and cannot be repeated. A selection of subject metadata schemas can be found in the textbox. More complete listings, with additional extensions and tools, are available from the Research Data Alliance (http://rd-alliance.github.io/metadata-directory/standards/) and DCC/JISC (http://rd-alliance.github.io/metadata-directory/standards/).

EXAMPLES OF METADATA SCHEMAS BY SUBJECT

Archaeology
ADS—Archaeology Data Service
http://guides.archaeologydataservice.ac.uk/g2gp/CreateData_1-2

Archives
EAD—Encoded Archival Description
http://www.loc.gov/ead/

Astronomy
Astronomy Visualization Metadata Standard
http://www.virtualastronomy.org/avm_metadata.php

Biology
DwC—Darwin Core
http://rs.tdwg.org/dwc/index.htm

Crystallography
CIF—Crystallographic Information Framework
http://www.iucr.org/resources/cif/spec

Ecology
EML—Ecological Metadata Language
https://knb.ecoinformatics.org/#external//emlparser/docs/index.html

Geography
ISO 19115 Geographic Information
https://geo-ide.noaa.gov/wiki/index.php?title=ISO_19115_Core_Elements

Microscopy
OME-XML—Open Microscopy Environment XML
http://www.openmicroscopy.org/site/support/ome-model/ome-xml/index.html

Social and Behavioral Sciences
DDI—Data Documentation Initiative
http://www.ddialliance.org/Specification/

Subject Headings and Other Standards

Librarians are very familiar with the use of subject headings or controlled vocabularies. Adding Medical Subject Headings (MeSH; https://www.nlm.nih.gov/mesh/) to articles in PubMed makes it easier to search for articles on a particular topic because all the phrases and synonyms of a term are pulled together by the subject heading. The same applies when adding documentation to data. While the readme file, or description field of a metadata record, can contain free text, the subject element of a metadata record should contain terms from a standardized listing of subject headings in order to make searching, and finding, easier. Often, controlled vocabularies are related to databases, such as the DAAI (Design and Applied Arts Index) Thesaurus or the Thesaurus of Psychological Index Terms for PsycINFO. Some controlled vocabularies exist outside of databases as well, such as the Gene Ontology (http://www.openmicroscopy.org/site/support/ome-model/ome-xml/index.html). In the absence of a specialized subject thesaurus, a general list, such as the Library of Congress Subject Headings (http://id.loc.gov/authorities/subjects.html), can be used.

As well as subjects, dates, chemical names, species names, and locations, to name a few, can have standard formats. Standards for these are usually maintained by societies and associations in the subject field. For example, the International Union of Pure and Applied Chemistry (IUPAC) has multiple nomenclature and terminology resources (http://www.iupac.org/home/publications/e-resources/nomenclature-and-terminology.html). As with metadata schema, the choice of subject headings or standards should be made based on the requirements of the repository researchers plan on using to store and share their data.

Key Points

Good documentation can increase the value of research data by ensuring that anyone looking at the data will understand it. Researchers will find it easier to work with their own data if they:

- Think about their organizational scheme
- Carefully document their projects and data
- Create long-term metadata for future use

Future use is especially important when researchers want to share their data, or are required to provide public access to their data. The next chapter will consider the ownership and licensing issues that need to be considered before data is shared or made publicly available.

References

Banks, Marcus. 2015. "Academic Librarianship: Three Wishes for 2016." Medium.com. https://medium.com/@marcusbanks/academic-librarianship-three-wishes-for-2016-8b1918f3e47c#.d8hc66g6y.

Borer, Elizabeth T., Eric W. Seabloom, Matthew B. Jones, and Mark Schildhauer. 2009. "Some Simple Guidelines for Effective Data Management." *Bulletin of the Ecological Society of America* 90, no. 2: 205–14.

Borgman, Christine L. 2015. *Big Data, Little Data, No Data: Scholarship in the Networked World.* Cambridge, Mass.: MIT Press.

Briney, Kristin. 2015. *Data Management for Researchers: Organize, Maintain and Share Your Data for Research Success.* Exeter, UK: Pelagic.

Burroughs Wellcome Fund and Howard Hughes Medical Institute. 2006. *Making the Right Moves: A Practical Guide to Scientific Management for Postdocs and New Faculty.* 2nd ed. Research Triangle Park, N.C.: Burroughs Wellcome Fund and Howard Hughes Medical Institute. http://www.hhmi.org/programs/resources-early-career-scientist-development/making-right-moves.

Carlson, Jake R. 2012. "Demystifying the Data Interview: Developing a Foundation for Reference Librarians to Talk with Researchers about Their Data." *Reference Services Review* 40, no. 1: 7–23.

Choudhury, Sayeed. 2013. "Open Access & Data Management Are Do-Able through Partnerships." Talk presented at ASERL Summertime Summit, Atlanta, August 6. https://smartech.gatech.edu/handle/1853/48696.

Collins, Francis S., and Lawrence A. Tabak. 2014. "Policy: NIH Plans to Enhance Reproducibility." *Nature* 505, no. 7485: 612–13.

Duke, Clifford S., and John H. Porter. 2013. "The Ethics of Data Sharing and Reuse in Biology." *Bioscience* 63, no. 6: 483–89. doi:10.1525/bio.2013.63.6.10.

Goodman, Alyssa, Alberto Pepe, Alexander W. Blocker, et al. 2014. "Ten Simple Rules for the Care and Feeding of Scientific Data." *PLoS Computational Biology* 10, no. 4: e1003542. doi:10.1371/journal.pcbi.1003542.

Hook, Les A., Suresh K. Santhana Vannan, Tammy W. Beaty, Robert B. Cook, and Bruce E. Wilson. 2010. *Best Practices for Preparing Environmental Data Sets to Share and Archive.* Oak Ridge, Tenn.: Oak Ridge National Laboratory Distributed Active Archive Center. http://daac.ornl.gov/PI/BestPractices-2010.pdf.

Kanare, Howard M. 1985. *Writing the Laboratory Notebook.* Washington, D.C.: American Chemical Society.

Krier, Laura, and Carly A. Strasser. 2014. *Data Management for Libraries.* Chicago: ALA TechSource.

Macrina, Francis L. 2014. *Scientific Integrity Text and Cases in Responsible Conduct of Research.* 4th ed. Washington, D.C.: ASM.

Metadata Working Group. 2015. "DataCite Metadata Schema for the Publication and Citation of Research Data." Version 3.1. DataCite. http://schema.datacite.org/meta/kernel-3.1/doc/DataCite-MetadataKernel_v3.1.pdf.

OSTP (Office of Science and Technology Policy). 2013. "Memorandum for the Heads of Executive Departments and Agencies." Executive Office of the President. Accessed June 9, 2015. https://www.whitehouse.gov/sites/default/files/microsites/ostp/ostp_public_access_memo_2013.pdf.

Pickard, Alison J. 2013. *Research Methods in Information.* 2nd ed. Chicago: Neal-Schuman.

Whitmire, Amanda, Kristin Briney, Amy Nurnberger, et al. 2015. "A Table Summarizing the Federal Public Access Policies Resulting from the US Office of Science and Technology Policy Memorandum of February 2013." http://Dx.Doi.Org/10.6084/M9.Figshare.1372041.

Zagorsky, Anna. 2013. "The Value of Record Keeping: Frederick Hammersley's Painting Books." *The Iris* (blog). November 13. http://blogs.getty.edu/iris/the-value-of-record-keeping-frederick-hammersleys-painting-books/.

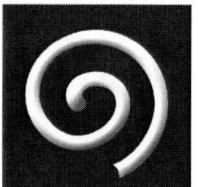

Publishing and Sharing Data

AFTER ALL THE WORK OF COLLECTING, storing, describing, cleaning, and analyzing data, researchers need to get credit for their work. Publishing an article shows their employer and funder that they have used their time and funds wisely. Sometimes, though, there is more data than can reasonably be included in an article, or there is raw data that could be valuable. While funders, such as NIH and NSF, have required sharing of data upon request, open data sharing or data publication have not been seen as worth the effort by many researchers. New funder policies that require public access to data are pushing researchers to share their data, and new peer-reviewed data journals make it easier for researchers to publish data and get credit for their work. Librarians can help by providing guidance on ownership and licensing of data, as well as directing researchers to appropriate journals and repositories for publishing and sharing of data. Libraries can help by providing institutional repositories for fields where there is no central, specialized, subject repository.

Preparing to Publish or Share Data

The reasons for data sharing and making data open are covered in the next section of this chapter, but even when data sharing is required by a funder, researchers should confirm the ownership of their data, making sure they are allowed to publicly share the data, and decide on a license to indicate to others how the data should be used and acknowledged. There are now options to have data sets peer reviewed through some data journals and repositories, which helps to legitimize the data set as scholarly output.

Data Ownership Issues

Data is governed by various laws, so some understanding of intellectual property laws is necessary. Copyright is actually a bundle of legal rights that allow the holder to publish, disseminate, create derivative works, publicly perform, and add term limits to these rights. Generally, copyright is given to works that are creative or the original expression of an idea, and work-for-hire laws often mean copyright rests with an employer. Copyright does not cover facts, so data is not subject to copyright, although a table or figure created to display data is covered by copyright. Data instead falls under other intellectual property laws, including those covered by patents. Intellectual property laws generally give ownership of things like patents and data to the funder of the work. In academia, this is often the federal government, and in 1980, the Bayh-Dole Act transferred the ownership of novel ideas and data to the institution that received the funding. At most academic institutions, copyright for scholarly works that are related to the research of an employee is given back to the employee, and while most institutions claim ownership of inventions and data, there are usually policies that share back net royalties if a patent proves fruitful and make researchers with grants the stewards of the data collected. Institutional, local, state, and federal agency regulations and policies may differ on data ownership, depending on what is collected, especially if it is human subject data, so reading the whole policy, contract, award notice, or regulation is important. Many institutions have employees, be they faculty, staff, or students, sign forms that indicate who controls intellectual property, and people often forget they have signed such a form because of all the other paperwork involved in starting a job.

A recent case highlights data ownership issues. Paul Aisen, MD, director of the Alzheimer's Disease Cooperative Study (ADCS) at the University of California, San Diego (UCSD), decided to move to the University of Southern California (USC) in June 2015. He had been in charge of the ADCS since 2007, and he was moving to become the founding director of USC's Alzheimer's Therapeutic Research Institute. He planned on taking the data from the ADCS, but UCSD immediately sued to maintain control of the large Alzheimer's study, which it established in 1991 and which receives an estimated $100 million per year in funding. A California Superior Court judge ruled in favor of UCSD in July, but there has been a countersuit filed by USC so the outcome is still uncertain (Hurley, 2015). In order to avoid cases like this, institutions have policies on data retention and transfer, as well as the need to comply with any federal policies on the transfer of grants. Most faculty moves will not be a problem, but when a valuable data set or a large grant are involved, policies and signed contracts can make the transition much easier.

Data librarians should be aware of the policies where they work and the policies and regulations of their locality, state, and federal award agencies, and they should be prepared to refer people to others in their institution who can help with legal matters. Most institutions have an office or department that takes care of intellectual property and patents and a university counsel who will deal with the legal issues surrounding these things. Supplying groups with the basics of these policies when teaching or presenting is very helpful. Often researchers do not realize that their data is owned by the institution, and students think they can just take their lab notebooks with them when they leave. The recognition of data as an asset has also spurred nongovernmental funders to include data ownership sections in their awards. Usually, this is to ensure that the data is available to others and that any discoveries, especially drug discoveries, are available to the public. But industry and business funders can be much more restrictive, so contracts from outside organizations should be inspected by university counsel before a researcher or student signs them.

Licensing

Data are facts, not novel ideas, so they cannot be copyrighted but they can be owned, as noted above, and data can be licensed. Of course, institutional intellectual property experts should be contacted first if there is some chance that a patent or other invention could be developed from the data. Licensing is one way to make data available for reuse, yet still have some control over what can be done with it, if the researcher is concerned about how others might use the data. Creative Commons licenses (https://creativecommons.org/licenses/) allow data owners to specify how their data can be used. Everything from a CC0 license, which waives all rights and puts the item in the public domain, to licenses that allow sharing with attribution, or don't allow commercial use or derivative works, are available. Researchers can use the license chooser to help decide on a license.

The Panton Principles (http://pantonprinciples.org/) were developed to specifically support open data, that is, making sure that data underlying published science is publicly available to freely download, copy, analyze, and reuse, with no legal, financial, or technical barriers. Panton Principles also support adding appropriate licensing to make sure it is clear the data is open. As well as suggesting a couple of Creative Commons licenses that are appropriate, Open Data Commons (http://opendatacommons.org/) has open licenses specific to data that can be added to any data publication.

Sensitive Data

There are many types of sensitive data: personal information, for example, social security numbers, personal health data, data that supports a patent; or confidential data for a government agency, for example, advanced technology research for NASA. There are legal issues surrounding different types of sensitive data, usually based on federal laws such as the Federal Information Security Management Act (FISMA), the Family Educational Rights and Privacy Act (FERPA), or the Health Insurance Portability and Accountability Act (HIPAA). If there is potentially sensitive data being collected and research is being done in another country, or if funds have come from another country, researchers should check the laws of those countries to be sure they have properly secured the necessary data.

The security of sensitive data was covered in chapter 5, but when sharing data, there needs to be further assessment. Researchers working with human subjects might think they can't share because of privacy issues, but many agencies are pushing to have more clinical trial data shared, especially negative data that is hard to get published.

The Institute of Medicine report *Sharing Clinical Trial Data: Maximizing Benefits, Minimizing Risk* (2015) recognizes that data sharing could improve patient care and contribute to further scientific discoveries, so they set out some principles for when and how trial data should be shared. As well as recommending the sharing of summary data for all trials, the report also recommends that raw patient data be made available, after cleaning and coding, for further analysis. The report recognizes that some data cannot be made publicly available, and policies will need to be developed to control access. The report also notes that the technology infrastructure and workforce are not yet in place for the robust sharing that should take place with clinical trial data. In the meantime, options such as registries or controlled-access databases are available if the researcher is interested in sharing or the funder requires sharing; for example, ICPSR has some data sets that require an application for use. The European Federation of Pharmaceutical Industries and Associations (EFPIA) has a clinical trial data portal gateway (http://transparency.efpia.eu/responsible-data-sharing/efpia-clinical-trial-data-portal-gateway) that links to portals at various drug companies where researchers can apply to get anonymized patient-level data and/or supporting documents from clinical studies to conduct further research.

Human studies that are not clinical trials face similar issues when considering data sharing. One potential resource is the local institutional review board (IRB) or ethics review board (ERB) that approves research protocols for human subject research. These boards are aware of the issues around confidentiality and privacy. Part of the review process looks at how data will be kept secure, so consulting with the local board will help ensure the proper security as well as any sharing constraints.

One way to share sensitive data without having to set up a controlled-access database is to anonymize or deidentify the data. In the United States, patient information is covered by the HIPAA Privacy Rule, which has two ways to deidentify data for sharing without requiring special permission, either "safe harbor" deidentification, removing eighteen types of identifiers (see "HIPAA Safe Harbor" textbox), or "expert determination," applying statistical and scientific principles and methods for rendering information not individually identifiable, with very small risk that the recipient could identify an individual. Researchers should also be aware of indirect identifiers that could be used in conjunction with each other or some knowledge of the individuals who might be in the data set, to reidentify individuals (see "Indirect Identifiers" textbox). The issue of privacy is very important and taken very seriously by HHS. Fines are regularly given out for data breaches. A stolen laptop and unencrypted backup media with records for fifty-five thousand current and former patients cost one patient care facility $750,000 (HHS Press Office, 2015). Research that involves surveys, interviews, questionnaires, and other social and behavioral research tools may not have the strict rules that govern clinical research, but there are privacy issues involved with any research that goes through a review board, and being aware of the identifiers covered by HIPAA and recognizing their importance can make the approval process easier.

HIPAA SAFE HARBOR

The following identifiers of the individual or of relatives, employers, or household members of the individual, are removed:

- Names
- All geographic subdivisions smaller than a state, including street address, city, county, precinct, ZIP code, and their equivalent geocodes, except for the initial three digits of the ZIP code if, according to the current publicly available data from the Bureau of the Census:
  (1) The geographic unit formed by combining all ZIP codes with the same three initial digits contains more than 20,000 people; and
  (2) The initial three digits of a ZIP code for all such geographic units containing 20,000 or fewer people is changed to 000
- All elements of dates (except year) for dates that are directly related to an individual, including birth date, admission date, discharge date, death date, and all ages over 89 and all elements of dates (including year) indicative of such age, except that such ages and elements may be aggregated into a single category of age 90 or older
- Telephone numbers
- Fax numbers
- Email addresses
- Social security numbers
- Medical record numbers
- Health plan beneficiary numbers
- Account numbers
- Certificate/license numbers
- Vehicle identifiers and serial numbers, including license plate numbers
- Device identifiers and serial numbers
- Web Universal Resource Locators (URLs)
- Internet Protocol (IP) addresses
- Biometric identifiers, including finger and voice prints
- Full-face photographs and any comparable images
- Any other unique identifying number, characteristic, or code

(http://www.hhs.gov/ocr/privacy/hipaa/understanding/coveredentities/De-identification/guidance.html)

Data might also be considered sensitive because of intellectual property issues surrounding proprietary or confidential information. Many government departments have confidential or sensitive information that cannot be shared. Or there may be export control laws or trade sanctions that impact sharing of data. This can be especially important to find out if a researcher is collaborating with colleagues in another country. Look for an institutional policy on compliance with U.S. export control laws, or find the department that deals with integrity and compliance. There are many laws and regulations, and they change regularly, so it is important to check with others if there is a question about the nature of the data. There are also privacy concerns about the sharing and storing of data between the United States and the European Union that may impact the sharing of data in the future, so it is very important to check with the security director for information technology if there is a chance that any type of sensitive data could be used internationally.

Publishing Data

John Kratz and Carly Strasser (2014) suggest that for data to be published, it must be available now and for the indefinite future, although there could be fees or an agreement for access; it must be adequately documented (see chapter 6); and it must be citable (see next section). Many researchers do not equate sharing their data in a repository as publication, but having data in a trusted repository (see textbox) or one that is recognized by journals or government agencies will ensure availability now and for the indefinite future. The data repository should provide a persistent identifier for the data set, so links used in citations to the data will always work. These repositories require documentation and metadata, so data sets will have the information needed to be cited. Some repositories are working to provide the curation and services needed for publication. A collaboration of the environmental data centers and Science Information Strategy (SIS) divisions of the Environmental Research Council in the UK is working to provide for formal data citations by including peer review and publication services (Callaghan et al., 2012).

If a researcher works at an institution that only recognizes journal publications for promotion and tenure, there are journals that provide peer review of data sets and publish the methods and description of the data set as an article, which has been described as a citable proxy (Lawrence et al., 2011). Generally, the data set resides in a trusted repository, the journal does not host the data set, and the description is in the journal. Some journals have added data papers as a new article type, for example, *F1000Research*, *Internet Archaeology*, and *GigaScience*, but there are also specialized data-only journals, for example, *Earth System Science Data*, *Scientific Data*, and *Open Health Data*. The Peer Review for Publication & Accreditation of Research Data in the Earth Sciences (PREPARDE) project's list of data journals (http://proj.badc.rl.ac.uk/preparde/blog/DataJournalsList) is a little out of date but helpful, because it includes some notes on scope and criteria. The list of data journals and journals that accept data papers is growing, so it is best to do an Internet search when looking for a place to publish data.

Data Citation

Getting promotion and tenure committees to recognize data as scholarly output is outside of the scope of most data librarians, but good data citation practice can be taught in classes and encouraged when working with researchers. The Force11 Joint Declaration of Data Citation Principles (https://www.force11.org/datacitation) have been developed to give the reasoning behind data citing and the need for some basic citation elements (see textbox). Bryan Lawrence et al. (2011) and Karen Patrias (2007) provide some suggested elements and formats for research that uses only parts of data sets or more complicated data sets. A specific citation format and researchers formally citing data sets they use, combined with data journals, all help to move toward the recognition of data as scholarly output.

MINIMAL DATA CITATION

Author(s)

Year

Data set title

Data repository or archive

Version

Global persistent identifier

◉ Encouraging Data Sharing and Open Data

Funding agencies, policy makers, journals, and many researchers are encouraging data sharing for various reasons, including accountability, reproducibility, transparency, and a "vast potential for scientific progress" (Fecher, Friesike, and Hebing, 2015). Scientists are slowly increasing their data sharing worldwide (Tenopir et al., 2015), but researchers are often reluctant to give up their role as "gatekeeper" of their data in order to provide public or open access to their data (Carlson, 2012). Libraries are trusted and neutral resources at most institutions, and they are known for organizing and describing materials to be found and shared, so helping researchers describe and share their data is a natural extension of library work. Data librarians can help by pointing out the many reasons for sharing data, besides compliance with funders or journals, and then help sort out ownership and licensing issues, as well as providing metadata advice, and suggesting suitable repositories for sharing data.

The open access movement has been working toward providing scholarly works "digital, online, free of charge, and free of most copyright and licensing restrictions" (Suber, 2012: 4). Open access is starting to take off because more institutions and funders are realizing that it is not fair to pay for the research to be done, and then pay again to acquire the articles about that research, or have publisher embargoes before the research can be shared. The open access movement has been focused on literature, but now funding agencies are helping to expand the focus to include other scholarly products, such as data or educational materials (Pinfield, 2015). Funding agencies have recognized in the past that data needs to be shared. The National Science Foundation (NSF) and the National Institutes of Health (NIH) have requirements for sharing of cell lines, specially bred animals, samples, DNA sequences, and so forth, as well as more traditional types of data found in lab notebooks or spreadsheets. Genomic sequence data, freely available now from the National Center for Biotechnology Information (NCBI), was one of the early fields where practitioners recognized that data must be shared for the field to grow and developed the Bermuda Principles in 1996 (Arias, Pham-Kanter, and Campbell, 2014). Now the Office of Science and Technology Policy memo (OSTP, 2013) will require public access to digital data that supports results in publications from researchers with grants from major U.S. federal funders, and many other funders and journals are requiring public access to data as well.

BENEFITS OF OPEN ACCESS

Researchers
- Increases readers' ability to find use relevant literature
- Increases the visibility, readership, and impact of author's works
- Creates new avenues for discovery in digital environment
- Enhances interdisciplinary research
- Accelerates the pace of research, discovery, and innovation

Educational Institutions
- Contributes to core mission of advancing knowledge
- Democratizes access across all institutions—regardless of size or budget
- Provides previously unattainable access to community colleges, two-year colleges, K–12 and other schools
- Provides access to crucial STEM materials
- Increases competitiveness of academic institutions

Students
- Enriches the quality of their education
- Ensures access to all that students need to know, rather what they (or their school) can afford
- Contributes to a better-educated workforce

Businesses
- Access to cutting-edge research encourages innovation
- Stimulates new ideas, new services, new products
- Creates new opportunities for job creation

Public
- Provides access to previously unavailable materials relating to health, energy, environment, and other areas of broad interest
- Creates better educated populace
- Encourages support of scientific enterprise and engagement in citizen science

Research Funders
- Leverages return on research investment
- Creates tool to manage research portfolio
- Avoids funding duplicative research
- Creates transparency
- Encourages greater interaction with results of funded research

(SPARC, 2015)

Even when researchers must share their data to comply with funder requirements, it can be helpful to point out some of the benefits of sharing and open access (see textbox). Some of the benefits are for the public good, such as promoting scientific integrity and debate, which improves research and leads to better science. But there are also reasons to share that benefit researchers directly, such as avoiding duplication of research or increased citations to papers with publicly available data (Piwowar, Day, and Fridsma, 2007; Dorch, Drachen, and Ellegaard, 2015).

Barriers to Data Sharing

Even with the many good reasons to share data, researchers will always have concerns about sharing it. Lisa M. Federer and colleagues (2015) found that while many researchers had shared data when asked by a potential collaborator, a colleague, or a junior researcher, they were less likely to deposit data in a repository. In the same study, those who hadn't shared data at all had many reasons, including lack of opportunity, human subject privacy, other privacy, and lack of knowledge about repositories and data preparation (see figure 7.1).

Carol Tenopir and colleagues conducted a baseline survey of scientists in 2011 and a follow-up in 2015 to learn about data sharing and data reuse practices and perceptions, and to track them over time. The 2015 survey found an increase in scientists' willingness to share at least some of their data without limitations since the baseline study. Many of the reasons for not sharing were similar to the Federer study: don't know of a repository, prohibited from sharing due to human subjects or other privacy issues, nobody would need or want the data, and don't know how to share. The lack of opportunity mentioned by Federer et al. (2015) could be similar to the lack of funds and insufficient time mentioned by Tenopir et al. (2015). Benedikt Fecher, Sascha Friesike, and Marcel Hebing (2015), in a systematic review of papers that surveyed academic data sharing, looked at hindering and enabling factors based on the categories of data donor, research organization, research community, norms, data recipients, and data infrastructure. They concluded that the efforts and risks of data sharing outweigh the potential individual benefits re-

	Scientific (n = 15)		Clinical (n = 5)		Total (n = 20)	
I would be willing to share my data, but I haven't had an opportunity to do so	8	53%	1	20%	9	45%
My data contains personally identifiable information and sharing would compromise my subjects' privacy	2	13%	5	100%	7	35%
I am prohibited from sharing my data for some reason other than subject privacy	2	13%	4	80%	6	30%
I don't know any repositories that accept the kind of data I produce	7	47%	2	40%	9	45%
It's too difficult to prepare my data and documentation for sharing with others	0	0%	0	0%	0	0%
I don't know how to prepare my data and documentation for sharing with others	6	40%	0	0%	6	30%
Repositories' requirements for format or description of data are too difficult to meet	0	0%	0	0%	0	0%
I don't feel I would get credit for sharing my data	1	7%	0	0%	1	5%
I put in a great deal of time and effort to gather my data, and I don't want to give it away	0	0%	1	20%	1	5%
I'm concerned that another researcher could beat me to publication if I share my data	1	7%	0	0%	1	5%
My data has commercial value, so I don't want to give it away for free	0	0%	0	0%	0	0%
I don't think anyone else would have any reason to use my data	4	27%	0	0%	4	20%
It isn't customary to share data in my research field	4	27%	3	60%	7	35%
I'm concerned another researcher might find errors in my data	0	0%	0	0%	0	0%
I'm concerned another researcher might misinterpret my data	1	7%	2	40%	3	15%

doi:10.1371/journal.pone.0129506.t016

Figure 7.1. Reasons for Not Sharing Data. *Source:* Federer et al., 2015

searchers expect. Their results indicate that researchers are mainly worried about their ownership of the data, giving them the right to publish first, and their need for control, especially the worry about data misuse.

Many of these barriers can be removed with the help of data librarians and institutional data management services. With the help of a data librarian, suitable repositories can be found, or institutional repositories can be used, and basic instruction in preparing data to share and adding metadata could be provided. If data management services have enough staff, the time factor could be removed by having personalized help to prepare data sets for sharing. Funders allow data management costs to be included in many awards, so making researchers aware of the option can help fund data management services. Data librarians can also help researchers learn how to anonymize or aggregate human subject data to help overcome any privacy issues. If there is no way to deidentify data, other options, such as registries with restricted access, could be set up to ensure only those with proper credentials can access data. Privacy issues that relate to patents should be referred to institutional intellectual property offices.

Getting Credit for Shared Data

Researchers actively try to publish their research because reward systems, such as promotion and tenure, recognize books and articles, and even posters and presentations, as scholarly output. NSF recognizes data sets as a product of research, and as more funders require public access to data, there is more chance for data reuse and data citation. In order for data and data sets to be shared widely, data must be recognized within scholarly reward systems (Costello, 2009). Tenopir et al. (2015) found that most researchers want data they provide to be acknowledged and cited in any work making use of the data. Table 7.1 shows frequencies and percentages of those who selected yes, no, or not sure to each proposed condition for the follow-up results only. As noted above, standards for data citation are being developed to allow for accurate citations, and more journals are starting to allow citations to data and other nonarticle or book resources.

In the social sciences, the field of political science encourages ethical research practices based on specific guidelines (American Political Science Association, 2012), including the obligation to facilitate the evaluation of their claims based on data. To support these practices, the Qualitative Data Repository (https://qdr.syr.edu/) at Syracuse University has been developing "active citation" methods, so data that is central to the author's argument, or data that supports contestable statements, will be annotated and linked to the supporting data sources (Moravcsik, Elman, and Kapiszewski, 2013). Other efforts to make sure credit is received for the data include the badges now being added for authors in *GigaScience* (http://www.gigasciencejournal.com/) based on Contributor Roles Taxonomy (CRediT). CRediT recognizes the myriad of skills needed when working on large collaborative projects by giving credit for roles such as data curation, formal analysis, methodology, project administration, validation, and visualization, as well as writing.

Journal Sharing Requirements

The OSTP memo requires public access to digital data that is "necessary to validate research findings including datasets used to support scholarly publication," so not all raw data needs to be shared. Publishing in a journal that supports linking the article to the supporting data set that has been deposited in a repository on the journal's acceptable

Table 7.1. Conditions for Use of Subjects' Data

	YES (%)	NO (%)	NOT SURE (%)
Co-authorship on publications resulting from use of the data	36.2	33.8	30.0
Acknowledgment of the data providers in all disseminated work making use of the data	87.7	5.5	6.8
Citation of the data providers in all disseminated work making use of the data	85.1	6.4	8.5
The opportunity to collaborate on a project using the data	58.7	19.7	21.7
Results based (at least in part) on the data could not be disseminated in any format without the data provider's approval	29.0	50.8	20.2
At least part of the costs of data acquisition, retrieval, or provision must be recovered	14.2	62.7	23.2
Results based (at least in part) on the data could not be disseminated without the data provider having the opportunity to review the results and make suggestions or comments, but approval not required	36.9	42.5	20.6
Reprints of articles that make use of the data must be provided to the data provider	46.8	38.6	14.6
The data provider is given a complete list of all products that make use of the data, including articles, presentations, educational materials, etc.	43.8	37.5	18.7
Legal permission for data use is obtained	33.4	45.4	21.1
Mutual agreement on reciprocal sharing of data	46.2	34.2	19.7
The data provider is given and agrees to a statement of uses to which the data will be put	44.2	32.5	23.3

Source: Tenopir et al., 2015.

list is one way to easily comply with OSTP memo policies. It is also possible to deposit data and provide a link to the data without it being a journal requirement, but researchers should note that data sets should be available at the same time as the article appears, so they can't delay deposit.

Researchers need to be aware that even if they haven't published in a journal that requires linked data, some journal policies require sharing of data for published articles when asked. Deevy Bishop (2015) writes about a young scientist who was contacted with a request for the data from an article. She was still working on the data and didn't want to share, but the requester complained to the journal, and the young scientist was contacted by PLOS and told sharing on request was part of the contract.

Open versus Public Data

When discussing journal articles, open access assumes that an article is free of cost to read; free to use or reuse, that is, no copyright or licensing restrictions; has no embargoes; and the author retains copyright. Public access on the other hand, as described in funder policies, allows for some restrictions. While the item must be free of cost to read online, or print out, people are not free to use or reuse the material in any way, for example, using a figure or table in another paper. Usually the version available is not the final version, and even that is often embargoed. And finally, the copyright is generally held by the journal. As noted in the section above, open data is freely available and allows for downloading, copying, analysis, and reuse. Public access to data, as proposed by the OSTP memo, applies to digitally formatted scientific data resulting from unclassified research, and includes storage plus the ability to search, retrieve, and analyze the data. Researchers are expected to make available the data that is necessary to validate research findings including data sets used to support scholarly publications. Ideally, the OSTP hopes that public access to the data will contribute to new scientific breakthroughs and spur innovation and entrepreneurial use of the discoveries, which will eventually enhance economic growth and job creation.

As of the end of 2015, most U.S. federal funders have not fully developed their data public access policies, so specific procedures are not known. It seems likely that the best way for a researcher to make data publicly available will be to deposit data sets into a repository—the specific repository will be determined by the funder or subject—and then either the researcher or the repository will provide metadata for a searchable database describing data sets that will be maintained by the funder. But, it still isn't clear, and there are many questions about who will be responsible for maintaining repositories and databases. Another scenario could be that the data is submitted to journals with the articles, and the publisher grants public access after an embargo and also provides metadata to the funder for a searchable database. Journals don't necessarily want to store all the data sets, so general repositories like Dryad or Figshare are partnering with journals to store data sets. And individual, searchable databases will fragment the available data, so a centralized database similar to Data.gov, a searchable database of U.S. government data, could be developed.

All over the world, sharing upon request is expected of researchers, but open data is now being encouraged or mandated. European Commission Horizon 2020 awards will require open access to scientific publications and research data (http://ec.europa.eu/research/participants/data/ref/h2020/grants_manual/hi/oa_pilot/h2020-hi-oa-pilot-guide_en.pdf); Research Councils UK has policies encouraging open data (http://www.rcuk.ac.uk/RCUK-prod/assets/documents/documents/RCUKCommonPrinciple-sonDataPolicy.pdf); and Canada has a draft statement that encourages researchers, to the fullest extent possible, to put their data in the public domain (http://science.gc.ca/default.asp?lang=En&n=83F7624E-1). Along with research data, government data of all levels is gradually becoming open as well, opening up new research areas combining the different data sets.

Depositing Data for Public Access

With or without a policy, any researcher who wishes to make their data public can make use of the many general, institutional, and subject-specific repositories that are available. Using the "Guidelines for Trusted Repositories" (see textbox earlier in this chapter) and the "Repository Considerations" (see textbox in chapter 5), researchers and data librarians can assess available repositories (see "Repository Lists" textbox) and decide on the most appropriate place for data deposit. Researchers should also check to see if they are expected to deposit some or all of their data in a specific government-funded repository (see examples in textbox).

REPOSITORY LISTS

- re3data.org (http://www.re3data.org/), run by DataCite and merged with Databib, now has more than 1,200 reviewed repositories and can be searched or browsed.
- Open Access Directory (OAD) Data repositories (http://oad.simmons.edu/oadwiki/Data_repositories), hosted by Simmons College, is a browsable list of open access data repositories arranged by subject.

Funder Repository Lists

- NIH Data Sharing Repository (https://www.nlm.nih.gov/NIHbmic/nih_data_sharing_repositories.html) is mainly for NIH-funded research, but some repositories allow other users.
- Biological and Chemical Oceanography Data Management Office (http://www.bco-dmo.org/data) accepts data from specific NSF-funded projects, but also allows access to that data for reuse.

Subject-specific repositories should be considered first because the data is more likely to be found and reused. There are often specific guidelines for data formatting, description, and metadata, to allow for easier reuse, that some researchers will find time consuming. General repositories such as Dataverse, Figshare, and Dryad, or institutional repositories are also options for providing open access to data. Clinical data should only be made open after anonymization. Usually some sort of a clinical or enterprise data warehouse, with controlled access, is used for electronic health record data. Depositing data in a secure registry or access-controlled database is a good way to make data available without having to send things out to every person who requests the data. Sensitive data is less likely to be available for sharing at any time, although researchers may need to work on documentation before submitting the data to the funder. Repository librarians familiar with the documentation and processes involved in depositing data and other materials can be very helpful guiding researchers through the necessary steps, including the addition of metadata and licensing decisions.

⊙ Key Points

Public or open access publishing of data should be the goal of most researchers.

- It increases the visibility of research and can lead to new collaborations and more citations.
- It supports efforts to make research transparent and reproducible.
- It allows others to reuse the data for new discoveries and innovations, thereby increasing the value of the funders' investment.

A researcher's plans for storing, preserving, describing, and sharing data all come together when it comes time to write a data management plan for a grant application, which is the focus of chapter 8.

⑥ References

American Political Science Association. 2012. *A Guide to Professional Ethics in Political Science.* Washington, D.C.: APSA. http://www.apsanet.org/Portals/54/APSA%20Files/publications/ethicsguideweb.pdf.

Arias, Jalayne J., Genevieve Pham-Kanter, and Eric G. Campbell. 2014. "The Growth and Gaps of Genetic Data Sharing Policies in the United States." *Journal of Law and the Biosciences* 2, no. 1. doi:10.1093/jlb/lsu032.

Bishop, Deevy. 2015. "Who's Afraid of Open Data." *BishopBlog*. Sunday, November 15. http://deevybee.blogspot.co.uk/2015/11/whos-afraid-of-open-data.html.

Callaghan, Sarah, Steve Donegan, Sam Pepler, et al. 2012. "Making Data a First Class Scientific Output: Data Citation and Publication by NERC's Environmental Data Centres." *International Journal of Digital Curation* 7, no. 1: 107–13.

Carlson, Jake R. 2012. "Demystifying the Data Interview: Developing a Foundation for Reference Librarians to Talk with Researchers about Their Data." *Reference Services Review* 40, no. 1: 7–23.

Costello, Mark J. 2009. "Motivating Online Publication of Data." *Bioscience* 59, no. 5: 418–27. doi:10.1525/bio.2009.59.5.9.

Dorch, Bertil F., Thea M. Drachen, and Ole Ellegaard. 2015. "The Data Sharing Advantage in Astrophysics." Conference Proceedings of Focus Meeting 3 on Scholarly Publication in Astronomy, November 29, 2015. http://arxiv.org/pdf/1511.02512v1.pdf.

Fecher, Benedikt, Sascha Friesike, and Marcel Hebing. 2015. "What Drives Academic Data Sharing?" *PLoS ONE* 10, no. l. 2: e0118053. doi:10.1371/journal.pone.0118053.

Federer, Lisa M., Ya-Ling Lu, Douglas J. Joubert, Judith Welsh, and Barbara Brandys. 2015. "Biomedical Data Sharing and Reuse: Attitudes and Practices of Clinical and Scientific Research Staff." *PloS One* 10, no. 6: e0129506. doi:10.1371/journal.pone.0129506.

HHS Press Office. 2015. "$750,000 HIPAA Settlement Emphasizes the Importance of Risk Analysis and Device and Media Control Policies." Department of Health & Human Services, last modified September 2. http://www.hhs.gov/about/news/2015/09/02/750%2C000-dollar-hipaa-settlement-emphasizes-the-importance-of-risk-analysis-and-device-and-media-control-policies.html.

Hurley, Dan. 2015. "When Academic Neurologists Leave, Who Owns Their Research? Sometimes, Not Always, It's a Tug of War between Institutions." *Neurology Today* 15, no. 19: 1, 31–36.

Institute of Medicine (IOM). 2015. *Sharing Clinical Trial Data: Maximizing Benefits, Minimizing Risk.* Washington, D.C.: National Academies Press.

Kratz, John, and Carly Strasser. 2014. "Data Publication Consensus and Controversies [Version 3; Referees: 3 Approved]." *F1000Research* 3, no. 94. doi:10.12688/f1000research.3979.3.

Lawrence, Bryan, Catherine Jones, Brian Matthews, Sam Pepler, and Sarah Callaghan. 2011. "Citation and Peer Review of Data: Moving towards Formal Data Publication." *International Journal of Digital Curation* 6, no. 2: 4–37.

Moravcsik, Andrew, Colin Elman, and Diana Kapiszewski. 2013. *A Guide to Active Citations. Version 1.8 for Pilot Projects.* Qualitative Data Repository (QDR), Center for Qualitative and Multi Method Inquiry, Syracuse University. https://qdr.syr.edu/guidance/acguide.

OSTP (Office of Science and Technology Policy). 2013. "Memorandum for the Heads of Executive Departments and Agencies." Executive Office of the President. Accessed June 9, 2015. https://www.whitehouse.gov/sites/default/files/microsites/ostp/ostp_public_access_memo_2013.pdf.

Patrias, Karen. 2007. *Citing Medicine: The NLM Style Guide for Authors, Editors, and Publishers.* Edited by Dan Wendling. 2nd ed. Bethesda, Md.: National Library of Medicine. http://www.ncbi.nlm.nih.gov/books/NBK7256/.

Pinfield, Stephen. 2015. "Making Open Access Work: The 'State-of-the-Art' in Providing Open Access to Scholarly Literature." *Online Information Review* 39, no. 5: 604–36. doi:10.1108/OIR-05-2015-0167.

Piwowar, Heather A., Roger S. Day, and Douglas B. Fridsma. 2007. "Sharing Detailed Research Data Is Associated with Increased Citation Rate." *PLoS ONE* 2, no. 3: e308. doi:10.1371/journal.pone.0000308.

SPARC (Scholarly Publishing and Academic Resources Coalition). 2015. "Why Open Access?" Accessed October 24, 2015. http://www.sparc.arl.org/resources/open-access/why-oa.

Suber, Peter. 2012. *Open Access*. Streaming edition. Boston: MIT Press. http://cyber.law.harvard.edu/hoap/Open_Access_(the_book).

Tenopir, Carol, Elizabeth D. Dalton, Suzie Allard, et al. 2015. "Changes in Data Sharing and Data Reuse Practices and Perceptions among Scientists Worldwide." *PLoS ONE* 10, no. 8: e0134826. doi:10.1371/journal.pone.0134826.

Writing Data Management Plans

A S DISCUSSED IN CHAPTER 1, data management involves the organization, storage, access, and preservation of data. It covers everything from the naming and organization of data, through the documentation of data, to the sharing and long-term preservation of data. A data management plan (DMP) pulls together all aspects of data management and the data life cycle and sets down how the various steps of data management will be done. In and of itself, a data management plan is helpful for researchers when they begin a project, because as you have seen in the chapters on documentation, sharing, and storage, knowing where your data will be stored and shared has an impact on how it will be collected and described. And, as funders and institutions start to realize the value of data, they are starting to require data management plans to show researcher accountability.

The Advantages of a Data Management Plan

Researchers will find that taking the time to organize their research and data collection before starting a project can have many benefits (see textbox). Throughout the chapters on documentation, sharing, and storage, it has been noted that data practices can differ by field of study, local resources, and the policies of the institution, state and federal agency, funder, or even journal of publication. Given all these considerations, a data management plan can prevent future headaches for researchers.

SUMMARY OF BENEFITS TO DATA MANAGEMENT PLANNING

- Data can be found and understood when it is needed.
- Data or notes are less likely to be missing when it comes time to process and analyze results.
- All project staff are aware of what they need to do when doing research and collecting data.
- There is continuity if project staff leave or new researchers join.
- Unnecessary duplication (e.g., recollecting or reworking data) is avoided.
- Permissions and ownership are understood so there should be no impediments to publication.
- Data underlying publications are maintained, allowing for validation of results.
- Data can be found if it is needed for sharing.
- Data is available if needed for Freedom of Information Act (FOIA) requests or to resolve intellectual property issues.

(Based on Jones, 2011; Krier and Strasser, 2014; Briney, 2015)

Because of the demand for DMPs by many funders, there are numerous templates and checklists available for use when writing grants (see below). While a funder template can be helpful to make sure all the specific funder requirements are addressed, it won't usually cover everything a researcher might need, and it won't take all local resources and discipline-specific standards into account. Using the reference skills covered in chapter 4, data librarians can help researchers with their data management plans by conducting a data interview with the general questions below to learn more about how the research is being done, fitting the needs with available resources, and then incorporating it all into a basic data management plan.

ⓖ General Data Management Planning

A data management plan should be thought of as a strategic plan for research data, not just another administrative duty (Corti et al., 2014). By working first with a general outline for a data management plan, researchers will find it easier to adapt the plan later for the various funding agencies that require DMPs. The textbox contains a list of topics and questions based on several different checklists and planning guides (Lamar Soutter Library, 2015; Corti et al., 2014; Briney, 2015; MIT Libraries, 2015). These questions can be used as is by a data librarian conducting an interview. Knowledge of the basics of data management covered in chapters 1 to 7 of this book will be needed to understand researchers' answers, and to ask pertinent follow-up questions for clarification if needed. The questions could also be used to create a checklist that can be used by researchers or students. If a more in-depth assessment is needed, DCC has an extensive "Checklist for a Data Management Plan, v4.0" (http://www.dcc.ac.uk/sites/default/files/documents/resource/DMP/DMP_Checklist_2013.pdf).

TOPICS AND QUESTIONS FOR DEVELOPING DATA MANAGEMENT PLANS

Data Collection
- What types of data will you be creating or capturing (experimental measures, observational or qualitative, model simulation, existing)?
- How will you collect and use the data (instruments and equipment, software, etc.)?
- Are standardized formats or templates used to collect data?
- Is the data digital only, or are there other formats?
- Who will be responsible for the data? (may depend on equipment or raw vs. processed data)

Data Description
- What file formats and naming conventions will you be using?
- How will files be organized?
- How will data be documented?
- What data collection methods have been used? Are they documented?
- Will any standards be used?
- Is there any future use, for example, journal article or mandatory repository, that requires specific metadata or formatting?

Storage
- Where and on what media will you store the data?
- What is your backup plan for the data?
- Who needs to access the data during the data collection process?
- How will you manage data security?

Protection or Privacy Needs
- How are you addressing any ethical or privacy issues (IRB, anonymization of data)?
- Who will own any copyright or intellectual property rights to the data?

Sharing and Access
- What restrictions need to be placed on reuse of your data?
- What type of license should be used for the data?
- What is the process for gaining access to your data?
- Will you need to provide public access to the data?

Preservation
- What is your long-term plan for preservation and maintenance of the data?
- How long does the data need to be preserved?
- Will funding be required to curate and preserve the data?

Early Data Sharing Policies in the United States

As early as 1997, reports such as *Bits of Power* were calling for the sharing of scientific data and access to publicly funded data (Committee on Issues in the Transborder Flow of Scientific Data, 1997). NSF developed data sharing requirements in 2001 (Borgman, 2007), and NIH had data sharing requirements for grants more than $500,000 starting in 2003 (http://grants.nih.gov/grants/policy/data_sharing/data_sharing_faqs.htm). Data sharing requirements commit funded researchers to making their data, cell lines, software, and so forth, available to other researchers upon request, at a reasonable cost. While there was no requirement for a full data management plan, proposals needed to include data management information that was necessary for data sharing. In 2005, the NIH Public Access Policy (https://publicaccess.nih.gov/) started requesting published articles funded by the NIH be deposited in PubMed Central. The policy became mandatory in 2008, and some grantees had funds withheld until they deposited articles in compliance with the policy. While not directly applicable to data, this policy has made some data available through access to articles, and it has shown that it is possible to manage and enforce a public access policy.

These policies have paved the way for future efforts to manage and share data collected with grant money. Along with recommendations on policies for the best use and management of scientific digital data, the Interagency Working Group on Digital Data (2009) suggested a list of elements that needed to be included in data management plans (see table 8.1). These elements form the basis for the data management plan criteria developed by U.S. federal funders that require DMPs. The report also recommends public access to the digital data being produced by funded research.

NSF Data Management Plan Requirements

In 2011, the National Science Foundation (NSF) started requiring DMPs with the majority of their grants. Eleven of sixteen Association of Research Libraries (ARL) libraries surveyed started offering research data management services in 2011 to help with this new requirement (Fearon et al., 2013), even though some institutions didn't have a large percentage of researchers with NSF grants (Akers, 2014). One of the complicating factors was that each directorate or division of the NSF was allowed to write its own guidelines. This allowed for discipline-specific elements to be included in the plan, but it also made the job of supporting researchers who need data management plans harder. Most divisions provide example plans, and some institutions have made example plans available publicly, so those new to writing data management plans can see what is expected.

The Office of Science and Technology and Data Plans

The latest U.S. federal initiative for data is the Office of Science and Technology Policy guidelines for "Increasing Access to the Results of Federally Funded Scientific Research" outlined in a February 2013 memo (OSTP, 2013). This policy outlines the requirement to provide public access to articles and digital data supporting those articles, but also has a data management plan requirement. As listed in Section 4(b) of the memo, agencies are required to "ensure that all extramural researchers receiving Federal grants and contracts

Table 8.1. Data Management Plan Elements Used to Formulate U.S. Federal Agency Policies

ELEMENT	DESCRIPTION
Description	Brief, high-level description of the digital scientific data to be produced.
Impact	Discussion of possible impact of the data within the immediate field, in other fields, and any broader, societal impact. Indicate how the data management plan will maximize the value of the data.
Content and Format	Statement of plans for data and metadata content and format, including description of documentation plans and rationale for selection of appropriate standards. Existing, accepted standards should be used where possible. Where standards are missing or inadequate, alternate strategies for enabling data re-use and re-purposing should be described, and agencies should be alerted to needs for standards development or evolution.
Protection	Statement of plans, where appropriate and necessary, for protection of privacy, confidentiality, security, intellectual property and other rights.
Access	Description of plans for providing access to data. This should include a description and rationale for any restrictions on who may access the data under what conditions and a timeline for providing access. This should also include a description of the resources and capabilities (equipment, connections, systems, expertise, etc.) needed to meet anticipated requests. These resources and capabilities should be appropriate for the projected usage, addressing any special requirements such as those associated with streaming video or audio, movement of massive data sets, etc.
Preservation	Description of plans for preserving data in accessible form. Plans should include a timeline proposing how long the data are to be preserved, outlining any changes in access anticipated during the preservation timeline, and documenting the resources and capabilities (e.g., equipment, connections, systems, expertise) needed to meet the preservation goals. Where data will be preserved beyond the duration of direct project funding, a description of other funding sources or institutional commitments necessary to achieve the long-term preservation and access goals should be provided.
Transfer of Responsibility	Description of plans for changes in preservation and access responsibility. Where responsibility for continuing documentation, annotation, curation, access, and preservation (or its counterparts, de-accessioning or disposal) will move from one entity or institution to another during the anticipated data life cycle, plans for managing the exchange and documentation of the necessary commitments and agreements should be provided.

Source: Interagency Working Group on Digital Data, 2009

for scientific research and intramural researchers develop data management plans, as appropriate, describing how they will provide for long-term preservation of, and access to, scientific data in digital formats resulting from federally funded research, or explaining why long-term preservation and access cannot be justified."

Other parts of the memo cover privacy, intellectual property (IP) rights, and citation of data sets, but there are three parts that must be considered when looking at research data and DMPs. The memo allows for the costs of data management to be included in funding proposals. Agencies need to evaluate data management plans, and agencies need to ensure researcher compliance with the submitted plan. It has been possible to include data storage costs on some grants, but agencies will now expand the availability of adding data storage and curation costs to grants. But, when grants have a specific budget limit, many researchers would rather put the whole budget toward things like reagents, equipment, or personnel that directly impact research. Institutions vary as to what is available for short- and long-term storage, but it can be helpful if there is a requirement or policy that covers the costs of storage, preservation, and public access to data. The evaluation and compliance recommendations will be the responsibility of the agencies. When agencies decide what and how DMPs will be evaluated, it should actually help researchers and data librarians, because there will be more concrete information about what needs to be in a DMP. In the UK, the Economic & Social Research Council (ESRC) provides guidance for peer reviewers of data management plans (http://www.esrc.ac.uk/files/funding/guidance-for-peer-reviewers/data-management-plan-guidance-for-peer-reviewers/). The NIH tying public access policy compliance to the withholding of funds is one model that may be used to encourage compliance with the creation of DMPs and the other memo requirements.

Data Policies outside the United States and in Nongovernment Organizations

The recognition of data as an asset and the push for research transparency and reproducibility has had an impact on government and private funders everywhere. In the UK, multiple government agencies require data deposit and open access and some form of data management plan based on the Research Councils UK Common Principles of Data Policy (http://www.rcuk.ac.uk/research/datapolicy/), and the UK Economic & Social Research Council (ESRC) requires a DMP that is peer reviewed (as noted above). The new EU Framework Programme for Research and Innovation Horizon 2020 (http://ec.europa.eu/research/participants/data/ref/h2020/grants_manual/hi/oa_pilot/h2020-hi-oa-pilot-guide_en.pdf) requires a DMP as well. In Canada, the Canadian Institutes of Health Research (CIHR), the Natural Sciences and Engineering Research Council of Canada (NSERC), and the Social Sciences and Humanities Research Council of Canada (SSHRC) have a data management plan requirement (http://www.science.gc.ca/default.asp?lang=En&n=83F7624E-1).

Nongovernmental organizations have started asking for DMPs and open access to data as well, for example, Wellcome Trust (http://www.wellcome.ac.uk/About-us/Policy/Policy-and-position-statements/WTX035043.htm), and the Gordon and Betty Moore Foundation (https://www.moore.org/docs/default-source/Grantee-Resources/data-sharing-philosophy.pdf).

Using Templates for Data Management Plan Writing

There have been studies looking at the DMP guidelines of various government agencies and nongovernment organizations to see how they compare (Thoegersen, 2015; Dietrich et al., 2012), but the only consistent element is access. Even when international policies are considered (such as ICPSR), access and sharing is still the major element; preservation is mentioned in most policies, followed by content and format, and then protection. Guidelines can change over time and elements vary from grant to grant, so researchers must check the pertinent sections of the most recent grant proposal guide and specific funding opportunity before writing a data management plan.

While there are differences, most guidelines can be loosely condensed into five items that need to be in most data management plans, making it a bit easier to conduct interviews to collect the information needed for a data management plan.

- Description of the data to be collected/created
- Standards/methodologies for data collection and management
- Ethics and intellectual property considerations
- Plans for data sharing and access
- Strategy for long-term preservation

(Research Data Oxford, 2016)

Using templates or outlines specific to funders' requirements is a good way to make sure all required elements of a data management plan are covered. Various organizations and libraries have developed materials to help with writing data management plans. ICPSR provides a framework for writing a DMP (http://www.icpsr.umich.edu/icpsr-web/content/datamanagement/dmp/framework.html), but it is not specific to a particular funder. MIT provides a list of questions (http://libraries.mit.edu/data-management/plan/write/) to be used in conjunction with funder requirements, and Leeds provides a similar list of what to include in each section for UK researchers (https://library.leeds.ac.uk/research-data-management-planning). With funder requirements changing regularly and new funders starting to require DMPs, using a collaborative template website is a good way to provide DMP services.

Multi-institution Template Projects

The DMPTool (https://dmptool.org/) was started in January 2011 to help with the data management requirements of funding of U.S. government agencies, such as NSF and NIH. Eight institutions partnered with contributions of personnel and development to create a collection of templates for writing data management plans (DMPTool, 2015). The first version of the DMPTool was released in September 2011, and as of November 2013, more than six thousand users from more than six hundred institutions have used the DMPTool. After securing further funding, a second version of DMPTool was released in May 2014. There is a long list of partner institutions that have joined with the original institutions, and once an institution is authenticated for the DMPTool online application, administrators at each institution can customize templates with their local resources. Specific information about local resources for storing data or using an institutional repository for sharing data can be added to the guidance boxes available for each section of a template, including boilerplate language about that resource.

Even if a researcher is from an institution that is not partnered, the DMPTool can be used to write and save plans. Some users have made their plans open, which can be a helpful tool when learning and writing DMPs. Data librarians will also find that the templates are up to date and are an ideal way to make sure they are not missing any part of a DMP.

DMP Online, developed by the DCC (http://www.dcc.ac.uk/resources/data-management-plans), includes all the UK funders who require DMPs, plus there is an EU template and the generic NSF format. DMP Assistant (https://portagenetwork.ca/), available from the Canadian Association of Research Libraries (CARL), is a version of DMP Online customized to the Canadian government policies and available in French and English. Both tools allow for generic templates and local customization (if the institution is a participant).

Many institutions provide consulting services for DMPs, but most places will not have enough trained staff to help with every researcher's data management plan, especially after the OSTP memo increases the number of researchers needing to write DMPs. Having a customized template service can help fill the gap, providing boilerplate language about local resources, and reaching researchers who do not know about library services. Template services are also helpful because they are always available for researchers who leave the DMP until just before the grant must be submitted. These group projects have the advantage of reducing the amount of programming support needed at the local level, while providing an interactive website with updated templates. In the case of the DMP-Tool, updating templates is a community effort as well, making it an ideal place to learn about updated funder requirements.

Problems with Data Management Plans

The varying requirements and lack of review (for NSF grants) of data management plans has led to some confusion about what must be included. Bishoff and Johnston (2015) conducted an analysis of some University of Minnesota DMPs and found that while there was reasonable attention to data sharing in DMPs, data retention was not mentioned often. And although data sharing was mentioned, the provisions for data sharing were inconsistent, with publication (nonspecific) and sharing by request most commonly mentioned. William H. Mischo, Mary C. Schlembach, and Megan N. O'Donnell (2014) found that for sharing, 44 percent of the DMPs reviewed mentioned publication of some sort, including traditional scholarly outputs such as journal articles, conferences, meetings, workshops, and posters, as a method for sharing and distribution of data. The guidance from NSF is not clear, but newer guidelines from the OSTP indicate that a table in a journal article is not adequate; the digital data used to create that table will need to be available. There is clearly a role for data librarians to help with policy compliance and data sharing options as each agency starts to enforce new policies.

Despite the benefits of templates, there can be problems with copying between DMPs from different researchers and outdated boilerplate language appearing in DMPs (Parham and Doty, 2012). Data librarians, or whoever at an institution is responsible for template maintenance, must be sure they take the time to regularly check the boilerplate sections of their templates. Researchers and grant offices need to be aware of updates as well, because often researchers share grant boilerplate language, and a researcher could pull an out-of-date resource without using the template program. There is also a problem when using boilerplate or copying if the resource, something like an institutional repository, has fees that are not included, or if the resource providers need to know ahead of time who will be sending data so they can plan for capacity. Opinion is divided as to whether it is better to require a consultation with a data librarian to get the boilerplate language so resource use and costs can be explained, or whether it will just push researchers to copy and paste from each other more because they don't have time for a consultation.

Improving data management plans is important for future research. Jacob Metcalf (2015) suggests that when it comes to DMPs "we need to find a sweet spot between 'check-box' compliance and unstructured open-endedness." One of his suggestions, developing a database to track and learn from DMPs, is actually now being done by a group of librarians. The DART Project, "Data Management Plans as a Research Tool" (http://dmpresearch.library.oregonstate.edu/), is a grant-funded effort to create an analytic rubric to standardize the review of DMPs that will help librarians understand DMP requirements and, more importantly, help libraries decide on the best services to support research efforts. While helping write data management plans has been a way for librarians to connect with researchers, learning more about the data management needs of researchers in order to help and provide resources throughout the research cycle is necessary if data librarians wish to continue to help with data at an institution.

Key Points

Data management plans help to pull together all the important aspects of collection, storing, sharing, and preserving data throughout a research project.

- DMPs can help a researcher keep organized and prevent data loss.
- Data interview skills are necessary to help a researcher develop a good DMP.
- DMPs will be required by more funders because of new OSTP policies.
- DMP templates can help ensure that researchers meet all grant requirements.

While helping with DMPs can be a good way to make contact with researchers and learn about their data management needs, it can also help libraries decide on future services training in the area of data management. Now that the basics of data management have been reviewed, the next chapter will describe how to start setting up data services in a library.

References

Akers, Katherine G. 2014. "Going Beyond Data Management Planning: Comprehensive Research Data Services." *College & Research Libraries News* 75, no. 8: 435–36.

Bishoff, Carolyn, and Lisa R. Johnston. 2015. "Approaches to Data Sharing: An Analysis of NSF Data Management Plans from a Large Research University." *Journal of Librarianship and Scholarly Communication* 3, no. 2. doi:doi.org/10.7710/2162-3309.1231.

Borgman, Christine L. 2007. *Scholarship in the Digital Age: Information, Infrastructure, and the Internet.* Cambridge, Mass.: MIT Press.

Briney, Kristin. 2015. *Data Management for Researchers: Organize, Maintain and Share Your Data for Research Success.* Exeter, UK: Pelagic.

Committee on Issues in the Transborder Flow of Scientific Data. 1997. *Bits of Power: Issues in Global Access to Scientific Data.* U.S. National Committee for CODATA, Commission on Physical Sciences, Mathematics, and Applications, and National Research Council. Washington D.C.: National Academy Press. http://www.nap.edu/catalog/5504/bits-of-power-issues-in-global-access-to-scientific-data.

Corti, Louise, Veerle Van den Eynden, Libby Bishop, and Matthew Wollard. 2014. *Managing and Sharing Research Data: A Guide to Good Practice.* London: Sage.

Dietrich, Dianne, Trisha Adamus, Alison Miner, and Gail Steinhardt. 2012. "De-mystifying the Data Management Requirements of Research Funders." *Issues in Science and Technology Librarianship* no. 70 (Summer). http://www.istl.org/12-summer/refereed1.html.

DMPTool. 2015. "About the DMPTool." Accessed December 25, 2015. https://dmptool.org/about.

Fearon, David, Jr., Betsy Gunia, Sherry Lake, Barbara E. Pralle, and Andrew L. Sallans. 2013. *SPEC Kit 334: Research Data Management Services.* Washington, D.C.: Association of Research Libraries, Office of Management Services.

Interagency Working Group on Digital Data. 2009. *Harnessing the Power of Digital Data for Science and Society.* Washington, D.C.: National Science and Technology Council. https://www.nitrd.gov/about/Harnessing_Power_Web.pdf.

Jones, Sarah. 2011. *How to Develop a Data Management and Sharing Plan.* Edinburgh: Digital Curation Centre.

Krier, Laura, and Carly A. Strasser. 2014. *Data Management for Libraries.* Chicago: ALA TechSource.

Lamar Soutter Library. 2015. "Creating a Simplified Data Management Plan (NECDMC Module 1)." University of Massachusetts Medical School. Accessed December 15, 2015. http://library.umassmed.edu/necdmc/necdmc_activity1b.docx.

Metcalf, Jacob. 2015. *Data Management Plan: A Background Report.* Council for Big Data, Ethics, and Society. http://bdes.datasociety.net/wp-content/uploads/2015/05/DMPReport.pdf.

Mischo, William H., Mary C. Schlembach, and Megan N. O'Donnell. 2014. "An Analysis of Data Management Plans in University of Illinois National Science Foundation Grant Proposals." *Journal of eScience Librarianship* 3, no. 1. http://dx.doi.org/10.7191/jeslib.2014.1060.

MIT Libraries. 2015. "Write a Data Management Plan." Accessed December 15, 2015. http://libraries.mit.edu/data-management/plan/write/.

OSTP (Office of Science and Technology Policy). 2013. "Memorandum for the Heads of Executive Departments and Agencies." Executive Office of the President. Accessed June 9, 2015. https://www.whitehouse.gov/sites/default/files/microsites/ostp/ostp_public_access_memo_2013.pdf.

Parham, Susan Wells, and Chris Doty. 2012. "NSF DMP Content Analysis: What Are Researchers Saying?" *Bulletin of the American Society for Information Science & Technology* 39, no. 1: 37–38. doi:10.1002/bult.2012.1720390113.

Research Data Oxford. 2016. "Data Management Planning." Accessed June 6, 2015. http://researchdata.ox.ac.uk/home/managing-your-data-at-oxford/data-management-planning/.

Thoegersen, Jennifer L. 2015. "Examination of Federal Data Management Plan Guidelines." *Journal of eScience Librarianship* 4, no. 1. http://dx.doi.org/10.7191/jeslib.2015.1072.

Starting Data Management Services

THERE IS NO ONE RIGHT WAY TO SET UP research data management (RDM) services in an organization. The need for RDM can come from individuals, research groups, departments, or higher levels of an organization, such as grants administration. The skills needed may be found throughout an organization, in areas such as institutional technology services, libraries, research offices, or data-intensive research. Models of research data services can be everything from an individual to a multidepartment committee, but the library, as a neutral partner in education and research, is a good place for RDM to start. Most researchers aren't even aware that there might be somebody out there who can help with data organization, data publishing, data management plans, and other related services, so data librarians need to be willing to get out there to market their expertise and promote awareness.

Establishing the Need for RDM

How does a library know when research data management services are needed? It isn't enough to decide that if RDM is a "Mid-Term Impact Trend" in the *Horizon Report* (Johnson et al., 2015), then it is time to set up a service. There needs to be more evidence.

For example, an analysis of reference desk questions could show that students are regularly looking for data sets to reuse for class or research, or librarians embedded in classes may have faculty asking about data for teaching or instruction in data management. Subject liaisons may have had data questions in their departments or heard researchers complaining about lost data or lack of guidance on data management plans. Maybe there have been questions about using the institutional repository for data sharing. Library administration may aspire to RDM services after comparisons with similar organizations, or they may see a place for library-based services after a recent study found researchers are least satisfied with processes for storing data beyond the life of the project and tools for preparing metadata (Tenopir et al., 2015). All these indicators point to the need for some sort of data service, but what exactly? In the previous chapters of this book, parts of the data life cycle have been explored. Planning, organizing, analyzing, storing, curating, preserving, describing, sharing, finding, and reusing are all data services that could be provided by a library or institution. Further exploration of the needs of the organization is necessary.

Setting Up a Committee or Task Force

While a committee may not be the final model for data services, it can be useful for information gathering. Involving people from multiple parts of the library, or even organization, can help keep the process open and ensure that everyone understands how the provision of new services will impact their area of service (see next section on change management). When setting up a committee, the goal should be clear, and the committee members should be able to help with that goal in some way. If the committee is trying to learn what other similar libraries are doing and how they are set up, a group of librarians and support staff from different departments with an interest in data and research, or knowledge of any of the many parts of data management, would be good. Maybe, library administration is committed to setting up data services and wants to understand institutional needs, so the committee needs to conduct some sort of survey or assessment of needs. Librarians who regularly work with researchers and already have some knowledge of data management will be good candidates for this type of committee. It is also helpful to consider adding archivists who understand preservation and long-term storage, and technology librarians who understand university IT structures. For a broader needs assessment, it is helpful to bring in people from outside the library who are potential users of data services or who will also provide some support for data services. Researchers are an obvious choice, but also consider information technology personnel who deal with security or storage, and grant or research support personnel (see chapter 10 on collaboration). Once the committee is set up, it can decide on the best methods to collect information.

Depending on the time frame or the culture of the institution, a committee or task force might not be feasible. Maybe library staff have too much going on or the institution does not encourage interdepartmental committees. A successful data service can still be set up without committee input, but there should be some input from outside the library and strong administrative commitment. Input from outside the library should include interviews with stakeholders in some of the relevant departments, such as research and grants office, institutional technology services, research deans, or data-intensive researchers. New data librarians need to be wary of taking on a position if the library has not ascertained the need for library-provided data services in any way.

Managing Change

Even in the early stages of assessing the need for data services, there will be people who question the need for the library and librarians to be part of institutional research data services. Hopefully, the first eight chapters of this book have shown that libraries and librarians are well suited to being part of any research data program, and that data is just another form of information. But some people still feel that libraries should focus on the local information needs of current library users, mainly faculty and students in an academic library, and not worry about helping with things like open access and other issues that have more to do with scholarly communication (Anderson, 2015). They may feel that the costs of preserving data are too high for a library to take on, or that the staff commitment would be too great. As with any change, it is important to communicate the need for change and how it will support the library going forward. Even when people are open to change, it is helpful to develop a transition plan that will allow people to stop doing some parts of their job and add in the new tasks involved in RDM services. William Bridges (2009) has some very helpful strategies and checklists for making it easier to manage change.

There is also concern about which department, at the institutional level, should be taking on the responsibility for research data management services—the library, the research office, or information technology. Eddy Verbaan and Andrew M. Cox (2014) found that while there was some jostling for position, at one institution, librarians tended to focus on preservation and advocacy, research office staff on compliance and research quality, and information technology staff on short-term data storage. Stakeholders at each institution will divide the various aspects of research data management in different ways, depending on the skills of the people in each department. For example, Verbaan and Cox found that the research office dealt with data management plans, but there are many examples of libraries taking care of that aspect of data policy (Bishoff and Johnston, 2015; Akers et al., 2014; Diekema, Wesolek, and Walters, 2014; Mischo, Schlembach, and O'Donnell, 2014; Akers and Doty, 2013).

Gathering Background Information

There are many ways an individual or committee can assess the research data management needs of an institution (see textbox). A literature review is usually a good start, since there is a range of articles about setting up data services, conducting surveys, and general overview articles to choose from. The second-mover advantage (Hoppe, 2000) suggests that there are informational spillovers when adopting new technology after innovators have tested new tools and techniques. Reviewing information about existing data services can help new data services avoid mistakes and move immediately to the appropriate tools. The review could focus on case studies to learn how others discovered a service was needed and how it was set up. Or it could focus on general articles that provide an overview of services and models for a data management service, or technical articles on setting up different types of repositories and collaborative work environments to help with the selection of technology.

SELECTED ASSESSMENT RESOURCES

Literature Review
- *Case studies:* Henderson and Knott (2015); Hiom et al. (2015); Knight (2015); Searle et al. (2015); Brandt (2014); Henry (2014); Jetten (2014); Steinhart (2014); Westra (2014); Shen and Varvel (2013); Wakimoto (2013); Wang (2013); Johnson, Butler, and Johnston (2012).
- *General overview:* Reeves Flores et al. (2015); Si et al. (2015); Akers et al. (2014); Coates (2014); Pinfield, Cox, and Smith (2014); Tenopir et al. (2014), Christensen-Dalsgaard et al. (2012); Reznik-Zellen, Adamick, and McGinty (2012); Tenopir, Birch, and Allard (2012).
- *Surveys:* Bishoff and Johnston (2015); Mattern et al. (2015); Weller and Monroe-Gulick (2015); Whitmire, Boock, and Sutton (2015); Averkamp, Gu, and Rogers (2014); Williams (2013); Westra (2010).

RDM Websites
- Cornell University Research Data Management Services Group
  http://data.research.cornell.edu/
- Johns Hopkins University Data Management Services
  http://dmp.data.jhu.edu/
- Purdue Libraries Research Data
  https://www.lib.purdue.edu/researchdata
- Purdue University Research Repository (PURR)
  https://purr.purdue.edu/
- University of California, San Diego, Research Data Curation Program
  http://libraries.ucsd.edu/services/data-curation/
- University of Edinburgh Research Data Management
  http://www.ed.ac.uk/information-services/research-support/data-management
- University of Maryland Libraries Research Data Services
  http://www.lib.umd.edu/data
- University of Michigan Library Research Data Services
  http://www.lib.umich.edu/research-data-services
- University of Oregon Research Data Management
  https://library.uoregon.edu/datamanagement
- University of Virginia Library Research Data Services
  http://data.library.virginia.edu/

Environmental Assessment Tools
- Collaborative Assessment of Research Data Infrastructures and Objectives (CARDIO)
  http://www.dcc.ac.uk/projects/cardio
- Data Asset Framework
  http://www.data-audit.eu/
- PEST—political, economic, social, and technological factors
  https://en.wikipedia.org/wiki/PEST_analysis

- Six Forces Model—competition, new entrants, end users, suppliers, substitutes, and complementary products
  https://en.wikipedia.org/wiki/Six_forces_model
- SWOT—strengths, weaknesses, opportunities, and threats
  http://ctb.ku.edu/en/table-of-contents/assessment/assessing-community-needs-and-resources/swot-analysis/main

An analysis of websites to find peer libraries with data services can be helpful when deciding on the types of services to offer. Try to find the organizational structure of the service and where it fits in the library and institution. Is the service staffed separately from other library services, or are the people working on data also working as liaisons or technical services staff? Is the data service affiliated with any departments outside the library? Contacting librarians who work in those data services is another source of potential background information. How did their service get started? How did they staff the service? How did the data librarians get their training? The information gathered can help library administration decide how to develop data services, but it can also show stakeholders outside the library that other institutions are providing data services, and usually it is the library organizing the service.

While resources at institutions usually differ, articles about surveys done to assess data needs at various institutions can contain useful information about the general needs of faculty or the specific needs of faculty in various disciplines. Many articles discussing survey results include the survey tools, which can provide a starting point and comparison for those who wish to conduct their own survey. There is also more general research on the information needs of researchers (Borgman, 2015; Wagner, 2008; Borgman, 2007). It is beneficial to consider all the services offered to researchers and consider how data services will fit with current services such as teaching, expert search services, bibliometric and altmetric consulting, or scholarly communications services. A literature review might also cover teaching of data information literacy (DIL), which includes data management and reuse of data sets for research and projects for all levels of learners (Wright et al., 2015; Carlson et al., 2011).

Environmental Assessment

An environmental assessment is an important step when setting up research data management services at an institution. Libraries need to assess the institutional environment as well as the resources and skills the library and its staff can provide related to the provision of data management services. There are many environmental assessment tools available (see "Selected Assessment Resources" textbox), some more complex than others, and the choice of tools will depend on the culture and formality of the library and institution. A simple SWOT analysis done by one or two librarians might be enough in some places, but other institutions may need a more in-depth and formal assessment done by a team that includes people outside of the library. It will also depend on where in the decision process the analysis takes place. A quick SWOT analysis in the beginning could be followed up by a data-specific analysis, such as CARDIO, when the data management service is set up. PEST analysis is especially appropriate for data management because of the political factor, the government mandates for data management plans, and public access to research data.

While a quick review of organization websites and department annual reports can provide enough basic information about the research being done and the data services available outside of the library to make some decisions, more in-depth information gathering is needed before finally setting up a service. This is where reference interview skills (chapter 4) and some of the survey questions from articles from the literature review will be helpful. It is important to try to interview some of the people connected with providing and/or using existing resources as you do your environmental scan. Try to learn about what they do, how they use data, and what services they can provide to others, to get a full picture of current institutional data needs and resources.

All organizations will have departments that deal with administrative and financial data, and while this is different from research data, there may be analysts or computer services contacts that can help in the future with research data. Grants offices will have analysts and data to indicate which funders contribute most to an institution, and this can help focus data management plan services. Academic medical centers will have patient data, as well as all the administrative data to deal with, and personnel familiar with managing that data. Educational institutions have student data, tracking courses and marks as well as financial records. In all cases, human resources will have personnel data that includes qualifications and licenses to practice. Find out what data exists and where, and look for the departments and people who are already caring for and using that data.

Many of the departments and people you learn about will be stakeholders who should be considered when starting data services. Some of them will be potential collaborators who might be concerned about competition. It is important to conduct these interviews carefully, and be ready to reassure people that the library is just exploring institutional services in order to fill in any gaps and act as a referral service. Other stakeholders could be groups that don't have anything to do with data but could help, such as administration. Make note of all these different groups and keep them in the loop as data management services start to develop. An important part of providing research data management services to a community, be it academic, corporate, or organization, is communication. You need to be able to listen to find out what is needed and what barriers stand in the way, and you need to explain what can be done in a way that prevents misunderstanding. Everyone's time and energy, and temper, will be saved if the people trying to set up RDM services are clear about what they want to do and what they can do. This is where the vocabulary in chapter 1 is important. Rather than making assumptions about the group you are talking with, make sure you include some clarification of common terms.

Librarian Skills Assessment

As mentioned above in the environmental assessment, learning about the current skills of librarians on staff is one way to plan for a new service. While past studies (Corrall, Kennan, and Afzal, 2013; Creamer et al., 2012) have found that there is a skills gap among librarians interested in RDM, the availability of new online and in-person educational opportunities covering RDM has increased (Goben and Raszewski, 2015a; Goben and Raszewski, 2015b), and there are more librarians ready to work with data. Archivists should not be neglected when looking for skilled staff. The digital preservation and curation skills of archivists fit well with research data (Akmon et al., 2011). While it is tempting to send out a survey asking current staff about their skills, using concept mapping to learn about the variety of skills and services already available might turn up librarians who are already helping with data (Vaughan et al., 2013). Concept maps, whether hand drawn or created with a program such as Cmap (http://cmap.ihmc.us/) are helpful because they can expose skills that are rarely used, or potential skills that librarians aren't yet using. And, they can also help generate a picture of all the different departments and contacts the library has through librarian activity and service. Plans and funding for continuing professional development for librarians taking on new roles in data management is integral for the quality of the service and should be included in discussions and plans for setting up the new service (Henderson, 2014; Tenopir, Birch, and Allard, 2012).

⑥ Planning Services

The information gathered from committees, task forces, assessments, and reviews should identify some data services of interest to the institution, as well as librarians with the skills to provide data services. As each of the following planning areas is considered (organization, services to offer, financing, promoting, and evaluating), it can be helpful to map out all the different areas in a business plan. The business plan can be as simple as filling in the boxes of a Business Model Canvas (http://www.businessmodelgeneration.com/canvas/bmc), which includes partners, activities, resources, customers, and so forth. The business plan could also be as extensive as the University of Edinburgh Research Data Management Roadmap (http://www.businessmodelgeneration.com/canvas/bmc), which gives a time frame for the completion of various objectives for the service. Or, the service could work on more of an entrepreneurial model, as outlined by Brian Mathews (2012).

Organization of Services

Cheryl A. Thompson, Chuck Humphrey, and Michael Witt (2015) have identified five models, or archetypes, found in data services in academic libraries. Data services might start with a nascent initiative, with one or two librarians testing a limited range of data management services. A dedicated working group could be set up using existing staff to form a team that collaborates to provide some data service, in addition to their other duties. Another way to start a data management services is to create a solo librarian position that takes on all data management roles, with no extra liaison, subject, teaching, or collection duties. The position might be filled by an existing staff member or a new hire. The library could also take an existing team, for example, scholarly communications or digital initiatives, and add data management activities to the duties of that team. The other model, specialized team, is less likely to be used at the start of data management services because it takes time to build up the expertise and users needed to warrant a dedicated team.

Potential RDM Services

As well as the structure of the service, there is a range of services that can be offered. Rebecca C. Reznik-Zellen, Jessica Adamick, and Stephen McGinty (2012) conducted an environmental scan of libraries providing data services and found there were three tiers of service: education, consultation, and infrastructure. They found that generally, institutions start by providing educational services, everything from educating administration and faculty on policies, to teaching how to write data management plans. Consultation services, directed at researchers and research groups, provide individualized help enhancing data collection and management. Reznik-Zellen, Adamick, and McGinty found only a few libraries that were able to offer infrastructure services, storage, or repository services, while most referred researchers to the appropriate campus entities or third-party providers. Spencer D. C. Keralis et al. (2013) broke the categories up a bit and looked at six areas where librarians could provide data services:

1. Informational—directing researchers to data management resources
2. Instructional—providing data management training
3. Infrastructural—providing space and resources for data storage and providing access to data
4. Cooperative—making tools and other resources available to researchers (e.g., DMPTool)
5. Collaborative—working with a researcher or group to develop sustainable data management practices
6. Archival—preserving and providing access to research data after a researcher leaves

Services don't have to follow such strict categories. Many libraries choose to organize services by using a data life cycle model, and fitting librarian skills into that model, similar to the University of Virginia Library's Research Data Services (http://data.library.virginia.edu/data-management/lifecycle/), which uses the following categories: Proposal Planning & Writing, Project Start Up, Data Collection, Data Analysis, Data Sharing, and End of Project. This type of organization has the advantage of teaching the data life cycle as researchers learn about services. Research Data Service at the University of Illinois at Urbana-Champaign (http://researchdataservice.illinois.edu/) simplifies the process further and organizes with the following categories: Plan, Organize, Save.

Paying for a New Service

Just as there are many models for providing research data services in a library, there are many ways to pay for that service. Initial RDM services provided by a library may avoid the expense of storage by focusing on DMPs and policy, and teaching best practices. Or maybe the library collections budget funds the purchase of data sets for reuse, for example, Inter-university Consortium for Political and Social Research (ICPSR). It is important to remember that even if there are only salary costs for the personnel providing the service, there are costs to RDM services that need to be considered by administration. The recovery of costs will depend on the culture of the institution, how the need for the service has developed, who will be providing which services, and what services are actually offered. Ricky Erway and Amanda K. Rinehart (2016) found eight strategies in use at U.S. institutions:

1. Institutional budgetary support
2. Charging grant budgets: direct funds
3. Charging grant budgets: indirect costs or overhead
4. Charging depositors (faculty or departments)
5. Charging data users

6. Endowment
7. Funding for data repository development
8. Making do: finding room in existing budgets

Unless there is a large number of data producing faculty willing to pay for a data manager, if a library wants to start RDM services, the personnel costs will need to be found within the library budget. At Purdue University and the University of Oregon, early data services were provided by a reconfiguration of existing positions, later supplemented by collaborations and grants (Brandt, 2014; Westra, 2014). Cornell had been developing technical expertise in digital services because of faculty needs, and then secured funding from government agencies, USDA, NIH, and NSF, to develop large databases, and that infrastructure has benefited faculty with data management needs (Steinhart, 2014). Most institutions staff data services with a combination of existing personnel who have some expertise and receive further training as needed, and also hire new staff with specialized skills to support the data management services being developed.

Outside of the United States, federal funders in other countries are requiring data management and open access to data, leading to national projects to provided shared research data expertise and networked resources in an effort to reduce costs. The Canadian Association of Research Libraries (CARL) has developed a library-based research data management network in Canada, called Portage, which has some funds from Research Data Canada. Plans include hiring staff and providing infrastructure, developing metadata guidelines and an aggregated discovery tool, and providing long-term preservation (Whitehead and Shearer, 2015). In Australia, the Australian National Data Service (http://ands.org.au/index.html) collects research resources, provides data management training and support, and supports discovery and reuse of data through Research Data Australia (https://researchdata.ands.org.au/). Some of these models could be used by existing consortia in the United States.

The most expensive part of any data service is the storage, backup, and preservation of data. Few places can stretch their existing budget to provide all the storage needed, so the other methods noted above need to be considered. The charges for data storage are compounded by the fact that research data needs to be stored for longer than the life of the grant that supported the research. And the costs of accessibility of the data, both providing adequate documentation for reuse and actual public access to the data, are hard to estimate. Some researchers recognize the need and value of data management and storage and are willing to add costs and personnel to their grant budgets when allowed by funders. Some universities, for example, the University of Leeds (https://library.leeds.ac.uk/research-data-policies), have policies that require plans for research data management to be reviewed and for direct costs to be included in funding requests when possible. On the other hand, there are researchers who think that if the institution owns their data (see chapter 7) then the institution should pay for the long-term storage of that data. Careful attention to the institutional climate around data and intellectual property is important when trying to decide how to fund data initiatives.

Funding long-term data retention will never be an exact science because of the varying costs of the technology involved in digital storage, but Serge J. Goldstein and Mark Ratliff (2010) looked at a couple of funding formulas for DataSpace at Princeton University and came up with a cost of $5.47 per gigabyte for long-term storage, and Beth Plale et al. (2013) calculated $5.56 for fifteen years of storage, so it is possible to set a reasonable cost for storage. But, in practice, when a repository is set up, the actual costs will probably be higher. Often, as in the case of MIT's DSpace, there are additional costs to identifying and managing collections that are not factored in to cost calculations (Royal Society, 2012).

Because research data management is an institutional issue, it is important to work with stakeholders throughout the institution to develop funding policies. All levels of administration, as well as researchers, should have input on developing acceptable funding models for each institution. Even if repositories are used, there are funding issues, because there are fees for many specialized repositories (Ember and Hanisch, 2013). Despite all the costing formulas and pricing structures (see textbox), data librarians should remember that data storage is an infrastructure issue (Bilder, Lin, and Neylon, 2015) and, as such, needs to be discussed at all levels of the institution. All the arguments for transparency and reproducibility of research apply to the need for open data storage that allows public access and provides documentation that makes the data set reusable. On the other hand, some institutions may choose to start with less expensive, scalable plans rather than trying to set up resource-intensive services before needs and funding are known (Schumacher et al., 2014).

RDM PRICING AND FUNDING EXAMPLES

- Archiving Services at Johns Hopkins University
  http://dmp.data.jhu.edu/preserve-share-research-data/archiving-services-we-offer/
- Calculating Data Management Costs (London School of Hygiene and Tropical Medicine)
  https://www.lshtm.ac.uk/research/researchdataman/plan/rdm_costs.html
- Costing Data Management: UK Data Service
  https://www.ukdataservice.ac.uk/manage-data/plan/costing
- Curation Costs Exchange
  http://www.curationexchange.org/
- Costing Research Data Management (Royal Veterinary College, University of London)
  http://www.rvc.ac.uk/research/about/research-data-management/before-a-project/costing-research-data-management
- PURR Project Space Allocation and Pricing
  https://purr.purdue.edu/aboutus/pricing

Promoting RDM Services

Starting data management services is similar to starting any business. It is necessary to go out and meet people and make them aware of the services being offered. A web page or guide that provides information about services offered and links to helpful materials is a good way to start creating an online presence for the new service. Make sure there are links from faculty or researcher library services pages to the guides. If the library is the sole provider of the service, the pages should fit with library branding to show that data management is an official library service. When other departments are collaborating, the pages should indicate their support. Brochures, cards, bookmarks, and other promotional materials that include contact information and the website URL, along with a description, are helpful to give out when meeting researchers and others around the institution. Library, department, or institutional newsletters or blogs can be used to notify researchers that a data management service is available.

Any public relations or marketing help available to the library should be used. Look for events that highlight services around the institution, such as a core facilities fair; make sure brochures or cards are out anytime the library has a table at an event; attend lectures and meetings that highlight data in different subject areas and hand out cards; and use events, such as Open Access Week or National Library Week, as an excuse to set up a table in high-traffic areas. Develop relationships with administrators in research divisions and use those contacts to offer presentations on writing DMPs or following policy to faculty and compliance officers. Rose Fortier and Emily Laws (2014) found that institutional repositories needed to market continuously and from multiple venues and viewpoints. The same can be said for the marketing of data services.

Evaluating and Refining RDM Services

It is a good idea to start thinking about what metrics will be used to measure data management services during the planning stages. Setting goals for the services being developed, based on the environmental assessment during planning, should lead to multiple types of evaluation options that will show if those goals are being met. It is not enough to just count how many people have asked for help. Just like there are classification schemes

EVALUATION AREAS

Process Including Product and Needs
- Does it work? Is resource use minimized?
- Does it attain longer-term goals?
- Is it pleasing to use?
- Are there any ethical/legal/safety issues for those who are involved?
- To what extent are the desired changes occurring? For whom?
- What are the potential barriers/facilitators?
- What is most appropriate development activity?

Outcome
- What are the desired changes in behavior or state?
- To what extent are these changes occurring?
- Are the changes effective? For whom?

Impact
- What are the unintended outcomes?
- To what extent have the intended benefits been achieved?
- What is the overall effect of the development activity?
- What are the cost benefits?
- What is the cost effectiveness of the development activity?

for reference questions (Ascher, 2014), there are different types and difficulty levels of service when helping with research data. Writing a data management plan for a grant is hard to compare to finding a data set for an undergraduate to reuse for a term paper. And the level of impact is very different as well. Helping with institutional data policies to ensure compliance with federal regulations can influence the whole organization while helping one graduate student develop a form for collecting data from an experiment generally affects fewer people. There should also be separate metrics for the service as a whole and the individuals providing the service.

There are three common areas that can be evaluated: process or product, outcome, and impact (Glenaffric Ltd., 2007). The questions related to each area in the textbox can help focus the evaluation.

Using a logic model to develop an evaluation is a good way to make sure all aspects of a program are included: resources, activities, outputs, and outcomes. Groups like Innovation Network (www.innonet.org/pointk), who help nonprofit groups with evaluation, have good online tools that can provide a framework for evaluation. Angus Whyte et al. (2014) have developed a logic model for evaluating research data management that takes context, inputs, activities, outputs, interactions, and outcomes into account. Each of the different aspects of the model has different components. For example, outcomes can be short or long term, direct or indirect, internal or external. The evaluation plan should also include information about timing, factors to evaluate, questions to address, method(s), and measure of success. Once a model is set up and goals considered, a measure to evaluate outcomes can be decided upon and a data collection method put into place.

It is important that assessment is an iterative process, so goals are adjusted based on the needs and gaps seen while working with researchers. Adjustment shouldn't have to wait until the end of an evaluation cycle. There are many outside forces to take into account when starting a data management service, and their impact cannot always be predicted. Realistic goals are very important with any new service.

Once evaluations are done, the results need to be communicated to library administration and institutional stakeholders. It is very important to include not only quantitative data from formal evaluations, but also stories about the impact the service has had with individuals (Albert, 2014). The Cornell University *Research Data Management Service Group Reports* (https://ecommons.cornell.edu/handle/1813/28575) include statistics on classes, consultations, and other work, but also goals, scope of service, and descriptions of the groups using the various services. This helps show where the service is having impact.

🌀 Key Points

Taking the time to plan is a very important part of setting up a new research data management service. Assessment, funding, service models, and marketing should all be considered along with potential services that might be offered.

- Involve stakeholders in and outside the library from early in the process.
- An environmental assessment can help pinpoint the services needed.
- Library and nonlibrary skills of librarians should be considered when staffing a new service.
- Evaluation should be planned when first developing the new service.

Having a good plan will make it easier to approach the institutional partners that will be considered in the next chapter.

References

Akers, Katherine G., and Jennifer Doty. 2013. "Disciplinary Differences in Faculty Research Data Management Practices and Perspectives." *International Journal of Digital Curation* 8, no. 2: 5–26.

Akers, Katherine G., F. C. Sferdean, Natsuko H. Nicholls, and Jennifer A. Green. 2014. "Building Support for Research Data Management: Biographies of Eight Research Universities." *International Journal of Digital Curation* 9, no. 2: 171–91. doi:10.2218/ijdc.v9i2.327.

Akmon, Dharma, Ann Zimmerman, Morgan G. Daniels, and Margaret Hedstrom. 2011. "The Application of Archival Concepts to a Data-Intensive Environment: Working with Scientists to Understand Data Management and Preservation Needs." *Archival Science* 11, no. 3: 329–49. doi:10.1007/s10502-011-9151-4.

Albert, Amanda B. 2014. "Communicating Library Value—the Missing Piece of the Assessment Puzzle." *Journal of Academic Librarianship* 40, no. 6: 634–37. doi:10.1016/j.acalib.2014.10.001.

Anderson, Rick. 2015. "A Quiet Culture War in Research Libraries—and What It Means for Librarians, Researchers and Publishers." *Insights* 28, no. 2: 21–27. doi:10.1629/uksg.230.

Ascher, Marie T. 2014. "Reference and Information Services in Health Sciences Libraries." In *Health Sciences Librarianship*, edited by M. Sandra Wood, 171–95. Lanham, Md.: Rowman & Littlefield.

Averkamp, Shawn, Xiaomei Gu, and Ben Rogers. 2014. *Data Management at the University of Iowa: A University Libraries Report on Campus Research Needs.* University of Iowa. http://ir.uiowa.edu./lib_pubs/153/.

Bilder, Geoffrey, Jennifer Lin, and Cameron Neylon. 2015. "Principles for Open Scholarly Infrastructures." *Science in the Open* (blog). February 23. http://cameronneylon.net/blog/principles-for-open-scholarly-infrastructures/.

Bishoff, Carolyn, and Lisa Johnston. 2015. "Approaches to Data Sharing: An Analysis of NSF Data Management Plans from a Large Research University." *Journal of Librarianship and Scholarly Communication* 3, no. 2: eP1231. doi:10.7710/2162-3309.1231.

Borgman, Christine L. 2007. *Scholarship in the Digital Age: Information, Infrastructure, and the Internet.* Cambridge, Mass.: MIT Press.

———. 2015. *Big Data, Little Data, No Data: Scholarship in the Networked World.* Cambridge, Mass.: MIT Press.

Brandt, D. Scott. 2014. "Purdue University Research Repository: Collaborations in Data Management." Chapter 16 in *Research Data Management: Practical Strategies for Information Professionals*, edited by Joyce M. Ray, 325–45. West Lafayette, Ind.: Purdue University Press.

Bridges, William. 2009. *Managing Transitions: Making the Most of Change.* 3rd ed. Philadelphia: Da Capo.

Carlson, Jacob, Michael Fosmire, C. C. Miller, and Megan Sapp Nelson. 2011. "Determining Data Information Literacy Needs: A Study of Students and Research Faculty." *Portal: Libraries and the Academy* 11, no. 2: 629–57.

Christensen-Dalsgaard, Birte, et al. 2012. *Ten Recommendations for Libraries to Get Started with Research Data Management: Final Report of the LIBER Working Group on E-Science / Research Data Management.* Ligue des Bibliothèques Européennes de Recherche (LIBER). http://libereurope.eu/wp-content/uploads/The%20research%20data%20group%202012%20v7%20final.pdf.

Coates, Heather L. 2014. "Building Data Services from the Ground Up: Strategies and Resources." *Journal of eScience Librarianship* 3, no. 1: e1063. doi:10.7191/jeslib.2014.1063.

Corrall, Sheila, Mary Anne Kennan, and Waseem Afzal. 2013. "Bibliometrics and Research Data Management Services: Emerging Trends in Library Support for Research." *Library Trends* 61, no. 3: 636–74.

Creamer, Andrew, Myrna E. Morales, Javier Crespo, Donna Kafel, and Elaine R. Martin. 2012. "An Assessment of Needed Competencies to Promote the Data Curation and Management Librarianship of Health Sciences and Science and Technology Librarians in New England." *Journal of eScience Librarianship* 1, no. 1: e1006. http://escholarship.umassmed.edu/jeslib/vol1/iss1/4/.

Diekema, Anne R., Andrew Wesolek, and Cheryl D. Walters. 2014. "The NSF/NIH Effect: Surveying the Effect of Data Management Requirements on Faculty, Sponsored Programs, and Institutional Repositories." *Journal of Academic Librarianship* 40, no. 3–4: 322–31. doi:10.1016/j.acalib.2014.04.010.

Ember, Carol, and Robert Hanisch. 2013. *Sustaining Domain Repositories for Digital Data: A White Paper*. Ann Arbor: University of Michigan, ICPSR. http://datacommunity.icpsr.umich.edu/sites/default/files/WhitePaper_ICPSR_SDRDD_121113.pdf.

Erway, Ricky, and Amanda K. Rinehart. 2016. *If You Build It, Will They Fund It? Making Research Data Management Sustainable*. Dublin, Ohio: OCLC Research. http://www.oclc.org/content/dam/research/publications/2016/oclcresearch-making-research-data-management-sustainable-2016.pdf.

Fortier, Rose, and Emily Laws. 2014. "Marketing an Established Institutional Repository: Marquette Libraries' Research Stewardship Survey." *Library Hi Tech News* 31, no. 6: 12–15. doi:10.1108/LHTN-05-2014-0038.

Glenaffric Ltd. 2007. *Six Steps to Effective Evaluation: A Handbook for Programme and Project Managers*. Bristol, UK: JISC. http://www.jisc.ac.uk/media/documents/programmes/reppres/evaluationhandbook.pdf.

Goben, Abigail, and Rebecca Raszewski. 2015a. "Policies and Background Literature for Self-Education on Research Data Management: An Annotated Bibliography." *Issues in Science and Technology Librarianship*, no. 82 (Fall).

———. 2015b. "Research Data Management Self-Education for Librarians: A Webliography." *Issues in Science and Technology Librarianship*, no. 82 (Fall).

Goldstein, Serge J., and Mark Ratliff. 2010. *DataSpace: A Funding and Operational Model for Long-Term Preservation and Sharing of Research Data*. Princeton, N.J.: Office of Information Technology, Princeton University. http://dataspace.princeton.edu/jspui/bitstream/88435/dsp01w6634361k/1/DataSpaceFundingModel_20100827.pdf.

Henderson, Margaret E. 2014. "New Roles and New Horizons for Health Sciences Librarians and Libraries." In *Health Sciences Librarianship*, edited by M. Sandra Wood, 403–18. Lanham, Md.: Rowman & Littlefield.

Henderson, Margaret E., and Teresa L. Knott. 2015. "Starting a Research Data Management Program Based in a University Library." *Medical Reference Services Quarterly* 34, no. 1: 47–59. doi:10.1080/02763869.2015.986783.

Henry, Geneva. 2014. "Data Curation for the Humanities: Perspectives from Rice University." Chapter 17 in *Research Data Management: Practical Strategies for Information Professionals*, edited by Joyce M. Ray, 347–74. West Lafayette, Ind.: Purdue University Press.

Hiom, Debra, Dom Fripp, Stephen Gray, Kellie Snow, and Damian Steer. 2015. "Research Data Management at the University of Bristol: Charting a Course from Project to Service." *Program* 49, no. 4: 475–93. doi:10.1108/PROG-02-2015-0019.

Hoppe, Heidrun C. 2000. "Second-Mover Advantages in the Strategic Adoption of New Technology under Uncertainty." *International Journal of Industrial Organization* 18, no. 2: 315–38. doi:10.1016/S0167-7187(98)00020-4.

Jetten, Mijke. 2014. "LIBER Case Study: Research Data Management at Radboud University." Association of European Research Libraries. http://libereurope.eu/wp-content/uploads/2014/06/LIBER-Case-Study-Radboud.pdf.

Johnson, Larry, Samantha Adams Becker, V. Estrada, and A. Freemen. 2015. *NMC Horizon Report: 2015 Library Edition*. Austin, Tex.: New Media Consortium. http://www.nmc.org/publication/nmc-horizon-report-2015-library-edition/.

Johnson, Layne M., John T. Butler, and Lisa R. Johnston. 2012. "Developing E-Science and Research Services and Support at the University of Minnesota Health Sciences Libraries." *Journal of Library Administration* 52, no. 8: 754–69. doi:10.1080/01930826.2012.751291.

Keralis, Spencer D. C., Shannon Stark, Martin Halbert, and William E. Moen. 2013. *Research Data Management in Policy and Practice: The DataRes Project*. Washington, D.C.: Council on Library and Information Resources. http://www.clir.org/pubs/reports/pub160.

Knight, Gareth. 2015. "Building a Research Data Management Service for the London School of Hygiene & Tropical Medicine." *Program* 49, no. 4: 424–39. doi:10.1108/PROG-01-2015-0011.

Mathews, Brian. 2012. *Think Like a Startup: A White Paper to Inspire Library Entrepreneurialism*. http://hdl.handle.net/10919/18649.

Mattern, Eleanor, Wei Jeng, Daqing He, Liz Lyon, and Aaron Brenner. 2015. "Using Participatory Design and Visual Narrative Inquiry to Investigate Researchers' Data Challenges and Recommendations for Library Research Data Services." *Program* 49, no. 4: 408–23. doi:10.1108/PROG-01-2015-0012.

Mischo, William H., Mary C. Schlembach, and Megan N. O'Donnell. 2014. "An Analysis of Data Management Plans in University of Illinois National Science Foundation Grant Proposals." *Journal of eScience Librarianship* 3, no. 1: e1060. http://dx.doi.org/10.7191/jeslib.2014.1060.

Pinfield, Stephen, Andrew M. Cox, and Jen Smith. 2014. "Research Data Management and Libraries: Relationships, Activities, Drivers and Influences." *PloS One* 9, no. 12: e114734. doi:10.1371/journal.pone.0114734.

Plale, Beth, Inna Kouper, Kurt Seiffert, and Stacy Konkiel. 2013. *Repository of NSF-Funded Publications and Related Datasets: "Back of Envelope" Cost Estimate for 15 Years*. http://hdl.handle.net/2022/16599.

Reeves Flores, Jodi, Jason J. Brodeur, Morgan G. Daniels, et al. 2015. "Libraries and the Research Data Management Landscape." In *The Process of Discovery: The CLIR Postdoctoral Fellowship Program and the Future of the Academy*, edited by John C. Maclachlan, Elizabeth A. Waraksa, and Christa Williford, 82–102. Washington, D.C.: Council on Library and Information Resources.

Reznik-Zellen, Rebecca C., Jessica Adamick, and Stephen McGinty. 2012. "Tiers of Research Data Support Services." *Journal of eScience Librarianship* 1, no. 1. http://dx.doi.org/10.7191/jeslib.2012.1002.

Royal Society. 2012. "Costs of Digital Repositories." https://royalsociety.org/topics-policy/projects/science-public-enterprise/digital-repositories/.

Schumacher, Jaime, Lynne M. Thomas, Drew VandeCreek, et al. 2014. *From Theory to Action: Good Enough Digital Preservation for Under-Resourced Cultural Heritage Institutions*. POWRR (Preserving digital Objects with Restricted Resources). http://commons.lib.niu.edu/handle/10843/13610.

Searle, Samantha, Malcolm Wolski, Natasha Simons, and Joanna Richardson. 2015. "Librarians as Partners in Research Data Service Development at Griffith University." *Program* 49, no. 4: 440–60. doi:10.1108/PROG-02-2015-0013.

Shen, Yi, and Virgil E. Varvel. 2013. "Developing Data Management Services at the Johns Hopkins University." *Journal of Academic Librarianship* 39, no. 6 (November): 552–57. doi:10.1016/j.acalib.2013.06.002.

Si, Li, Wenming Xing, Xiaozhe Zhuang, Xiaoqin Hua, and Limei Zhou. 2015. "Investigation and Analysis of Research Data Services in University Libraries." *Electronic Library* 33, no. 3: 417–49. doi:10.1108/EL-07-2013-0130.

Steinhart, Gail. 2014. "An Institutional Perspective on Data Curation Services: A View from Cornell University." In *Research Data Management: Practical Strategies for Information Professionals*, edited by Joyce M. Ray, 303–23. West Lafayette, Ind.: Purdue University Press.

Tenopir, Carol, Ben Birch, and Suzie Allard. 2012. *Academic Libraries and Research Data Services: Current Practices and Plans for the Future: An ACRL White Paper.* Association of College and Research Libraries. http://www.ala.org/acrl/sites/ala.org.acrl/files/content/publications/ whitepapers/Tenopir_Birch_Allard.pdf.

Tenopir, Carol, Elizabeth D. Dalton, Suzie Allard, et al. 2015. "Changes in Data Sharing and Data Reuse Practices and Perceptions among Scientists Worldwide." *PLoS ONE* 10, no. 8: e0134826. http://dx.doi.org/10.1371%2Fjournal.pone.0134826.

Tenopir, Carol, Robert J. Sandusky, Suzie Allard, and Ben Birch. 2014. "Research Data Management Services in Academic Research Libraries and Perceptions of Librarians." *Library & Information Science Research* 36, no. 2: 84–90. doi:10.1016/j.lisr.2013.11.003.

Thompson, Cheryl A., Chuck Humphrey, and Michael Witt. 2015. "Exploring Organizational Approaches to Research Data in Academic Libraries: Which Archetype Fits Your Library?" Research Data Alliance Sixth Plenary Meeting, Paris, September 23–25.

Vaughan, K. T., Barrie E. Hayes, Rachel C. Lerner, et al. 2013. "Development of the Research Lifecycle Model for Library Services." *Journal of the Medical Library Association* 101, no. 4 (October): 310–14.

Verbaan, Eddy, and Andrew M. Cox. 2014. "Occupational Sub-Cultures, Jurisdictional Struggle and Third Space: Theorising Professional Service Responses to Research Data Management." *Journal of Academic Librarianship* 40, nos. 3–4: 211–19. doi:10.1016/j.acalib.2014.02.008.

Wagner, Caroline S. 2008. *The New Invisible College: Science for Development.* Washington, D.C.: Brookings Institution Press.

Wakimoto, Jina Choi. 2013. "Developing Research Data Management Services." *EDUCAUSE Review Online.* http://er.educause.edu/articles/2013/2/developing-research-data-management-services.

Wang, Minglu. 2013. "Supporting the Research Process through Expanded Library Data Service." *Program* 47, no. 3: 282–303. doi:10.1108/PROG-04-2012-0010.

Weller, Travis, and Amalia Monroe-Gulick. 2015. "Differences in the Data Practices, Challenges, and Future Needs of Graduate Students and Faculty Members." *Journal of eScience Librarianship* 4, no. 1. doi:10.7191/jeslib.2015.1070.

Westra, Brian. 2010. "Data Services for the Sciences: A Needs Assessment." *Ariadne: A Web & Print Magazine of Internet Issues for Librarians & Information Specialists* 30, no. 64: 13–13. http://www.ariadne.ac.uk/issue64/westra.

———. 2014. "Developing Data Management Services for Researchers at the University of Oregon." Chapter 18 in *Research Data Management: Practical Strategies for Information Professionals,* edited by Joyce M. Ray, 375–91. West Lafayette, Ind.: Purdue University Press.

Whitehead, Martha, and Kathleen Shearer. 2015. *Portage: Organizational Framework April 7, 2015.* Prepared by Martha Whitehead and Kathleen Shearer. Portage. http://www.carl-abrc. ca/uploads/SCC/Portage%20Organizational%20Framework,%20April%207,%202015.pdf.

Whitmire, Amanda Lea, Michael Boock, and Shan C. Sutton. 2015. "Variability in Academic Research Data Management Practices: Implications for Data Services Development from a Faculty Survey." *Program: Electronic Library and Information Systems* 49, no. 4. http://dx.doi. org/10.1108/PROG-02-2015-0017.

Whyte, Angus, Laura Molloy, Neil Beagrie, and John Houghton. 2014. "What to Measure? Towards Metrics for Research Data Management." Chapter 14 in *Research Data Management: Practical Strategies for Information Professionals,* edited by Joyce M. Ray, 275–300. West Lafayette, Ind.: Purdue University Press.

Williams, Sarah C. 2013. "Using a Bibliographic Study to Identify Faculty Candidates for Data Services." *Science & Technology Libraries* 32, no. 2: 202–9. doi:10.1080/0194262X.2013.774622.

Wright, Sarah J., Jake R. Carlson, Jon Jeffryes, et al. 2015. "Developing Data Information Literacy Programs: A Guide for Academic Librarians." In *Data Information Literacy: Librarians, Data, and the Education of a New Generation of Researchers,* edited by Jake R. Carlson and Lisa R. Johnston, 205–30. West Lafayette, Ind.: Purdue University Press.

Leveraging Partnerships

DATA MANAGEMENT SERVICES cannot exist in a vacuum. Interactions with other departments and people throughout the organization are necessary to provide needed services. Consulting with the research office and information technology services while developing RDM services should lead to ongoing connections that can be used to support RDM. But there are many others who can help. Look for groups with similar goals or related services. Find people with lots of connections who will recommend data services when discussing research with others. Keep in touch with administrators who will advocate for recognition of data as an institutional asset deserving of funds for preservation. Any connection has the potential to contribute to the success of RDM, so data librarians need to be ready to explain RDM to anyone they meet.

Finding Partners

Data management and research touch on many departments and people at most institutions. While it is possible for one person to start offering some data management services without connecting to other groups around the institution, there is more chance of success if an effort is made to engage with the community at large. Chapter 9 mentioned a few interested groups, faculty, research office, technology services, in connection with finding committee members or interviewees to help with setting up a data management service, but there are many more potential partners around the institution. At the Midwest Data Librarians Symposium, Brianna Marshall led a session on creating partnerships. The first task of the group was to brainstorm all the potential partners they thought could contribute to data management services. The list was longer than anyone expected (see textbox) and serves as a useful starting point when looking for partners.

POTENTIAL PARTNERS FOR DATA MANAGEMENT

- Researchers
- Provosts
- Campus IT/academic IT
- Lab/department IT
- Research office
- Grant office/admins
- Subject librarians
- Library administrators
- Research deans
- Research integrity office/IRB [institutional review board]
- Campus legal
- Info security office
- High performance computing/research core
- Tech transfer/economic development office
- PR/marketing
- Archives/records/museums
- Grad school
- Undergraduate research
- Teaching centers
- Research centers
- University senate (research, faculty, governing body)
- Visualization center
- Campus committees
  - Tech
  - Policy
  - Promotion & tenure
- LIS school
- Program officers for national agencies
- Professional associations
- Donors/trustees
- Student groups
- Emeritus faculty

(Marshall and MDLS15 participants, 2015a)

Environmental Assessment

If an environmental assessment wasn't part of the planning process, as outlined in chapter 9, now is the time to conduct one in search of partners. People and resources that are already involved with various aspects of data collection, use, and management are usually the first partners people think of, but making a data management service successful requires contact with people in other areas as well. Don't neglect the various administrative groups around the institution. Learning which administrative groups make budget decisions and which influence researchers' choices of collaborators can help with funds and promotion. Look into the organizing structure of the institution to learn how ideas, funds, grants, and even power, move from group to group. This will help identify those who can help with influence and are in a position to pass on information about data services to those in need of it. Research support services, such as laboratory or equipment services, image or art services, computer services, or any group that contributes to research, can refer people to new data services and could have helpful information about providing a research service at the institution.

Data Life Cycle

In conjunction with the environmental assessment, finding partners that contribute to the data life cycle can be a good way of fitting new data services in with old. In a university setting, there is often a statistical analysis service affiliated with a math, business, or biostatistics department. They may prefer to only deal with data analysis and find it difficult to work with a researcher to organize their data enough to analyze it. Or they may realize that a researcher needs to describe and add metadata to their data before the raw data and analysis can be published. Data analysts will probably be thrilled to be able to refer researchers to a data management librarian for help in these areas. But, as mentioned in chapter 9, these are the collaborators who need to be approached cautiously. Reassure these groups that any new data services will be filling in gaps, not trying to lure away research collaborators.

Making Connections

Data librarians are not the first type of specialized librarian to start new services at an organization, or to use their expertise for more than traditional reference service. Embedded librarians have been working their way into classrooms, offices, and virtual spaces for many years now, as traditional reference desk transactions have gone down and the value of knowledge has gone up (Shumaker, 2012). In health sciences libraries, a systematic review of the literature and job ads identified various embedded roles, such as liaison librarian, informationist, clinical informationist, bioinformationist, public health informationist, and disaster information specialist, as well as new activities such as participating in systematic reviews, finding and teaching emerging technologies (which includes user experience librarian), and involvement with continuing medical education, grants development, and data management (Cooper and Crum, 2013). Through outreach efforts, librarians can become involved in many projects around their institutions. Barbara I. Dewey (2004) suggests librarians reach out to many different groups, campus governance, chief academic officer, chief student affairs officer, institutional research and assessment, and many others. In fact she suggests that librarians can and should get involved everywhere:

Librarians are in a unique position to become involved in core activities and initiatives throughout the university. The fact that we are generalists and devoted to all disciplines and all sectors of the academic user community gives us a special insight on ways to advance the university and achieve its mission. However, in order to be productive and effective throughout the campus, librarians must strategically and energetically seek and accept leadership roles. Central administrators may not automatically consider that a librarian should be tapped or invited to participate on campus-wide projects. Thus, librarians must take it upon themselves to establish an acute sense of important campus agendas and propose involvement including reasons why their perspective is important. A proactive approach is essential in getting one or more seats at the right tables rather than waiting to be asked. (Dewey, 2004: 11)

As well as efforts to make connections with people around the institution, it is important not to forget people within the library. Hopefully, librarians and library staff interested in data management have been involved in the planning, but there may be people with needed skills or the potential to help who didn't get involved early on. The Purdue University Libraries Research Data group developed a new organizational structure that led to increased collaborations (Zilinski et al., 2015). A metadata specialist in the technical services/cataloging environment had to learn the additional requirements needed to add metadata to data. User interface design for DMPTool was enhanced with the work of a digital user experience specialist. And the molecular biosciences information specialist worked on education, research, and reuse of data, and encouraged researchers to use the Purdue University Research Repository (PURR) as a workspace for data projects. Regular outreach to all librarians who interact in any way with faculty and researchers is important because if they know what data management services can do, they can refer people to the service when needed, and they can mention the service when giving orientation talks. A concept map of one librarian's interactions shows that just one liaison can interact with many department heads, faculty, students, and groups, with many different communication strategies (in person, guides, newsletters, social media, etc.), all of which can be used to share data management services information (Pasek, 2015).

Planning for Partnerships

Once partners are identified, a strategy needs to be in place for contacting and engaging the person or group. Some people will not understand the concept of data management, or understand it to be something different, as discussed in chapter 1. Others will wonder why you are contacting them, and what you want from them. Thinking beforehand about why you wish to engage certain people or groups, and how you can help them and they can help you, will make interactions go much smoother.

Roles for Partners

Graham Pryor (2014) sees a three-way division of potential collaborators: university management, support and administrative services, and researchers/data producers. By combining Pryor's groups and their responsibilities with the brainstormed partners mentioned earlier in this chapter, potential roles to discuss with partners can start to emerge (table 10.1).

Table 10.1. Roles for Potential Partners of Academic Libraries

GROUP	RESPONSIBILITIES/ROLES	EXAMPLES
University Management	• champion to advocate for RDM • set up a representative, balanced steering group that • reflects interest of stakeholders • appraise and approve plans • support budgets • advise of strategic issues • support RDM policy for institution	• provost • research deans • library administrators • university senate (research, faculty, • governing body) • donors, trustees

Support and Administrative Services	• function as part of RDM team or steering group
	• analyze policy requirements at national, funder, and
	• institutional level
	• identify current status of institutional data sets
	• identify services and gaps
	• plan and budget for RDM services
	• plan for the acquisition of skills to support RDM services
	• plan an advocacy program to promote RDM services
	• facilitate RDM training for managers, support staff, and
	• researchers
	• bring units together to work as a seamless RDM service
		• campus IT/academic IT
		• lab/dept IT
		• research office
		• grant office/admins
		• subject librarians
		• research integrity office/IRB
		• campus legal
		• info security office
		• high performance computing/research core
		• tech transfer/economic dev office
		• graduate school
		• PR/marketing
		• archives/records/ museums
		• campus committees
		  • tech
		  • policy
		  • promotion & tenure

Researchers/Data Producers	• contribute views to steering group • collaborate as requirements are collected and RDM • services, e.g., storage, curation, are tested • clearly articulate discipline needs around data • champion adoption of approved RDM services • support training initiatives	• student groups • emeritus faculty • research centers • grad school • teaching centers • visualization center • high-performance computing/research core

Approaching Potential Partners

Before approaching any potential partners, whether you know them already or not, it is helpful to think a little about the motivations of the person and what you would like to talk about with him or her. In the same session that produced the list of potential partners listed at the start of this chapter, Brianna Marshall also had symposium participants develop a persona (see textbox) for a partner, although a shortened version was used due to time constraints. Each group wrote a brief summary of the role of the partner, then came up with three goals and three frustrations that the partner might have. It was very important that the groups think sympathetically about the partner and try to consider how others might view new services such as research data management.

PERSONAS

Personas are archetypes used to help in areas such as marketing and user interface design. Creating personas can help design teams and developers understand all the different groups that might use their product or service. These articles provide some basic information on creating personas.

Calabria, Tina. 2004. "An Introduction to Personas and How to Create Them." StepTwo.com. March 2. http://www.steptwo.com.au/papers/kmc_personas/.

Churruca, Silvia. 2013. "Introduction to User Personas." *UX Lady* (blog). June 27. http://www.ux-lady.com/introduction-to-user-personas/.

O'Connor, Kevin. 2011. "Personas: The Foundation of a Great User Experience." *UX Magazine*. Article No: 640, March 25. http://uxmag.com/articles/personas-the-foundation-of-a-great-user-experience.

U.S. Dept. of Health & Human Services. 2006. "Personas." In *The Research-Based Web Design & Usability Guidelines*, enlarged/expanded edition. Washington: U.S. Government Printing Office. http://www.usability.gov/how-to-and-tools/methods/personas.html.

Once a persona was created, the groups developed a thirty-second elevator speech that highlighted the ways data management services could help with the goals, or ease the frustrations, of the potential partner (Marshall and MDLS15 participants, 2015b). Ideas ranged from asking a dean of graduate studies to sponsor a data management workshop because the skills will help graduate students with future grants and job prospects, to approaching campus IT services to work together because data security is important to data management services and IT, and both groups having a unified message about security and storage will help data management throughout the institution.

Even if personas and elevator speeches are not developed (although an elevator speech can be very helpful), learning about potential partners and thinking about why they might be good partners for data management services ahead of time will lead to a more successful interaction. Does the partner share goals with the library and data management services? Then maybe he or she can be an advocate or program advisor. Does the potential partner have specialized skills that can help with data management, such as legal knowledge? Then that partner might be a consultant who contributes when needed. Do the services of the partner contribute to data management? Then that group will be collaborators, maybe even joint providers as part of an extended data management services team. The more people who understand what is going on as data management services develop, the better the chance for the service to succeed. Those who know share information with others, and their advocacy will help get the word out about the service.

External Partners

There are a few potential partners in the list at the start of the chapter that do not fall into the groups above. These are external partners: LIS schools, program officers for national agencies and funders, and professional associations. Disciplinary repositories and collaborative services, such as ICPSR (https://www.icpsr.umich.edu/) or the Data Conservancy (http://dataconservancy.org/), could also be included in the list of potential external partners. Depending on the needs of the library, these groups can help with training, information, resources, and advice. Contact with people in external organizations can be very helpful if there are problems when trying to establish data management services. By providing a larger picture view of the need for data management services and access to experts in various aspects of the data management life cycle, external partners support data management services everywhere.

Working with Partners

There is a broad range of partners available to help libraries setting up research data management services. Once useful partners are identified and approached, data librarians need to make sure their efforts are coordinated and acknowledged. Different types of partnerships require different strategies for engagement and participation. Relationship-building activities that are used by liaisons and embedded librarians, such as sending brief e-mails with items of interest in their research field or sending personal invitations to events, should be included in any type of partnership. If acknowledgment of partnerships is part of the library's annual report, data management services should make sure any partners are included.

Advocates and Advisors

Advocates and advisors are those people who will champion data management services to others or provide insight into the workings or the organization, or even suggestions on how to move the service forward. These are people who usually have shared goals for an institution or a commitment to the same strategic plan as the library. They need to be kept up to date on what is happening with data management services so they have current information to pass on to their contacts. Send a thank-you message for any referrals from advocates or advisors, and acknowledge any other help they might provide, to strengthen and promote the relationship.

Consultants

Consultants help with their expertise. Relationships with consultants will depend on things like institutional culture, departmental politics, and whether or not the person is external to the organization. In some universities, departments must pay for faculty from outside the department to teach if they wish to use their expertise for a whole course. And salary support for experts is often included in grant applications. On the other hand, university counsel may be available to everyone, but it might take some time to get an answer. If a particular relationship is needed to acquire expert information, acknowledge that there might be some cost involved and be prepared to discuss the preferred method of compensation. Often, a nascent data management service has no budget, or planned grants or publications where the consultant could be included, to offer as an incentive to collaborate. Explaining how data management services will advance the institutional mission and why their expertise is needed might be enough to engage some people. Even if an agreement cannot be reached, keep consultants informed about the progress of the program. It may be at some future date they will want to help voluntarily, or the service will have a budget, but they might also become an advocate if they think the service is worthwhile.

Collaborations—Teams and Workgroups

Basic leadership and management skills are useful if a data librarian is trying to bring together many partners and needs to be able to create teams to do the necessary planning and work. Because the data librarian organizing things is usually not the supervisor of the other team members, leadership will involve guiding the group based on shared goals and teamwork. James M. Kouzes and Barry Z. Posner (2007) have found five practices that indicate exemplary leadership:

1. Model the way.
2. Inspire a shared vision.
3. Challenge the process.
4. Enable others to act.
5. Encourage the heart.

These are all important when bringing together a diverse team. Show respect for all collaborators and value their input. Remind the group of the shared institutional goals you are working toward, even though data management as an organized service is new to the organization. Trust others to move the development of data management services forward in their areas. Recognize the contribution of all members and share progress to develop a sense of community. As Pryor (2014: 57) has written, "The success of an RDM service will, quite evidently, rest upon the inclusivity and connectivity of its human infrastructure. It will call for some considerable management talent."

As well as having good leadership, teams at Google have found five team dynamics that lead to successful teams (Rozovsky, 2015):

1. Psychological safety: Team members should feel comfortable taking risks.
2. Dependability: Team members should be able to count on each other to do good work on time.
3. Structure and clarity: Goals, roles, and plans should be clear.
4. Meaning of work: The goals of the team should be important to everyone.
5. Impact of work: Everyone should believe the work is important to the organization.

These leadership skills and suggestions, combined with active listening and some of the other communication skills covered in chapter 4, should provide the librarian trying to organize a collaborative workgroup or team with a solid starting point for a successful team.

Collaborative Teaching

In the Data Information Literacy (DIL) project, librarians interacted with faculty in a different form of partnership (Wright et al., 2015). Through several projects in multiple locations, librarians with DIL training worked with individual faculty members and research groups to tailor DIL training for students. The initial contacts were "low-hanging fruit"—faculty the librarians already had good relationships with or courses librarians were already helping with. These contacts progressed to "coming to an understanding," a point where librarians interviewed faculty and students to decide on the issues that needed to be addressed and started to consider strategies for training. When the collaboration continued beyond informal conversations, it was considered a "working relationship" between the faculty and a team of librarians. One of the most important characteristics of the teams was flexibility. In order to make projects work, teams had to be able to find work-arounds to time constraints or changing needs and strategies. When it came to engaging with faculty, it was very important for librarians to know about disciplinary norms for data management and research ahead of time, including the disciplinary repositories, grant requirements, metadata, and organizations and journals that relate to data for that discipline. Being prepared in this way, and being clear about what was needed from faculty, were important parts of successful DIL projects.

⑥ Key Points

Developing good relationships with relevant partners around an institution is important for any service, but especially for new services like data management. Good collaborations will help spread the word about new data services available in the library.

- Finding and developing partnerships is important for the success of a data management service.
- Developing relationships with people at all levels and in all areas of the organization is critical to success.
- Be prepared to explain concisely what data management services are and how they can help the person you are talking to.
- Learn leadership, not management, and treat collaborators as trusted associates, not subordinates.

In the next chapter, partnerships are just one of the ways that will be considered when it comes time to expand data management services.

⑥ References

Cooper, I. Diane, and Janet A. Crum. 2013. "New Activities and Changing Roles of Health Sciences Librarians: A Systematic Review, 1990–2012." *Journal of the Medical Library Association* 101, no. 4 (October): 268–77.

Dewey, Barbara I. 2004. "The Embedded Librarian: Strategic Campus Collaborations." *Resource Sharing & Information Networks* 17, no. 1: 5–17. doi:10.1300/J121v17n01_02.

Kouzes, James M., and Barry Z. Posner. 2007. "The Five Practices of Exemplary Leadership." In *The Jossey-Bass Reader on Education Leadership*, 2nd ed., 63–72. San Francisco: Wiley.

Marshall, Brianna, and MDLS15 participants. 2015a. "Outline of Partnerships Session: Topic 3: Forming Partnerships on Campus." Midwest Data Librarians Symposium. University of Wisconsin, Milwaukee. UWM Digital Commons. http://dc.uwm.edu/mdls/2015/partnerships/8/.

———. 2015b. "Topic 3: Forming Partnerships on Campus." Midwest Data Librarians Symposium. University of Wisconsin, Milwaukee. UWM Digital Commons. http://dc.uwm.edu/mdls/2015/partnerships/.

Pasek, Judith E. 2015. "Organizing the Liaison Role." *College & Research Libraries News* 76, no. 4: 202–5.

Pryor, Graham. 2014. "Who's Doing Data? A Spectrum of Roles, Responsibilities and Competences." In *Delivering Research Data Management Services: Fundamentals of Good Practice*, edited by Graham Pryor, Sarah Jones, and Angus Whyte, 41–58. London: Facet.

Rozovsky, Julia. 2015. "The Five Keys to a Successful Google Team." *Re:Work* (blog). https://rework.withgoogle.com/blog/five-keys-to-a-successful-google-team/.

Shumaker, David. 2012. *The Embedded Librarian: Innovative Strategies for Taking Knowledge Where It's Needed*. Medford, N.J.: Information Today.

Wright, Sarah J., Jake R. Carlson, Jon Jeffryes, et al. 2015. "Developing Data Information Literacy Programs: A Guide for Academic Librarians." In *Data Information Literacy: Librarians, Data, and the Education of a New Generation of Researchers*, edited by Jake R. Carlson and Lisa R. Johnston, 205–30. West Lafayette, Ind.: Purdue University Press.

Zilinski, Lisa D., Amy Barton, Tao Zhang, et al. 2015. "Research Data Integration in the Purdue Libraries." *Bulletin of the Association for Information Science & Technology* 42, no. 2: 33–37. doi:10.1002/bul2.2016.1720420212.

Expanding RDM Service

ONCE A LIBRARY STARTS OFFERING basic research data management services, there will soon be requests for many other services related to data and data management. It is tempting to try to do everything, but it is very important to consider scalability and sustainability when adding any new library service. Offering classes is one way to share data management expertise with more people (chapter 12). And supporting the reuse of data, from purchased data sets or open data, can help many researchers and students (chapter 13). But there are other individualized services, such as data input form development, helping with data analysis, and helping with specialized data, such as GIS or patient data, that require time and expertise. Each library and institution must assess whether or not the resources to provide these services are available, no matter what the perceived need.

Making the Decision to Expand Services

As mentioned at the end of chapter 9, evaluation of data management services should be ongoing and used to refine the scope of service as an iterative process. There is no guarantee that the initial services developed, based on the needs that were found through the various steps of the startup process, will be used. For example, there may be many students asking for help to find data for projects, but they may not be willing to attend library workshops, so the data librarian might need to find out if the instructor will be willing to give up class time for a lecture on finding data. It should be an ongoing process to check that the goals developed for the RDM service are being met. Whether the goals were based on numbers reached, departments reached, increased collaborations, or administrative awareness, there should be a point where all goals have been met and it is time to consider expansion of services.

Using Statistics

Before trying to add new services, it is helpful to show that current services are at capacity and there is a need for more. Using some sort of training management system that can keep track of participants in classes with their rank and department, combined with a waiting list option, is important to show the need for more classes. Keeping track of numbers of consultations is also important, and the system used for this should have rank and department as well, and include space for the initial question or intended use of the information. Comparing data management plan consultations and DMPTool usage to the total number of grants with DMPs submitted might also be a helpful statistic. Along with participation statistics, data librarians should keep track of time spent preparing for classes and consultations, time spent teaching or in meetings, and any time needed for follow-up activities. Meetings with administrators, faculty, and other stakeholders should also be documented to show the time spent in relationship and collaboration-building activities.

Using Evaluations

As discussed in chapter 9, evaluations sent out to class participants and researchers using consulting services can be used to show that instructional sessions meet expectations and data librarians provide helpful information, as well as showing impact and value. Surveys should also allow respondents to suggest further areas where they need instruction or consulting services, which can be used to show the need for new services. Just as surveys can be used when starting RDM services, surveys can be sent to people who haven't used existing data management services to find out why they haven't and learn which services would be useful. New and updated interviews could also be used to find out what services and resources are still needed for teaching and research. Informal evaluations, thank-you notes, or comments from collaborators can also be used as a chance to ask about what more could be done.

Another potential evaluation resource is data management plans from grants. DMPs have been used to find out how researchers plan on sharing and storing their data at several institutions (Bishoff and Johnston, 2015; Mischo, Schlembach, and O'Donnell, 2014; Parham and Doty, 2012). The authors then used the information to target specific disciplines, plan sharing and storage services, develop consistent language about repository services, and improve faculty knowledge of sharing options. Steven Van Tuyl and Amanda L. Whitmire (2016) assessed the success of sharing plans by checking if data was available as planned in a data management plan or required by a publisher. They found that data sharing was not usually carried out and when data was shared, it was of questionable usability. They offer recommendations for sharing data that can be used to support educational efforts based on DMP evaluations. The DART Project (http://dmpresearch.library.oregonstate.edu/) is creating a rubric that will help with DMP analysis to assist data librarians providing research support.

Staffing and Funding

Finding resources to expand data management services can be difficult, even when evaluations and statistics indicate that more services are needed. The same options that are available for starting a service apply when expanding. Assessing resources and services throughout the library to see what can be eliminated, moving positions from departments that have changed because of new technology, or changing duties because of a change in library or institutional goals are all possibilities. Even within the data management service, it is important to look at how time is being spent. After a couple of years of DMPTool training and customization, there may be very few consultation requests, so time could be devoted to new services. And once policies and training curriculum have been developed, it will take less time keep them up to date, so there is time for other activities. Referral to external resources is also an option to expand resources (Si et al., 2015). There are extensive RDM training resources available on the Internet (Goben and Raszewski, 2015) that can be shared, and DMPTool is available to everyone, even when an institution doesn't participate.

It is important to remember that research data is an institutional asset and requires the support of many departments around the institution. Approaching the provost or Office of Research for support with funds, or contracting with a specific department with data intensive research might be suggested. It might be helpful to explore how core facilities and specialized services operate around the institution. When data policies are developed, it could be a requirement for data management funds to be included in grants. Working with collaborators identified in chapter 10 is important to continue the growth of data management services. Cosponsoring training or formalizing referral services expands data management services without many additional resources. It is also possible to share expertise with collaborators and stakeholders. The University of Melbourne Library and UKLON Informatics developed a capacity building immersiveInformatics research data management training program for staff in the library and other university departments to help with development of skilled staff to provide support to researchers (Shadbolt et al., 2014).

What If You Can't Expand?

It is possible that even after showing the need for more services, the decision will be made not to add data services and people to the library. Whoever is providing the service, be it a single data librarian or a team where data management is just one job duty, will need to assess the commitment of the library to providing research data management services. Is there one or more people who still need convincing of the role of libraries in providing data services? Or maybe it is just a budget or hiring freeze, and expansion can be explored again when conditions are better. Maybe one more year of sustained interest would convince people that a data management service is feasible. Depending on the institutional interest in data management, maybe research data management needs to move into another department. Not every institution locates data services in the library. The position could be in the research office, a specific school in the dean's office, or even a particular department. If there are enough interested collaborators and champions, it should be possible to explore other models for providing data management services.

⊚ Adding Services throughout the Data Life Cycle

There are many potential services in research data management and related areas such as data science that could be offered in libraries. The services relate to various steps in the data life cycle, but there are also some disciplines where services could be provided throughout the data life cycle if the expertise is available. Table 11.1 is an extensive, but not exhaustive, list of services that could be offered by libraries or in collaboration with other departments. Further information on some of these services can be found below.

Table 11.1. Potential Services to Consider as Data Management Services Grow (Not a Comprehensive List)

DATA LIFE CYCLE STEP	EXPANDED SERVICES
Plan	DMP consultation and review Laboratory notebooks/electronic lab notebooks (ELNs) Note taking and organization
Collect	Development of forms for data input Reference service for census, statistical, and government data Web scraping for data Workflow consults
Describe	Metadata Readme file customization forms
Process and Analyze	Database creation Data cleaning Data mining/text mining Statistics Teaching code Visualization
Publish and Share	Compliance Institutional repository Scholarly communication (see chapter 14) Specialized repository
Preserve	Institutional data catalog Infrastructure Legacy data Repositories (see chapter 5)
Reuse	See chapter 13
All—Disciplinary Data	Astrophysics Digital humanities GIS Patient/health data Weather and ocean data
All—Specialized Services	Data policy (federal, institution, journal) Citizen science/crowdsourced projects Embedded librarians or informationists Interface design Teaching data information literacy (see chapter 12)

Plan

Helping with data management plans has been discussed as one of the first services for a library because funder requirements make DMPs important to many faculty and the grants office. Along with setting up and customizing DMPTool and offering consultations with researchers, studying submitted DMPs can help improve future grants (see the studies and DART Project in the "Using Evaluations" section above). As with many services that can be offered through consultations, teaching the topic to groups and classes can be part of the service. Grant writing is often a component of writing courses or workshops sponsored by the Office of Research, so data librarians should seek out these types of opportunities to offer classes that cover using DMPTool or writing data management plans for funders.

Laboratory notebooks or electronic lab notebooks (ELNs) and note taking and organizing systems are essentially the same thing but for different disciplines (see the textbox for digital examples). Both involve planning and organizing the collection and retrieval of collected research data or information. Note taking and managing information are major activities of serious researchers (Tancheva et al., 2016), and data librarians can help researchers of all disciplines plan ahead to ensure that data from fieldwork or lab work, research notes or collected information, are all easy to find in whatever digital or paper system they use. A *Library Journal* Research report (2015) found that 84 percent of faculty feel that support for faculty research is an "essential" or "very essential" service for libraries to provide, and 63 percent think the same about the library coordinating research data services, but they probably don't think of RDM as a service that can help

---

DIGITAL NOTE TAKING SYSTEMS

Electronic Laboratory Notebooks
- ELN guide from University of Utah Libraries
  http://campusguides.lib.utah.edu/ELNs
- LabArchive
  http://www.labarchives.com/
- Open Science Framework (OSF)
  https://osf.io/
- RSpace
  http://www.researchspace.com/

Note Taking Programs
- Research Support: Productivity and Citation Tools from University of North Carolina, Ashville
  http://library.unca.edu/researchsupport/productivity
- Evernote
  https://evernote.com/
- OneNote
  https://www.onenote.com/
- Scrivener
  http://www.literatureandlatte.com/scrivener.php

---

with the organization of nonquantitative research materials. This may be another area where teaching, especially to students, is a good option.

Collect

When data librarians are familiar with research in different disciplines, helping improve data collection can be another area of service. Creation of templates or forms to aid data or information collection can provide researchers with a good way to ensure consistent data input, which is then easier to search and analyze. Forms or templates can include reminder notes so dates are entered correctly and explain how measurements should be taken, including the proper units to use. Cerys Willoughby, Thomas A. Logothetis, and Jeremy G. Frey (2016) have shown that structured templates can improve the completeness of information captured, and customized templates could be beneficial when complying with specific guidelines from funders. In a similar way, using templates and forms to structure workflow can ensure that all necessary steps are followed and data or notes are saved in an organized and easy-to-follow manner that can be replicated.

Data librarians with programming experience might want to consider offering web scraping consultations and classes. The web contains large amounts of digital data that aren't always in a form that can be easily downloaded. Web scraping, with a program like Python, can gather data for different types of research projects. Knowing that there are other methods to get data can be helpful when trying to answer a question that seems to have no data in the usual sources. Web scraping expands the resources that can be considered for data collection. Interested data librarians should investigate further training in a course such as Data Scientist Training for Librarians (http://altbibl.io/dst4l/).

Describe

As mentioned in chapter 6, librarians' familiarity with cataloging and ontologies is a big help when working with researchers trying to add metadata and descriptions to their research data. Rather than trying to keep up with all the different schemas available, review major funders used by researchers at your university and keep track of the requirements for the repositories recommended in their policies. Many researchers will find it difficult to add formal metadata, that is, machine-readable files, to all their data, so promoting readme files may be an easier way to start encouraging documentation. Templates for readme files that are customized for a research group or project can make it easier to collect the necessary information for data reuse and, if necessary, add metadata (see chapter 6 for basic fields).

Process and Analyze

Most of the expanded services related to processing and analyzing data require specialized software or computer programming training. Programs range from being free and fairly easy, such as cleaning spreadsheets with OpenRefine (http://openrefine.org/), to more complex, but still freely available, like Python (https://www.python.org), to expensive programs, such as SPSS (http://www-01.ibm.com/software/analytics/spss/). Digital humanities has some specialized tools to process data. Digital Research Tools (DiRT, http://dirtdirectory.org/) has a growing list of tools for scholarly use. Tools can be browsed by what the researcher wants to do, for example, analyze, interpret, or model data; or by the type of data, for example, text file, polls, or sheet music.

Most institutions already have one or two other departments that provide these services, which should have turned up during the environmental assessment (see chapter 9), and the departments involved should be approached as collaborators. Institutional IT departments usually support site licensing for many of these programs, and many IT departments provide technical support, training classes, or access to online training videos. The type of service provided by the library should fill the gaps left by other departments, unless of course a department would like to stop a particular service. Rutgers University Libraries provided statistical analysis services and statistical software workshops for graduate students, in the absence of these services being available elsewhere on campus (Wang, 2013). Even if no services are offered, it is very helpful for data librarians to know about and understand these tools for consultations and when making referrals.

Publish and Share

New funder policies have made publishing and sharing data an important activity for libraries to manage. It is important for researchers to know that journal and OSTP policies only require the sharing of digital data that supports a published paper, but the NIH and NSF will expect other types of data and research products, including cell lines and software, to be shared as well. Helping researchers keep track of what they need to share, and making sure the supporting documentation is clear, is an important data management service. Not all researchers will be publishing in journals that specify where data should be deposited, so libraries should provide a list of discipline-specific repositories that fit with the major research areas of the institution. Researchers should be aware that even if a journal does not have a requirement to publish or deposit data at the time of article publication, and they don't have a grant that requires data sharing, the journal may have a policy that requires data be shared upon request. There are also papers that have been retracted when data to support suspect figures is not available, even when the original institution has closed and the paper is more than ten years old (Palus, 2016).

Institutional repositories can be used to publish, share, and preserve data. Rutgers University Libraries surveyed thirty-five repositories to assess their policies, staffing, workflows, and so forth, to develop a plan for working with data that includes making sure the institutional data policy clearly acknowledges ownership, protects confidential and sensitive data, provides adequate staffing, creates a workflow for mediated and self-deposit of data, and provides guidance for those who work with data (Palumbo et al., 2015).

Some libraries have used their knowledge of repositories to work with discipline-specific groups to develop subject repositories. Cornell University's Mann Library worked with several USDA agencies to develop the USDA Economics, Statistics and Market Information System (ESMIS, http://usda.mannlib.cornell.edu/), which holds reports and USDA data, some of which is updated yearly. If a university conducts enough research in a specific area, it is possible to get grants to make the data publicly available. The University of Guelph Library has received funding from the Ontario Ministry of Agriculture, Food, and Rural Affairs Knowledge Translation and Transfer program (OMAFRA-KTT) to develop a special agri-environmental research data repository for research data from agriculture and environmental research projects conducted at the university (http://dataverse.scholarsportal.info/dvn/dv/ugardr).

Preserve

Libraries are a natural place to provide preservation of materials, and many libraries have experience with digital collections and the ways they differ from print collections. Data requires further expertise to deal with the varied formats and a good infrastructure to deal with some of the large file sizes (Sweetkind-Singer and Schwarzwalder, 2010). Even if the library has responsibility for the development and provision of services for data storage and sharing, it is difficult to develop a sustainable infrastructure for data and research. It needs more than just storage of data, so a strong institutional commitment is necessary to support research cyberinfrastructure (Li et al., 2014). When a library does plan on developing a data repository, for preservation or for publishing and sharing (see above), it is important to make sure the repository will meet certification requirements, for example, Trustworthy Repositories Audit & Certification: Criteria and Checklist (TRAC) (http://www.crl.edu/archiving-preservation/digital-archives/metrics-assessing-and-certifying/trac) from the Center for Research Libraries (CRL).

A data catalog or registry to keep track of institutional research data is an option if an institution cannot store and preserve all of the data collected by researchers. This will make it easier to show funders that data has been shared in the appropriate disciplinary repository or explain why it can't be shared. The University of Melbourne used grants and publications to start collecting information about data sets produced at the university, and used the semantic web application Vitro to link data sets, publications, and authors (Porter and Shadbolt, 2010). The New York University School of Medicine Health Sciences Library was able to help the Department of Population Health increase usage of the many large, externally funded data sets, for example, census and public health data sets, by creating a data catalog that includes access information and connects interested researchers to expert researchers (Read et al., 2015). The data catalog will expand to include internally generated data sets to promote data sharing and reuse within the institution.

Some libraries actively seek out data sets to curate as special projects to help promote the use of library data services and illustrate best practices for those currently collecting data. A project to understand and manage a faculty member's legacy data set served as a learning experience for a group of librarians, as well as providing a chance to collaborate with institutional IT and develop guidelines for future projects (Marshall et al., 2013). Aaron Collie and Michael Witt (2011) proposed the inclusion of data when processing electronic theses and dissertations (ETD). Many universities have started institutional repositories using theses and dissertations, and collecting the data supporting these could help with developing institutional data collections. The article includes an augmented ETD workflow to show how data could be incorporated into the typical process used to deposit a dissertation.

Disciplinary Data

Focusing data management services is also an option, whether starting, adjusting, or expanding a service. Disciplines that have historically had large amounts of data, such as weather forecasting, ocean monitoring, astronomy, or genomics, have been early adopters of digital data storage and management practices. The John G. Wolbach Library (http://library.cfa.harvard.edu/) of the Harvard-Smithsonian Center for Astrophysics provides the usual academic library services such as print and electronic book and journal access, interlibrary loan services, reference services, and access to databases. But training events include sessions on GitHub and programming, there is a telescope and virtual reality headsets to borrow, and there is a library team working on the Astronomy Dataverse Network (https://dataverse.harvard.edu/dataverse/cfa) and the Unified Astronomy Thesaurus (http://astrothesaurus.org/). The library director, Chris Erdmann, was the organizer for the first Data Science Training for Librarians course (http://altbibl.io/dst4l/), which teaches librarians how to use collect and analyze data from various sources. Knowing how to find and process data with specialized software is also important for librarians dealing with data from geographic information systems (GIS). The Branner Earth Sciences Library & Map Collections at Stanford University provides GIS support services and training for the entire university (http://library.stanford.edu/libraries/branner/about).

A broader specialization is providing services for digital humanities (DH) projects. While there are questions about how much libraries should invest in digital humanities and whether the library is the best place to host a digital humanities center (Schaffner and Erway, 2014), the digital collections and scholarly publishing initiatives of many academic libraries make libraries natural collaborators and participants in digital humanities projects. As with other data management services, being aware of the resources that can help, such as the collaboration hub DHCommons (http://dhcommons.org/) or the DiRT directory of digital tools for scholarly research (http://dirtdirectory.org/), is a good way to start supporting projects. Libraries or archives that use Omeka for online exhibits (https://omeka.org/) might offer classes in using the program to support students and faculty interested in DH projects. As with large data sets, the preservation and long-term access to DH projects will require collaboration and resources outside of the library. John W. White and Heather Gilbert (2016) provide some guidance as to how to make DH projects sustainable.

With most of these specialized data services, librarians are working with researchers, starting with data management planning and help with DMPs on grants, to making sure the final product is preserved properly and available for sharing. These projects need the skills of librarians in all departments; subject liaisons, metadata specialists, archivists, and technology and systems librarians all have a role in supporting these projects. By focusing on a single discipline, the librarians involved will find it easier to collect the resources, ontologies, schemas, and so forth, and learn the skills, R or Python programming, that are necessary for data management. A discipline-specific project could be used as proof of concept for library involvement in data management, or to gauge the impact of data services on the resources of the library and institution. At a specialized institution, such a project may be necessary to position the library as an integral part of the organization.

Specialized Data Services

Other services related to data management can be considered when trying not only to expand data services but also to increase the relevancy of the library within the institution. Data librarians need to be creative about how they can contribute to the research of the institution and even outside of the institution. Adhering to policies is important to ensure funding and avoid repercussions, such as retraction of research papers. Being the expert on funder and journal policies regarding data can lead to librarian involvement with policy development and quality assurance guidelines (Schmidt and Dierkes, 2015), and knowledge of data sharing can also help with the development of policies (Higman and Pinfield, 2015).

Librarians involved with user interface design can also get involved in data services. Creating intuitive forms for the input of data can help ensure data accuracy, and developing good data searching tools will be important as more data is made available for sharing. As these new interfaces are developed, it is important to keep accessibility in mind (Walker and Keenan, 2015). Interfaces for depositing data sets need to be easy to use as well, and librarians should be prepared to help with adequate metadata so data sets can be found and used.

Data librarians are in a good position to become embedded with the groups they are assisting. A *Financial Times*/SLA report (2013) that surveyed corporate information services found that 45 percent had information providers embedded within various departments. More embedded librarians are seen in higher education and health sciences libraries as well (Shumaker, 2012). Data librarians are also becoming embedded with different groups. A data librarian and a subject librarian worked together to provide subject-specific services and became successfully embedded in an earth and environmental sciences department (Wang and Fong, 2015). And the National Library of Medicine has a successful program of administrative supplements for informationists, most of whom are providing data-related support to researchers with NIH grants (https://www.nlm.nih.gov/ep/InfoSplmnts.html).

Working with data—especially open government data—to improve communities is being done by many groups for many reasons (Tauberer, 2014). Many groups provide resources to help make access to open government data easier and help with analysis of the data, including libraries. Boston received a Knight News Challenge grant that allowed the city to work with its libraries to develop an interface and catalog to make finding city data sets easier and then to work with the libraries to provide introductory classes and data challenges to increase the use of the data (http://www.cityofboston.gov/open/home.asp). New York Public Library Labs has hosted a Civic Data Hack Day to make data sets more usable, design better interfaces for exploring data sets, and create reusable tools to anyone can work with data (http://www.nypl.org/events/programs/2015/02/07/nypl-labs-civic-data-hack-day). With more universities encouraging community engagement, it is probable that more libraries will become involved in civic open data efforts such as the work between the Western Pennsylvania Regional Data Center (http://www.wprdc.org/) and the University of Pittsburgh and its library system (Brenner et al., 2015). Even without an official data management service, this sort of community engagement is something that librarians with an interest in data could explore.

🎧 Key Points

Research is becoming more data intensive. More journals and funders are requiring data deposit and sharing. Institutions are starting to realize that they must keep track of the data produced by their employees. With all these trends, libraries with data management services should be prepared to see more demands for service.

- Create assessment metrics when starting a data management service that will support the need for new or expanded services in the future.
- There are many different services corresponding to the steps of the data life cycle that can improve support for researchers and strengthen collaborations.

- Providing services throughout the data life cycle for a particular discipline or department can also be a means of expanding services and supporting key institutional programs.
- Providing a few specialty data services is also an option when there is expertise in areas that are of interest to the library, institution, or community.

Most libraries will not have enough staff to provide one-on-one help with data management, so the next chapter will cover various ways to teach data management.

References

Bishoff, Carolyn, and Lisa R. Johnston. 2015. "Approaches to Data Sharing: An Analysis of NSF Data Management Plans from a Large Research University." *Journal of Librarianship and Scholarly Communication* 3, no. 2: eP1231. doi:doi.org/10.7710/2162-3309.1231.

Brenner, Aaron, Bob Gradeck, Michael Bolam, and Eleanor Mattern. 2015. "Libraries Will Be an Asset for Us: Emerging Roles for Academic Libraries in Civic Data Partnerships." Coalition for Networked Information. Fall Membership Meeting, Washington, D.C., December 15. https://www.cni.org/wp-content/uploads/2015/12/CNI_libraries_brenner.pdf.

Collie, Aaron, and Michael Witt. 2011. "A Practice and Value Proposal for Doctoral Dissertation Data Curation." *International Journal of Digital Curation* 6, no. 2: 165–75.

Financial Times/SLA. 2013. *The Evolving Value of Information Management: And the Five Essential Attributes of the Modern Information Professional. Financial Times.* http://www.sla.org/wp-content/uploads/2014/03/FT-SLA-Report.pdf.

Goben, Abigail, and Rebecca Raszewski. 2015. "Research Data Management Self-Education for Librarians: A Webliography." *Issues in Science and Technology Librarianship*, no. 82 (Fall). http://istl.org/15-fall/internet2.html.

Higman, Rosie, and Stephen Pinfield. 2015. "Research Data Management and Openness: The Role of Data Sharing in Developing Institutional Policies and Practices." *Program* 49, no. 4: 364–81. doi:10.1108/PROG-01-2015-0005.

Li, Wilfred W., Richard L. Moore, Matthew Kullberg, et al. 2014. "Developing Sustainable Data Services in Cyberinfrastructure for Higher Education: Requirements and Lessons Learned." *E-Science Technology & Application* 5, no. 1: 16. doi:10.11871/j.issn.1674-9480.2014.01.002.

Library Journal Research. 2015. *Bridging the Librarian-Faculty Gap in the Academic Library. Library Journal.* https://s3.amazonaws.com/WebVault/surveys/LJ_AcademicLibrarySurvey2015_results.pdf.

Marshall, Brianna, Katherine O'Bryan, Na Qin, and Rebecca Vernon. 2013. "Organizing, Contextualizing, and Storing Legacy Research Data: A Case Study of Data Management for Librarians." *Issues in Science and Technology Librarianship*, no. 74 (Fall). doi:10.5062/F4K07270.

Mischo, William H., Mary C. Schlembach, and Megan N. O'Donnell. 2014. "An Analysis of Data Management Plans in University of Illinois National Science Foundation Grant Proposals." *Journal of eScience Librarianship* 3, no. 1: e1060. doi:10.7191/jeslib.2014.1060.

Palumbo, Laura B., Ron Jantz, Yu-Hung Lin, et al. 2015. "Preparing to Accept Research Data: Creating Guidelines for Librarians." *Journal of eScience Librarianship* 4, no. 2: e1080. doi:10.7191/jeslib.2015.1080.

Palus, Shannon. 2016. "'We Are Living in Hell': Authors Retract 2nd Paper due to Missing Raw Data." *Retraction Watch* (blog). February 23. http://retractionwatch.com/2016/02/23/we-are-living-in-hell-authors-retract-2nd-paper-due-to-missing-raw-data/.

Parham, Susan Wells, and Chris Doty. 2012. "NSF DMP Content Analysis: What Are Researchers Saying?" *Bulletin of the American Society for Information Science & Technology* 39, no. 1: 3–38. doi:10.1002/bult.2012.1720390113.

Porter, Simon, and Anna Shadbolt. 2010. "Creating a University Research Data Registry: Enabling Compliance, and Raising the Profile of Research Data at the University of Melbourne." International Association of Scientific and Technological University Libraries, 31st Annual Conference, Purdue University, West Lafayette, Ind., June 23: Paper 3. http://docs.lib.purdue.edu/iatul2010/conf/day3/3/.

Read, Kevin, Jessica Athens, Ian Lamb, et al. 2015. "Promoting Data Reuse and Collaboration at an Academic Medical Center." *International Journal of Digital Curation* 10, no. 1: 260–67.

Schaffner, Jennifer, and Ricky Erway. 2014. *Does Every Research Library Need a Digital Humanities Center?* Dublin, Ohio: OCLC Research. http://www.oclc.org/content/dam/research/publications/library/2014/oclcresearch-digital-humanities-center-2014.pdf.

Schmidt, Birgit, and Jens Dierkes. 2015. "New Alliances for Research and Teaching Support: Establishing the Göttingen eResearch Alliance." *Program* 49, no. 4: 461–74. doi:dx.doi.org/10.1108/PROG-02-2015-0020.

Shadbolt, Anna, Leo Konstantelos, Liz Lyon, and Marieke Guy. 2014. "Delivering Innovative RDM Training: The immersiveInformatics Pilot Programme." *International Journal of Digital Curation* 9, no. 1: 313–23.

Shumaker, David. 2012. *The Embedded Librarian: Innovative Strategies for Taking Knowledge Where It's Needed.* Medford, N.J.: Information Today.

Si, Li, Wenming Xing, Xiaozhe Zhuang, Xiaoqin Hua, and Limei Zhou. 2015. "Investigation and Analysis of Research Data Services in University Libraries." *Electronic Library* 33, no. 3: 417–49. doi:10.1108/EL-07-2013-0130.

Sweetkind-Singer, Julie, and Robert Schwarzwalder. 2010. "Making the Transition from Text to Data Repositories." International Association of Scientific and Technological University Libraries, 31st Annual Conference, Purdue University, West Lafayette, Ind., June 23: Paper 2. http://docs.lib.purdue.edu/iatul2010/conf/day3/2.

Tancheva, Kornelia, Gabriela C. Gessner, Neely Tang, et al. 2016. *A Day in the Life of a (Serious) Researcher: Envisioning the Future of the Research Library.* Ithaka S+R. http://sr.ithaka.org?p=277259.

Tauberer, Joshua. 2014. *Open Government Data: The Book.* 2nd ed. https://opengovdata.io/.

Van Tuyl, Steven, and Amanda L. Whitmire. 2016. "Water, Water, Everywhere: Defining and Assessing Data Sharing in Academia." *PLoS ONE* 11, no. 2: e0147942. doi:dx.doi.org/10.1371%2Fjournal.pone.0147942.

Walker, Wendy, and Teresa Keenan. 2015. "Going Beyond Availability: Truly Accessible Research Data." *Journal of Librarianship and Scholarly Communication* 3, no. 2: eP1223. doi:doi.org/10.7710/2162-3309.1223.

Wang, Minglu. 2013. "Supporting the Research Process through Expanded Library Data Services." *Program* 47, no. 3: 282–303. doi:10.1108/PROG-04-2012-0010.

Wang, Minglu, and Bonnie L. Fong. 2015. "Embedded Data Librarianship: A Case Study of Providing Data Management Support for a Science Department." *Science & Technology Libraries* 34, no. 3: 228–40. doi:10.1080/0194262X.2015.1085348.

White, John W., and Heather Gilbert. 2016. *Laying the Foundation: Digital Humanities in Academic Libraries.* West Lafayette, Ind.: Purdue University Press. Knowledge Unlatched Open Access Edition. http://docs.lib.purdue.edu/purduepress_ebooks/33/.

Willoughby, Cerys, Thomas A. Logothetis, and Jeremy G. Frey. 2016. "Effects of Using Structured Templates for Recalling Chemistry Experiments." *Journal of Cheminformatics* 8, no. 9. doi:10.1186/s13321-016-0118-6.

Teaching Data

IT IS CLEAR FROM ALL THE DIFFERENT ASPECTS of data management and research data covered in the first eleven chapters of this book that there are many aspects of data management that could be taught and many different groups that need instruction. The basics of data management, something based on good lab notebook habits, could be taught in high school and undergraduate courses. More complex data cleaning and analysis classes are of use to many different disciplines. It might also be necessary to provide specialized data classes on GIS or clinical trial data. Researchers with grants will need to know how to write a data management plan and share data. Data librarians might need to teach liaison librarians the basics of data management to help with consultations and referrals. And at a more general level, data information literacy is important for all people. So when contemplating data education services, it is important to figure out what needs to be taught and to which groups.

Before You Teach

Teaching people how to find information has long been a part of librarianship (Hopkins, 1982). Like many other disciplines, at the university or college level, librarian teaching and instruction skills are usually learned on the job (Westbrock and Fabian, 2010), so it is important to consider some basics about teaching when developing classes. Theresa Westbrock and Sarah Fabian (2010) also found in their survey that of the twelve Association of College & Research Libraries (ACRL) standards (2007), planning and instructional design skills were considered the most important for instruction librarians. Data librarians working at an academic institution will probably find that there is faculty development assistance for teaching available, sometimes even as a special program. Or there may be classes on instruction and working with adult learners available from a school of education nearby or online. And many library associations offer classes and workshops on teaching as continuing education for members.

Library Instruction Formats

There are several ways library instruction sessions can be delivered:

- One-shot—These are usually short, one hour or less, sessions where the librarian teaches the group how to use the resources necessary for a particular class or gives an orientation. The name refers to the fact that a librarian has one shot to get the students to think about the library. These classes are usually done for students in a course setting. Single-session classes outside of a course setting are considered workshops or seminars (see below).
- Course-integrated—Some faculty may feel that multiple sessions from a librarian are needed for a particular course. For example, a science writing course to prepare students to write their dissertation might include two librarian-led sessions, one on database searching and one on citation management.
- Curriculum-integrated—Programs that have a standard curriculum that includes multiple courses over the duration of the program could have library instruction built into several classes, so students can build on what they are learning and they get a chance to practice their skills. An example of this might be a nursing program that teaches basic PubMed searching in the first year, adds knowledge of Medical Subject Headings (MeSH) the next year, followed by learning how to correctly formulate a search strategy from a patient problem.
- Workshop or seminar—Like a one-shot session, these are usually short classes that are offered outside of a specific class. These can cover many topics based on the needs of the institution and the skills of the librarians. More intensive, longer workshops can also be offered if there is interest. The boot camp format, providing intensive training on a topic for a day or more, is another option that can work for some subjects. A good example of this format is the New England Science Boot Camp for Librarians (http://esciencelibrary.umassmed.edu/professional-educ/science-boot-camp).
- Online—Library instruction for any of the above types of sessions could also be online. Anything from an online tutorial on how to search a database with subject examples for a specific class, to an asynchronous class using a course management system (CMS) that fits in with a particular curriculum, to a MOOC (massive open online course) that anyone could take.
- Supporting (Just in time)—Librarians can also provide instruction on an as-needed basis. Some people might not consider a reference interview an instruction session, but it can be if the librarian explains how things work as the question is

answered. Being embedded in a class, whether in person or in a CMS, provides students with ready access to a librarian's help for questions related to course materials (Shumaker, 2012). LibGuides, or other research guide programs, can also be used to pull together short tutorials, handouts, instructions, and resources and act as a supplement to the other types of instruction.

- For-credit course—Depending on the academic institution, librarians can be the instructors or coinstructors of for-credit classes. It takes commitment to get a for-credit course developed, with proposal forms and administrative review needed in most places, so it helps to work with a faculty member when trying to start a course. And it takes time to prepare, instruct, and have office hours for students, so careful planning is necessary when thinking of credit-bearing courses.

Learning Paradigms

Teacher-centered learning is often what most people think of when they think about taking a class. Based on a lecture format, sometimes called "sage on the stage," this type of instruction only works with an engaging instructor. Audience response systems, through clickers or a phone app, can provide some interaction and break up a lecture. Various types of student-centered learning have been developed to encourage students to become active participants in their classes. Small groups of students work together on a specific problem or case, depending on the subject, or there could be a team of students working on different components of a project. These techniques require extra planning and preparation on the part of the instructor but can lead to better outcomes for the students. It is clear from teaching medical students that their understanding of evidence-based medicine improved when they finally had to search for information for a specific patient their team was treating. The different types of student-centered learning are also part of the flipped classroom. In this method, students do background readings and listen to lectures before class, and spend class time on exercises, projects, or discussions. As with other student-centered methods, the flipped classroom requires a lot of preparation by the instructor, and students need to take the time to prepare properly or they will not benefit from the classroom activities.

Instructional Design Models

Instructional design is the process of deciding on learning objectives, developing activities to reach those objectives, and developing an appropriate assessment. Most models for instructional design are based on cognitive, learning, and behavioral psychology. Choice of a model will depend on the length of time of the instruction session, the time available to prepare, the amount of information from the course instructor (e.g., does the instructor have a specific goal or has he or she just indicated that students need to search a particular database?), and the pedagogical leanings of the librarian. Because librarians usually have to fit a class into an existing course or curriculum, or teach a stand-alone session on a topic, following every step in a model may be difficult or impossible. Instead, these models should be thought of as a framework to help guide the development of instruction sessions.

Lesson Planning

Whichever model is used, creating a lesson plan to map out the class will ensure that all objectives are covered. A well-developed lesson plan is helpful if multiple people need to teach the same materials to multiple sections of a course, if a class is new or infrequently taught, or as a backup in case a librarian is unable to teach a class. Just as there are numerous instructional design models, there are many lesson plan templates available. Some components of these templates will help with library instruction, but others won't apply in every situation, so the lesson plan components listed (see textbox) should be used as needed.

One component that should be in every lesson plan is the learning outcomes, objectives, or goals. What should the students know at the end of a class? A common way to consider objectives is using the six levels of the cognitive domain in Bloom's Taxonomy: Knowledge, Comprehension, Application, Analysis, Synthesis, and Evaluation (https://en.wikipedia.org/wiki/Bloom%27s_taxonomy). There are many tables and visual representations of Bloom's Taxonomy online that suggest verbs for each level that can be used to create learning objective statements. For example, a Knowledge-level objective for a data management class might be, "Students should be able to list the steps in the data life cycle." And an Analysis-level objective for the same class might be, "Students should be able to distinguish between data storage and data preservation." When planning the class content, it helps to consider the skills necessary to accomplish the goals or objectives that have been set for the class, and then develop a lesson that covers those skills.

Motivation

An important consideration when developing any sort of library instruction is the motivation of the people in the class. As noted at the opening of this chapter, there are many different groups and types of classes that a data librarian could be teaching. An undergraduate being taught to find some census data to use in an essay will not approach the subject in the same way as a faculty member who needs to comply with data management plan requirements for a grant, or a researcher who has had a retraction because of lost data. And students who willingly attend a data boot camp because they are getting ready to do graduate research will be more receptive than students who must find data for a required assignment in a required course. It usually isn't too hard to teach to a group that knows why they need data management skills. But, it may be necessary to use a few data disaster scenarios based on experience, or found online through a list such as *Retraction Watch* blog (http://retractionwatch.com/), to give some students a reason to be interested in what they are doing.

Data Instruction

Much library instruction is based on teaching information literacy. This means not just the mechanics of one database or the specific resources and citation style of one subject should be taught, but students should have an understanding of the various ways to find information when it is needed and how to evaluate and use what is found. The competency standards and framework developed by the ACRL (2006; 2015) help librarians develop library instruction sessions by ensuring they cover the skills needed to encourage understanding and lifelong learning. Data information literacy (DIL) competencies (see the textbox) were developed through an assessment of faculty and student needs and review of the literature to provide a similar framework for teaching a broad range of data management skills (Carlson et al., 2011). A general DIL Guide for developing programs in academic libraries is available online, made possible by an Institute of Museum and Library Services (IMLS) grant (http://www.datainfolit.org/dilguide/). The guide includes discussion of approaches, tips, references, recommendations for working with faculty and graduate students, and more. IMLS has also funded a program on data literacy for high school librarians (http://datalit.sites.uofmhosting.net/) that has useful ideas for developing programs that promote an understanding of data and statistics in everyday life.

TWELVE CORE DIL COMPETENCIES

- Databases and data formats: Learn the structure of databases, such as relational databases, and the different formats and types used in the discipline.
- Discovery and acquisition of data: Locate a disciplinary repository and search for a data set. Evaluate the data set, retrieve it, and ready it for use.
- Data management and organization: Understand the data life cycle and create data management plans. Develop documentation.
- Data conversion and interoperability: Migrate data to other forms, and understand standard formats. Understand risks of loss and corruption when reformatting data.
- Quality assurance: Recognize and fix different problems with data sets. Document and add metadata to data sets to enable reproduction of research.
- Metadata: Understand and annotate with metadata. Read and interpret disciplinary metadata. Understand ontologies.
- Data curation and reuse: Recognize data that might have long-term value. Understand the process of planning and executing data curation. Understand data citation.
- Cultures of practice: Recognize practices of field and how they relate to data throughout the life cycle, and understand data standards of field.
- Data preservation: Recognize benefits, best practices, and resources needed for data preservation. Understand long-term value of some data and the need for preservation policies.
- Data analysis: Understand use of data analysis and processing tools for discipline, and how they affect data.
- Data visualization: Use basic visualization tools appropriately and avoid misleading or ambiguous presentations of data.
- Ethics, including attribution: Understand intellectual property, ownership, privacy, and so forth, as they relate to data. Acknowledge data sources appropriately.

(Adapted from Carlson et al., 2013; Carlson, Johnston, and Westra, 2015; Carlson et al., 2015)

Available Curricula

Creating a course or class in data management can be a daunting task, especially when added to the many other tasks a data librarian must carry out. Several groups have made it easier by making lesson plans for multimodule curricula freely available. Most are licensed so they can be used as is or adapted. These courses were often developed to use with a specific group, such as librarians or researchers, or for a specific discipline, such as environmental science, but most cover the basics and therefore can be adapted for any subject or audience. It can be very helpful when first teaching data management to have a class outline to see how much time it takes to cover the materials for different objectives. For example, it is helpful knowing that it can take a whole fifty-minute class to teach grad-

DATA MANAGEMENT CURRICULA AND COURSES

- Data Management Course for Structural Engineers
  http://z.umn.edu/datamgmt
  Seven web-based lessons developed for graduate engineering students
- Data Management Short Course for Scientists
  http://commons.esipfed.org/datamanagementshortcourse
  Aimed at researchers in environmental sciences but includes some good case studies that can be used as examples
- Data Management Workshop Series
  https://sites.google.com/a/umn.edu/data-management-workshop-series/home-1
  A five-session, flipped classroom course with available videos and other teaching materials
- DataONE
  https://www.dataone.org/education
  Includes modules with slides that can be downloaded plus additional webcasts, tutorials, and data stories
- Essentials 4 Data Support
  http://datasupport.researchdata.nl/en/
  An online introductory course for librarians, information technology staff, and research support staff
- Fundamentals of Research Data Management
  https://canvas.uw.edu/courses/889213
  Syllabus, modules, and class videos available from a pilot of the NECDMC curriculum
- MANTRA
  http://datalib.edina.ac.uk/mantra/
  Research data management training for students, researchers, faculty, and information professionals. Includes a DIY training kit for librarians
- New England Collaborative Data Management Curriculum (NECDMC)
  http://library.umassmed.edu/necdmc/index
  A seven-module framework with exercises and slide sets with scripts. Includes tips on teaching with materials. Module one can be used as a stand-alone introductory lecture.
- Research Data Management Syllabus and Lesson Plans
  https://figshare.com/articles/GRAD_521_Research_Data_Management_Syllabus_and_Lesson_Plans/1003834
  Syllabus and lesson plans for a series of lectures from a ten-week, two-credit graduate-level for-credit course in research data management
- RDM Rose
  http://rdmrose.group.shef.ac.uk/
  Learning materials for information professionals that can be adapted for different groups

uate students to understand the concept of metadata and what constitutes a basic record (Whitmire, 2014). New materials are being developed through Big Data to Knowledge (BD2K; https://datascience.nih.gov/bd2k) training grants from the National Institutes of Health, and other IMLS programs, so it is always a good idea to check for new materials when starting to develop classes.

Assessment of Needs and Outcomes

As with running a data management service, assessment is important when it comes to teaching. Whether it be conducting a survey to determine what training is needed by a particular group or giving pre- and postassessment tests of student learning outcomes, it is important to know that any teaching done is meeting the needs of the community and actually having an effect. Jacob Carlson and colleagues (2011) used surveys with faculty and students to develop the twelve data information literacy (DIL) competencies. The surveys are available in the Data Information Literacy Toolkit (http://docs.lib.purdue.edu/dilsymposium/2013/interviewinstruments/1/) and could be used to assess training needs of targeted groups around campus. Lisa M. Federer, Ya-Ling Lu, and Douglas J. Joubert (2016) assessed the needs of biomedical researchers at the National Institutes of Health using nine survey-based data literacy skills (available with the online version of the article). The survey showed that the library instruction priorities should be visualization, which was highly relevant to the work of many people, and ontology and data management planning, which had the lowest overall median expertise ranking.

For classes, workshops, and other types of training that is not for credit, formative assessment helps monitor what students have learned and where there are still gaps. A postsurvey that checks if students have learned what was planned in the class outline can help confirm that activities are helpful. The questions could be self-reporting of understanding, or actual questions to answer based on the class. A more rigorous test of the instruction session would be a pre- and posttest to see if student understanding has improved. Christopher Eaker (2014) had students complete a preworkshop survey and seven postmodule surveys (available with the online article) throughout the day of workshops based on the New England Collaborative Data Management Curriculum (http://library.umassmed.edu/necdmc/index) and found that the modules were generally effective. If the class is for credit, a summative assessment to evaluate student performance will be needed. For her graduate-level course on RDM, Amanda L. Whitmire (2015) used a combination of several types of formative assessment, anonymous surveys, targeted questions, and active learning exercise results, and a summative assessment based on student performance on an assignment to write a data management plan. Reasonable and realistic learning outcomes can make it easier to carry out any type of assessment.

One-Shot Classes

It can be difficult to teach data management to some groups because data management plans, including things like metadata, sharing, storage, and preservation, don't really start to make sense until the student has data to manage. So a good starting point for introductory classes is good lab notebook habits, which can be adapted for field notebooks or even research notes in the humanities (Purrington, 2015). Barbara A. Reisner, K. T. L. Vaughan, and Yasmeen L. Shorish (2014) added data management instruction into a one-credit required course for chemistry majors. Their Literature & Seminar course introduced information resources used by practicing chemists, and one class covered data management using a card sort exercise. Finding disciplinary-specific data sources is another one-shot class that would fit into many types of courses. Students often need data to back up statements in papers, and the availability of data or statistics on some subjects is limited or hard to find.

Course-Integrated Instruction

As part of undergraduate economics research at Haverford College, students are taught a protocol for documenting their research to allow for replicability. All data files used must be preserved, metadata thoroughly explaining the raw data must be included, and documentation should include files of the commands for all the steps of data processing and analysis done by the statistical software (Ball and Medeiros, 2012).

While not specifically part of a course, librarians at Rutgers University provided required data management training for graduate students in a department, starting with a data seminar in the departmental weekly seminar series, a data profile form the students filled out, and a three-hour workshop during a graduate student annual retreat (Fong and Wang, 2015). The workshop was developed to help students with the challenges they reported on their data profile forms. This type of assessment can be helpful to any librarian trying to develop relevant content for courses.

Marianne Bracke and Michael Fosmire (2015) developed a series of DIL workshops for the graduate students in a lab group that gave context to the work the students were doing. They interviewed the faculty member in charge and the students to decide on the data management skills to cover. The workshops were held during lab meetings, and checklists for data collection and management were developed with the help of the students. This model could easily be used when working with faculty to develop a series of classes within a course. Some of the workshops, seminars, and for-credit classes mentioned below could also be adjusted to fit as lecture and lab components for courses in multiple disciplines.

Curriculum-Integrated Instruction

Getting librarians involved throughout a multiyear curriculum in a greater capacity than orientations and the odd one-shot session is a bit more difficult than providing workshops or helping with a course. Medical librarians have become an integral part of the evidence-based medicine (EBM) curriculum in many medical schools (Maggio, Durieux, and Tannery, 2015). Librarians who were interviewed were involved in developing content, creating supporting materials, teaching classes, and sequencing EBM sessions within the larger medical school curriculum. Not every field of study has the structured curriculum of a health sciences professional school, but there are other ways to develop a curricular approach.

A syllabus review was done by librarians to help identify information literacy (IL) and DIL opportunities in undergraduate and graduate nutrition science and political science programs at Purdue University. Analysis procedures were adapted from methods used for grounded theory research. For each theme the analysis found in a syllabus review, the team listed associated IL and DIL activities and sources. For example, the main theme of the graduate syllabus in nutrition science was "Engaging as a Scholar." The data-related activities were visualizing data for a poster and presenting a seminar, both using the students' own original data. The IL-related activities involved summarizing and critiquing articles, finding and evaluating scholarly literature, and technical writing, all using information from the scholarly literature. The findings of these reviews helped the liaisons develop a holistic understanding of the programs and provided the information needed to suggest to faculty IL and DIL services that will support the students through the curriculum (Maybee et al., 2015).

Workshops, Seminars, and Boot Camps

Workshops, seminars, and boot camps of all sorts can be used to provide instruction when it is just not possible to provide integrated instruction, to provide special training, or to test the waters for data services. There is a range of program types. Single-session workshops (usually less than two hours) can help introduce students to basic practices of data management or analysis (Adamick, Reznik-Zellen, and Sheridan, 2012; Konkiel, Marshall, and Polley, 2013; Valentino and Boock, 2015). Longer workshops and workshop series can cover more aspects of the data management life cycle (Coates, 2013; Muilenburg, Lebow, and Rich, 2014). A program such as a symposium can raise awareness of library services and develop institutional relationships by having speakers from around the institution discuss data management (Reed, 2015).

Researchers and faculty members who must write a data management plan for a grant probably never learned how to write one during their undergraduate or graduate training, so it is important to offer workshops or departmental seminars on the topic. It is very easy for a data librarian to be overly enthusiastic about the intricacies of a complete data management plan and pack too much into a class. Focusing on what funding agencies really want to see in a data management or sharing plan is the best way to make sure the class content is manageable. Lisa R. Johnston, Meghan Lafferty, and Beth Petsan (2012) used a discussion-based workshop format to train researchers (materials available https://www.lib.umn.edu/datamanagement/workshops/dataplan). The discussions focus

POTENTIAL NSF DATA MANAGEMENT PLAN ITEMS

1. Types of data, samples, physical collections, software, curriculum materials, and other materials to be produced in the course of the project
2. Standards to be used for data and metadata format and content (where existing standards are absent or deemed inadequate, this should be documented along with any proposed solutions or remedies)
3. Policies for access and sharing including provisions for appropriate protection of privacy, confidentiality, security, intellectual property, or other rights or requirements
4. Policies and provisions for re-use, re-distribution, and the production of derivatives
5. Plans for archiving data, samples, and other research products, and for preservation of access to them

(Source: NSF Grant Proposal Guide, January 2016, Section 2: http://www.nsf.gov/pubs/policydocs/pappguide/nsf16001/gpg_2.jsp#IIC2j)

on the list of potential data management plan inclusions suggested by the National Science Foundation in the Grant Proposal Guide (see textbox). More than three hundred researchers and faculty attended either walk-in sessions or department-based workshops. The response to the classes was very good and had a positive impact on the libraries' position on campus as a source of help for data management needs.

Bringing an intensive boot camp or workshop to an institution can help a library gain an audience for data services. The event could be taught by data librarians, collaborators on campus, or outside experts, or a combination. The Virginia Data Management Bootcamp, which started at two universities and has spread to seven, has been providing instruction to faculty, staff, and students at all the schools for four years (Henderson, 2015). The boot camp combines the teaching expertise of all the institutions by using distance education technology to share instructors, and hands-on activities are arranged ahead of time so all locations can gain experience with data management techniques. Tracy K. Teal and colleagues (2015) developed Data Carpentry workshops based on the Software Carpentry workshop model (http://software-carpentry.org/) to train researchers with little experience to analyze their data. The workshops use one domain-relevant data set through the whole workshop to show the complete data life cycle. Data and Software Carpentry hands-on workshops last two days to allow researchers a chance to develop the needed skills. In a similar vein, the University of Toronto held a two-day DataFest (https://utorontodatafest.wordpress.com/) where undergraduate teams worked to solve data analysis problems. The event was one of many sponsored by the American Statistical Association (https://www.amstat.org/education/datafest/).

Online Classes

Online instruction in data management has the potential to be used in many ways. Lisa R. Johnston and Jon Jeffryes (2015) developed a seven-module noncredit online course to support civil engineering graduate students (http://z.umn.edu/datamgmt), based on interviews with the research group, that was later opened up to all STEM graduate students. Students had to complete a data management plan to finish the course. Many students did not finish the course, and follow-up surveys showed that setting aside time for self-education was difficult. The course was adjusted to create a five-week, once-a-week, one-hour session, flipped course, where students watched a video before attending class and worked on practical exercises in class. More students were able to finish this course. Being able to repurpose course materials and allowing students to revisit modules as needed were benefits to the development of the online course.

Supporting Data Assignments and Projects

Kristin Partlo (2009) has found that a teaching reference interview and a data reference worksheet are helpful when dealing with undergraduate data requests that suggest students aren't quite sure what kind of data they need and what they should do with it for their assignment. It can be very helpful to track data questions that make their way to the library, whether through phone, chat, in-person, or whatever venue for questions a library might have. Not only can the statistics be used to show the need for library data services (see chapter 9), but follow-up with instructors can be helpful to learn more about current and future service needs. It can also be helpful to find out if the instructor expects the students to do all the work themselves.

DIL can also be embedded in data-intensive courses, just as reference and information literacy can be embedded in all types of courses in any subject area (Shumaker, 2012). Purdue had a DIL team embedded in an undergraduate engineering software design project course. Embedded data librarians worked with graduate assistants and students to improve documentation included with student code so it could be used by the next group of students working on the project. A rubric was developed so students understood what they needed to include in their documentation, and graduate assistants were better able to evaluate projects. This kind of embedded support is very labor intensive. It requires a good relationship with faculty, intensive planning to set up, and continuing investment of time to support students as they progress through the course. Although in-person contact was worth the effort to better understand the course environment and build relationships, it was often difficult to schedule around the other responsibilities of the embedded librarians (Carlson and Nelson, 2015).

Data librarians who cannot commit the time to an embedded course often provide course-specific guides to help students focus on the resources needed for a particular course. Through course management systems (e.g., Blackboard), resource guide platforms (e.g., LibGuides), or a series of web pages, many librarians have developed collections of resources, tutorials, helpful hints, and direct links to e-mail or chat for reference help to support students in a variety of disciplines. By working with the instructor to ensure students are using the correct resources for their work, a course guide can help take care of repetitive reference questions, leaving the data librarian more time to help with faculty and student research projects. It is important to update not only the resource links in a course guide, but also to check the content with the instructor regularly in case the syllabus has changed.

For-Credit Class

During faculty interviews, Michael Witt and colleagues (2009) found that not only did faculty often feel that students lacked data management skills, they also didn't feel prepared to train their students. Along with workshops (see above), for-credit classes, either general or discipline specific, are being developed by libraries to help support students who are doing or plan on doing any sort of research. Some of the materials in the "Data Management Curricula and Courses" textbox earlier come from for-credit classes or have been adapted into for-credit classes. But finding a curriculum or syllabus to follow or adapt is only part of the work of setting up a for-credit course. Depending on institutional policies, even if librarians are faculty, they might not be able to offer a for-credit course without pairing up with another department or school. And there is usually a process for adding new courses that must be followed. Librarians not familiar with the whole process should look for help from experienced colleagues or check if the institution has a faculty teaching center that can help, not only with the process but with the development of the syllabus and course materials. Having an experienced teaching expert to help with instructional design, lesson plans, learning outcomes, and assessment can make the course development process easier.

Course goals need to be realistic and suited to the audience. At Cornell, a DIL interviews with a faculty member, a former graduate student, and a lab technician identified many essential competencies for graduate students (Wright and Andrews, 2015). The faculty member didn't see cultures of practice as an essential competency but the other two did, and follow-up interviews indicated that it would be very helpful for students to be aware of this. Student assessments of the course were positive, and most realized how important it was to know about data management. The feedback discussed for this course also shows the pull between theory and skills with specific tools. While it is helpful to have an understanding of the data life cycle and why data should be interoperable, students tend to focus on the skills they need to use the tools to complete the project at hand. This debate between theory and skills is common for many subjects, and there is no good general answer, so it is helpful if course descriptions and objectives are clear about what students will learn.

In order to address more specifically what graduate students find relevant in a data literacy program, Jake R. Carlson and Marianne S. Bracke (2015) used an authentic learning approach to develop their class. The course framework was based on DIL competencies, but lesson plans were developed weekly so the lessons could be adjusted to incorporate students' areas of interest or to review more challenging concepts. Ongoing assessments were critical for the approach taken to the course. Another strength of the course was allowing students to use their own data set for the course exercises, although providing some good and bad examples of data sets, DMPs, and other data practices was helpful as well. Most of the students were interviewed six months after the last session of this course. The course helped the students understand the value of good data management practices, and the specifics they had almost all used were file naming conventions and incorporating metadata.

Observations such as those made by Carlson and Bracke are important for all data management training. Data management doesn't occur in a vacuum, and students may not get support from the rest of the research group, including their advisor, when trying to improve data management practices. As they note, "This balance between empowering individual students and the desire to foster change in lab culture and practices is another area that needs to be carefully navigated for both the student and the data literacy instructor" (2015: 105).

Key Points

Providing training in data management and data information literacy is an important role for data librarians. There are many different ways to provide data management training. Depending on the institution, they can be used to start or expand data services.

- Understanding of instructional design and pedagogy is helpful when developing classes.
- Data information literacy (DIL) competencies can help provide a framework for different types of data management instruction.
- Many data management curricula have been developed and are free to use as a basis for any class or course.
- They are many ways to provide training and support for research and projects that require data collection, management, and analysis.

Finding and reusing a data set for research completes the data life cycle and will be covered in the next chapter.

⑥ References

ACRL (Association of College & Research Libraries). 2006. *Information Literacy Competency Standards for Higher Education.* Chicago: American Library Association. http://www.ala.org/acrl/standards/informationliteracycompetency.

———. 2007. *Association of College and Research Libraries Standards for Proficiencies for Instruction Librarians and Coordinators.* Chicago: American Library Association. http://www.ala.org/acrl/standards/profstandards.

———. 2015. *Framework for Information Literacy for Higher Education.* Chicago: American Library Association. http://www.ala.org/acrl/standards/ilframework.

Adamick, Jessica, Rebecca C. Reznik-Zellen, and Matt Sheridan. 2012. "Data Management Training for Graduate Students at a Large Research University." *Journal of eScience Librarianship* 1, no. 3: e1022. doi:10.7191/jeslib.2012.1022.

Ball, Richard, and Norm Medeiros. 2012. "Teaching Integrity in Empirical Research: A Protocol for Documenting Data Management and Analysis." *Journal of Economic Education* 43, no. 2: 182–89. doi:10.1080/00220485.2012.659647.

Bracke, Marianne, and Michael Fosmire. 2015. "Teaching Data Information Literacy Skills in a Library Workshop Setting: A Case Study in Agricultural and Biological Engineering." In *Data Information Literacy: Librarians, Data, and the Education of a New Generation of Researchers*, edited by Jake R. Carlson and Lisa R. Johnston, 129–48. West Lafayette, Ind.: Purdue University Press.

Carlson, Jacob, Michael Fosmire, C. C. Miller, and Megan Sapp Nelson. 2011. "Determining Data Information Literacy Needs: A Study of Students and Research Faculty." *Portal: Libraries and the Academy* 11, no. 2: 629–57.

Carlson, Jake R., and Marianne S. Bracke. 2015. "Planting the Seeds for Data Literacy: Lessons Learned from a Student-Centered Education Program." *International Journal of Digital Curation* 10, no. 1: 95–110. doi:doi:10.2218/ijdc.v10i1.348.

Carlson, Jake R., Lisa Johnston, and Brian Westra. 2015. "Developing the Data Information Literacy Project: Approach and Methodology." In *Data Information Literacy: Librarians, Data, and the Education of a New Generation of Researchers*, edited by Jake R. Carlson and Lisa R. Johnston, 35–50. West Lafayette, Ind.: Purdue University Press.

Carlson, Jake R., Lisa Johnston, Brian Westra, and Mason Nichols. 2013. "Developing an Approach for Data Management Education: A Report from the Data Information Literacy Project." *International Journal of Digital Curation* 8, no. 1: 204–17. doi:10.2218/ijdc.v8i1.254.

Carlson, Jake R., and Megan Sapp Nelson. 2015. "Addressing Software Code as Data: An Embedded Librarian Approach." In *Data Information Literacy: Librarians, Data, and the Education of a New Generation of Researchers*, edited by Jake R. Carlson and Lisa R. Johnston, 101–28. West Lafayette, Ind.: Purdue University Press.

Carlson, Jake R., Megan Sapp Nelson, Marianne Stowell Bracke, and Sarah Wright. 2015. *Data Information Literacy Toolkit.* V1.0. Last updated April 6. Purdue University Libraries/ Distributed Data Curation Center. doi:10.5703/1288284315510.

Coates, Heather L. 2013. "Developing a Data Management Lab: Teaching Effective Methods for Health and Social Sciences Research." Paper presented at Data Information Literacy Symposium, Purdue University, West Lafayette, Ind., September 23–24.

Eaker, Christopher. 2014. "Planning Data Management Education Initiatives: Process, Feedback, and Future Directions." *Journal of eScience Librarianship* 3, no. 1: e1054. doi:dx.doi.org/10.7191/jeslib.2014.1054.

Federer, Lisa M., Ya-Ling Lu, and Douglas J. Joubert. 2016. "Data Literacy Training Needs of Biomedical Researchers." *Journal of the Medical Library Association* 104, no. 1 (January): 52–57. doi:10.3163/1536-5050.104.1.008.

Fong, Bonnie L., and Minglu Wang. 2015. "Required Data Management Training for Graduate Students in an Earth and Environmental Sciences Department." *Journal of eScience Librarianship* 4, no. 1: e1067. doi:dx.doi.org/10.7191/jeslib.2015.1067.

Henderson, Margaret E. 2015. "Virginia Data Management Bootcamp: A Collaborative Initiative in Data Education." Poster presented at New England eScience Symposium, University of Massachusetts Medical School, Worcester, Mass., Thursday, April 9. http://escholarship.uma-ssmed.edu/escience_symposium/2015/posters/5/.

Hopkins, Frances L. 1982. "A Century of Bibliographic Instruction: The Historical Claim to Professional and Academic Legitimacy." *College & Research Libraries* 43, no. 3: 192–98.

Johnston, Lisa R., and Jon Jeffryes. 2015. "Teaching Civil Engineering Data Information Literacy Skills: An E-learning Approach." In *Data Information Literacy: Librarians, Data, and the Education of a New Generation of Researchers*, edited by Jake R. Carlson and Lisa R. Johnston, 149–78. West Lafayette, Ind.: Purdue University Press.

Johnston, Lisa R., Meghan Lafferty, and Beth Petsan. 2012. "Training Researchers on Data Management: A Scalable, Cross-Disciplinary Approach." *Journal of eScience Librarianship* 1, no. 2: 79–87. doi:10.7191/jeslib.2012.1012.

Konkiel, Stacy, Brianna Marshall, and David E. Polley. 2013. "Integrating Data Management Literacies with Data Visualization Instruction: A One-Shot Workshop." Paper presented at Data Information Literacy Symposium, Purdue University, West Lafayette, Ind., September 23–24.

Maggio, Lauren A., Nancy Durieux, and Nancy H. Tannery. 2015. "Librarians in Evidence-Based Medicine Curricula: A Qualitative Study of Librarian Roles, Training, and Desires for Future Development." *Medical Reference Services Quarterly* 34, no. 4 (October–December): 428–40. doi:10.1080/02763869.2015.1082375.

Maybee, Clarence, Jake R. Carlson, Maribeth Slebodnik, and Bert Chapman. 2015. "'It's in the Syllabus': Identifying Information Literacy and Data Information Literacy Opportunities Using a Grounded Theory Approach." *Journal of Academic Librarianship* 41, no. 4: 369–76. doi:10.1016/j.acalib.2015.05.009.

Muilenburg, Jennifer, Mahria Lebow, and Joanne Rich. 2014. "Lessons Learned from a Research Data Management Pilot Course at an Academic Library." *Journal of eScience Librarianship* 3, no. 1: e1058. doi://dx.doi.org/10.7191/jeslib.2014.1058.

Mullins, Kimberly. 2014. "Good IDEA: Instructional Design Model for Integrating Information Literacy." *Journal of Academic Librarianship* 40, nos. 3–4: 339–49. doi:10.1016/j.acalib.2014.04.012.

Partlo, Kristin. 2009. "The Pedagogical Data Reference Interview." *IASSIST Quarterly* 33, no. 4: 6–10.

Purrington, Colin B. 2015. "Maintaining a Laboratory Notebook." ColinPurrington.com. http://colinpurrington.com/tips/lab-notebooks.

Reed, Robyn B. 2015. "Diving into Data: Planning a Research Data Management Event." *Journal of eScience Librarianship* 4, no. 1: e1071. doi:10.7191/jeslib.2015.1071.

Reisner, Barbara A., K. T. L. Vaughan, and Yasmeen L. Shorish. 2014. "Making Data Management Accessible in the Undergraduate Chemistry Curriculum." *Journal of Chemical Education* 91: 1943–46. doi:10.1021/ed500099h.

Shumaker, David. 2012. *The Embedded Librarian: Innovative Strategies for Taking Knowledge Where It's Needed.* Medford, N.J.: Information Today.

Teal, Tracy K., Karen A. Cranston, Hilmar Lapp, et al. 2015. "Data Carpentry: Workshops to Increase Data Literacy for Researchers." *International Journal of Digital Curation* 10, no. 1: 135–43. doi:10.2218/ijdc.v10i1.351.

Valentino, Maura, and Michael Boock. 2015. "Data Management for Graduate Students: A Case Study at Oregon State University." *Practical Academic Librarianship* 5, no. 2: 77–91.

Westbrock, Theresa, and Sarah Fabian. 2010. "Proficiencies for Instruction Librarians: Is There Still a Disconnect between Professional Education and Professional Responsibilities?" *College & Research Libraries* 71, no. 6: 569–90.

Whitmire, Amanda L. 2014. *Lesson Plan: GRAD 521—Research Data Management.* Oregon State University. http://ir.library.oregonstate.edu/xmlui/bitstream/handle/1957/47005/GRAD521_lessonPlans_2014.pdf.

———. 2015. "Implementing a Graduate-Level Research Data Management Course: Approach, Outcomes, and Lessons Learned." *Journal of Librarianship and Scholarly Communication* 3, no. 2: eP1246. doi:10.7710/2162-3309.1246.

Witt, Michael, Jacob Carlson, D. Scott Brandt, and Melissa H. Cragin. 2009. "Constructing Data Curation Profiles." *International Journal of Digital Curation* 4, no. 3: 93–103.

Wright, Sarah J., and Camille Andrews. 2015. "Developing a For-Credit Course to Teach Data Information Literacy Skills: A Case Study in Natural Resources." In *Data Information Literacy: Librarians, Data, and the Education of a New Generation of Researchers*, edited by Jake R. Carlson and Lisa R. Johnston, 73–99. West Lafayette, Ind.: Purdue University Press.

Reusing Data

MAKING DATA PUBLICLY AVAILABLE HELPS promote transparency and reproducibility of research, but funders also want to make data available for reuse. As stated in the Office of Science and Technology (OSTP) memo, "Policies that mobilize these publications and data for re-use through preservation and broader public access also maximize the impact and accountability of the Federal research investment. These policies will accelerate scientific breakthroughs and innovation, promote entrepreneurship, and enhance economic growth and job creation" (2013: 1). Governments and funders hope that having research data—not just the article summary, but the actual raw data—available for others to use in new ways will lead to new discoveries and inventions. And there is a realization that everyone should be able to have access to that data, not just collaborators in academia or industry. Along with research data, governments around the world, at all levels, are making data about communities and infrastructure open as well. Reusing these different types of data can be the focus of an undergraduate research project, the work of an environmental group trying to save an endangered species habitat, or part of the decision-making process for a new business. Finding and using relevant data is also an important part of the evidence-based decision and policy process in all disciplines for businesses, organizations, and governments.

Much of the focus of this book has been on helping researchers organize, describe, preserve, and deposit research data, and while this makes it easier for researchers to reanalyze and rework their own data and hopefully conduct better research, there is great interest now in having them share that data publicly. Research data can be combined with data from other sources to provide new insights, or reanalyzed with new techniques to answer new questions. Using existing data may be the only way to work with data that is difficult or expensive to collect, such as large-scale surveys or data from the Large Hadron Collider at CERN (European Organization for Nuclear Research, http://opendata.cern.ch), or impossible to collect again, as in the case of historic data (Corti et al., 2014). More and more studies are showing that researchers with open practices, such as open access articles and data, have more citations, media coverage, collaborations, funding, and other benefits (McKiernan et al., 2016; Tennant et al., 2016). Articles reusing data are still in the minority. A study of articles from the top ten journals in biology, chemistry, math, and physics found that overall only 14.7 percent reused data, although it was as high as 36 percent in physics (Womack, 2015).

Health Care Data

Sharing research data related to health care and basic biomedical research is very important for advancing cures for many diseases. Shared genetic sequences and related information on genes and proteins from the National Center for Biotechnology Information (NCBI) are integral to biomedical research worldwide. For example, medical researcher Atul Butte has mined NCBI databases to find correlations between gene activity and sequence in tissues from different species. His research has led to the discovery of new gene targets for diseases and new uses for existing drugs (Goldman, 2012). Butte has given a TEDMED talk and NCBI lecture that are both useful when learning or teaching about data reuse (see textbox below, "Health Care Data Sharing Resources and Examples"). Genome data is so important that during outbreaks of virulent diseases, such as Ebola and the Zika virus, the sharing of genome data is essential to learning about the spread of the disease and how it can be treated. But, while human genome data is shared according to the Bermuda Agreement of 1996, other genomes are not covered, so Nathan L. Yozwiak, Stephen F. Schaffner, and Pardis C. Sabeti (2015) have proposed a model for the sharing of data during global health emergencies and made their own genomic data freely available immediately. In 2016, the World Health Organization set up the Zika Open Project (http://www.who.int/bulletin/online_first/zika_open/en/) to make data and papers about the Zika virus freely available, and one research group is sharing research data in real time (Butler, 2016).

In January 2016, the White House Cancer Moonshot Task Force (Obama, 2016) was established to increase efforts to make progress toward prevention, treatments, and cures for all types of cancer by providing extra funding in specific areas for five years. One of the areas of focus is the vice president's Exceptional Opportunities in Cancer Research Fund, which will fund projects that encourage scientists, cancer physicians, advocates, philanthropic organizations, and representatives of the biotechnology and pharmaceutical industry to work together and share data to generate new ideas and new breakthroughs (The White House, Office of the Press Secretary, 2016). Along with genomic data, clinical trials data will be an important part of this effort. There are several open access platforms for clinical trials data, but a study of these platforms showed that only 15.5 percent of available trials had been requested for further analysis (Navar et al., 2016). The goals of reanalysis vary. Some proposed studies looked at the secondary analysis of a treatment effect, such as duration of response, and some at secondary disease state analysis, such as complications. There were also studies looking at placebo effect, reevaluation of end point, meta-analysis of treatments, or proposals looking at statistical or trial methodology.

Health data from survey and long-term studies is also available for reuse, although much of it requires an application with a research proposal before access is given to the data. Data from large cohort, long-term prospective studies can be mined for new insights, especially when a broad range of questions or measurements are collected. The Framingham Heart Study, started in 1948, now includes a third generation of participants. The study has identified several risk factors for cardiovascular disease, including high blood pressure, high blood cholesterol, smoking, obesity, diabetes, and physical inactivity. Some of the data collected is already available through dbGaP and BioLINCC, but researchers can apply to use genetic data, clinical data, and biospecimens. Another prospective study,

HEALTH CARE DATA SHARING RESOURCES AND EXAMPLES

- Atul Butte: TEDMED talk
  http://www.tedmed.com/speakers/show?id=6614
  Translational Bioinformatics: Transforming 300 Billion Points of Data
  https://youtu.be/o4KNG7nd938
- Biologic Specimen and Data Repository Information Coordinating Center (BioLINCC) of the National Heart, Lung and Blood Institute (NHLBI)
  https://biolincc.nhlbi.nih.gov/home/
- Centers for Disease Control and Prevention (CDC) Data & Statistics
  http://www.cdc.gov/DataStatistics/
- Clinical Trial Data Portal Gateway, European Federation of Pharmaceutical Industries and Associations (EFPIA)
  http://transparency.efpia.eu/responsible-data-sharing/efpia-clinical-tri-al-data-portal-gateway
- ClinicalStudyDataRequest.com
  https://www.clinicalstudydatarequest.com/
- Framingham Heart Study
  http://www.framinghamheartstudy.org/
- Genotype and Phenotype database (dbGaP) at NCBI
  http://www.ncbi.nlm.nih.gov/gap
- NCBI Tools to analyze biological data
  http://www.ncbi.nlm.nih.gov/home/analyze.shtml
- NIH Data Sharing Workbook
  http://grants.nih.gov/grants/policy/data_sharing/data_sharing_workbook.pdf
- Nurses' Health Study
  http://www.nurseshealthstudy.org/
- Yale University Open Data Access Project (YODA)
  http://yoda.yale.edu/

the Nurses' Health Study (http://www.nurseshealthstudy.org/), started in 1976, has been investigating the risk factors for major chronic diseases in women. Another source of data and statistics that can be reused for health research is the Centers for Disease Control and Prevention (CDC) (http://www.cdc.gov/DataStatistics/).

Climate Data

Some disciplines already have a robust data sharing network in place because data must be compiled over time and geography in order to produce results. Climate data not only covers time and geography but also brings in data from many different disciplines. Temperature and weather are only part of the picture. Data comes from multiple sources, such as radar and satellite, covering many different indicators, like ice sheets, soil, drought, and air quality. As well as the data, tools to read, analyze, and map the data have been made available (see textbox). Worldwide data is collected into reports about climate change, available from the U.S. Global Change Research Program (http://www.globalchange.gov/) or the Intergovernmental Panel on Climate Change (IPCC, http://www.ipcc.ch/).

CLIMATE DATA RESOURCES

- Climate Change Knowledge Portal (CCKP) from the World Bank
  http://sdwebx.worldbank.org/climateportal/
- Climate.gov (NOAA) Maps & Data
  http://nsidc.org/data
- Climatic Research Unit, University of East Anglia
  http://www.cru.uea.ac.uk/data/
- Goddard Institute for Space Studies (GISS) National Aeronautics and Space Administration (NASA)
  http://data.giss.nasa.gov/
- IPCC Data Distribution Centre, Observational Record
  http://www.ipcc-data.org/observ/index.html
- National Centers for Environmental Information (NCEI) National Oceanographic and Atmospheric Administration (NOAA)
  https://www.ncdc.noaa.gov/data-access
- National Snow & Ice Data Center
  http://nsidc.org/data
- U.S. Global Change Research Program data
  http://www.globalchange.gov/browse/datasets

Other Research Data Uses

The examples above show research data being reused to further the goal of the original data, namely, health care and climate science, but data gets reused for other reasons. For example, many people are finding ways to creatively reuse research data sets, code, and application program interfaces (APIs) that NASA has collected and developed, and now made openly available via a website (https://open.nasa.gov/). In an effort to learn more about the orbital mechanics involved in the Apollo missions, Martin Vézina (2013) used data from NASA to create an orrery that can be adjusted and run on any computer (http://mgvez.github.io/jsorrery/). NASA satellite imaging was combined with open data and crowdsourced information to create Global Forest Watch (GFW, http://www.global-forestwatch.org/), an interactive online forest monitoring and alert system that provides the information needed to better manage and conserve forests.

Another way to reuse data is in the reproduction of research results using the data and information provided in an article or report. This has led to many changes in research. When looking at a particular research paper, reproducibility is "the ability to recompute data analytic results given an observed dataset and knowledge of the data analysis," and replicability is "the chance that an independent experiment targeting the same scientific question will produce a consistent result" (Leek and Peng, 2015). John P. A. Ioannidis (2005) claims that most biomedical research findings are false, which has led to proposed changes in how research is conducted and reviewed. Francis S. Collins and Lawrence A. Tabak (2014) suggest that improving research design and understanding of statistical analysis can help improve the reproducibility of research papers, and the Reproducibility Project: Cancer Biology (https://osf.io/e81xl/) is trying to replicate a number of cancer biology studies. The NIH has developed a module to help with the understanding of making research reproducible (https://www.nih.gov/research-training/rigor-reproducibility), and the NIH has a requirement for all grant applications to address rigor and reproducibility in all grant applications and progress reports (http://grants.nih.gov/reproducibility/index.htm).

Reproducibility and replication are issues in all disciplines that use statistics and other computational methods for analysis. Thomas Herndon, Michael Ash, and Robert Pollin (2014) tried to reproduce the results of a famous economics paper (Reinhart and Rogoff, 2010), using the same data sets and methods, and found a very different relationship between GDP growth and public debt. Andrew C. Chang and Phillip Li (2015) were only able to replicate twenty-two of sixty-seven economic papers (33 percent) without contacting the authors. And even after contacting authors, only 49 percent of papers studies could be replicated. To promote better economic research, ReplicationWiki (http://replication.uni-goettingen.de/wiki/index.php/Main_Page) is sharing the results of replication studies and encouraging researchers to replicate the work of others. And in psychology, Martin Schweinsberg and colleagues (2016) have proposed Pre-Publication Independent Replication (PPIR) as a method for ensuring study reliability. Other researchers are using Run My Code (http://www.runmycode.org/home) to deposit the data and code from their publications to increase the transparency of their research.

Government and Organization Data

There is a lot of data being collected by many groups that is not part of a specific project to answer a research question. Governments collect demographic and other population data to help with the provision of services. Financial data is collected by banks and other organizations. Health data is collected by hospitals and insurance companies. Social networks and businesses acquire data about those who use their services. Consumer purchasing choice data is collected by retailers. Historical data sets are being digitized by interested groups. While some of this data can be found using the Registry of Research

Data Repositories (http://www.re3data.org/), there are also many other sites that make different types of data available, such as:

- Data.gov (https://www.data.gov)—Searching and access to fourteen areas of U.S. government data
- Data USA (http://datausa.io/)—Creates visualizations with U.S. government data
- Minnesota Population Center (https://www.ipums.org/)—Public access to many types of demographic data, including historical series and health data
- Census Reporter (http://beta.censusreporter.org/)—Knight News Challenge-funded project, finds and visualizes data from the decennial census and the American Community Survey
- Sunlight Foundation (http://sunlightfoundation.com/)—Works to get more access to government data and provide tools to analyze the data for new insights

Research with Government or Organization Data

The data collected by governments and organizations is used in many ways. Government health data can be the basis for research; for example, Karen A. Kuhlthau and colleagues (2016) used data from the 2010–2014 National Health Interview Survey (NHIS) to compare health insurance coverage and health care access and affordability for a national sample of adult childhood cancer survivors (CCS) to adults without cancer. Multiple government data sources, federal and state, were used to show that a reduction of officers in a police force led to an increase in traffic injuries and fatalities (DeAngelo and Hansen, 2014). Linda D. Lowry (2015) conducted an analysis of business master's theses and found that most (72 percent) relied on government or commercial data sets for data.

Reusing some types of government data raises ethical and legal issues. Even with deidentification or anonymization, studies that use federal tax forms combined with individual educational data (Chetty et al., 2011) or some kinds of genetic data could potentially expose personal data and pose an invasion to privacy. Groups around the world are trying to find a balance between privacy and the benefits of health, economic, and educational research conducted with personal data (Hayden, 2015).

Other Uses of Government and Organization Data

The uses for government and organization data are as varied as the groups collecting and analyzing the data. The Police Foundation has made local and national law enforcement and public safety open data sets available through the Public Safety Open Data Portal (http://publicsafetydataportal.org/) for people to access, visualize, and analyze the data in support of transparency in policing and community engagement. The Education Dashboard (http://educationdashboard.org/#/) uses open data from the government of Tanzania, prepared using open tools, OpenRefine, Fusion Tables, and qGIS (see textbox below, "Data Analysis Tools"), to provide citizens with search or map access to test scores and student-teacher ratios around the county.

Businesses can use public data to decide where to locate or set up new locations, for example, the New York City Business Atlas (https://maps.nyc.gov/businessatlas/), and public data can also be part of their product. For example, Trulia uses data from NOAA, U.S. Forest Service, U.S. Geological Survey's earthquake map, FEMA's flood map, and U.S. Census data, combined with real estate data, school information, and crime statistics to provide information about properties for sale.

Data is also used in teaching. Statistics, especially, can help students bolster their argument in a research paper, but any data can be a primary source for a research paper. Data sets are also necessary when teaching the skills needed for processing, analyzing, and visualizing data. While it is possible to fabricate a spreadsheet or other data to use for an exercise, students will always find it more interesting to use a real-world scenario. Searching for and downloading data can also be included in cases where the students will be called upon to find their own data in the future.

Citizen groups and organizations around the world are using whatever open data they can find to help effect change in their communities. The Open Data Impact Map (http://opendataenterprise.org/map.html) is a searchable database of open data use cases from around the world. One use case is Edmonton, Alberta, Canada, where the public library has hosted hackathons to find uses for open data from the city (http://www.epl.ca/browse_program/open-data-day/), and the city provides a dashboard to show how government agencies are performing (https://dashboard.edmonton.ca/). Open Data Barometer (http://opendatabarometer.org/3rdEdition/report/) collects information on the status of open data from governments around the world and helps work toward United Nations Sustainable Development Goals (https://sustainabledevelopment.un.org/sdgs). These goals, which include eliminating poverty and promoting clean water and good sanitation, show how collecting and analyzing data can be used to change communities and even countries for the good.

Skills and Tools for Data Reuse

Requests for data to reuse can come from people with varying experience for a variety of reasons. As discussed in chapter 4, starting with a reference interview to learn more about what is needed, how it will be used, and how much the person knows about working with data is important before suggesting a data set or searching for data. If the person is a novice at using data and isn't even sure how to work with a spreadsheet, finding data that has already been cleaned and analyzed will be important (Partlo, 2009). A student might be flexible about his or her topic, as long as the data is easy to use. On the other hand, a researcher may need specific data and be prepared to do cleanup and analysis. However, researchers will be more satisfied if the data is comprehensive, easy to obtain and use, and credible (Faniel, Kriesberg, and Yakel, 2016).

Finding Data

There is no way to know about all data sources for all subjects, but data librarians should familiarize themselves with the data sources the institution or library purchases, general repositories (see textbox below, "General Repositories"), and subject repositories specific to the disciplines covered by the library. Purchased resources tend to be those requested by researchers or heavily used at the institution, so it is helpful to have an understanding of what data they contain, how to download the data, and best practices for working with the data. Purchased data resources can vary. IBISWorld (http://www.ibisworld.com/) synthesizes data from many sources and provides reports, which include data, on industry market size, competitors, forecasting, business valuations, and benchmarking. ICPSR (Inter-university Consortium for Political and Social Research, http://www.icpsr.umich.edu/) is the world's largest archive of behavioral and social science research data, but the data comes from many sources and knowledge of statistical software is needed to analyze the data. Usually the subject librarians in a discipline are already aware of these resources and probably know how to use them, so it can be very helpful to consult with colleagues when learning about specialized resources.

These are the two main sources to search for general and specialized data repositories:

- Re3data.org (http://www.re3data.org/), run by DataCite and merged with Databib, now has more than 1,200 reviewed repositories and can be searched or browsed.
- Open Access Directory (OAD) Data repositories (http://oad.simmons.edu/oad-wiki/Data_repositories), hosted by Simmons College, is a browsable list of open access data repositories arranged by subject.

Also available is Data Citation Index from Web of Science (http://wokinfo.com/products_tools/multidisciplinary/dci/). This subscription service is not yet as comprehensive as some of the repository lists, but as more data sets are cited, it will become a useful tool for finding data and analyzing data use. Maura L. Valentino (2013) provides a good overview of the variety of other methods that can be used to find data for library patrons.

Data quality varies from database to database, so it is important to read over accompanying documentation and review the data to be sure it is useful before finishing up with a researcher or student. Check the licensing or look for a data usage agreement as well. Some data owners may be fine with any type of usage, but others may not want commercial usage of data, so a researcher who is being paid to write a report for a business may not be able to use the data in the report.

Sometimes, researchers find a data set through a published article and want to acquire a data set that is not publicly available. It is legitimate to request the data, especially if the article is published in a journal that requires data sharing or if the research was funded by a government agency, such as NSF or NIH, which requires data sharing. Check for any notes or supplements to the article that might lead to or contain the data. Check for any restrictions that might be noted, or look for a link to a registry or request form, where the researcher might need to apply to acquire the data. If there is no discernable process

GENERAL REPOSITORIES

- Dataverse http://dataverse.org/
  Search for data in repositories worldwide that use Dataverse.
- Dryad
  http://datadryad.org/
  Curated resource that makes the data underlying scientific publications discoverable, freely reusable, and citable.
- Figshare
  https://figshare.com/
  All types of research outputs can be stored and become citable, shareable, and discoverable. Options for publishers and institutions.
- Zenodo
  https://zenodo.org/
  Share and preserve any research outputs in any size, any format, and from any science.

to request the data, Christian Kreibich (2015) has some suggestions on how to approach a researcher and ask for the data. The most important points are: make your purpose clear, make your affiliation clear, show that you know what you are asking for and how to responsibly use it, and be respectful.

Analyzing Data

Finding data is usually a basic skill for a data librarian, but as discussed in chapters 9 and 11, providing help with data processing, analysis, and visualization will depend on the training of the people in the data service and the resources of the library. As well as familiarity with the software programs needed for data cleaning and analysis, some disciplinary knowledge is also useful when providing specialized services. Teaching basic classes covering analysis and visualization tools may be an option if there is enough expertise but not enough time to offer individual consultations.

Before doing anything with data that has been located, it is helpful to read over any documentation that comes with the data set and then check over the data to see if there is enough information to actually use the data. If the data is not ready to use as is, could it be cleaned up using suggestions from Jeffrey T. Leek (2013) and Hadley Wickham (2014), or using OpenRefine. It may be that filtering the data with OpenRefine to find and standardize name variations will be enough to help with analysis. Data librarians should also be ready to refer people to other services at their institution, such as those found during the environmental scan (see chapter 9), and as always, keep track of the number of requests received for analysis and visualization help so a case can be made to add services in the future.

DATA ANALYSIS TOOLS

- csvkit
  https://csvkit.readthedocs.org/en/0.9.1/
  Suite of utilities for converting and working with CSV files
- Digital Research Tools (DiRT)
  http://dirtdirectory.org/
  Searchable collection of digital research tools for scholarly use
- *Exploring Big Historical Data*
  http://www.themacroscope.org/2.0/
  Online book with links to many tools and instructions on how to use them
- Free Statistical Tools on the Web
  http://gsociology.icaap.org/methods/statontheweb.html
  Collection of links to tools and resources for statistics and statistical analysis
- Google Books Ngram viewer
  https://books.google.com/ngrams
  Word and phrase searching across books

- Google Fusion Tables
  https://www.google.com/fusiontables/data, https://datasense.withgoogle.com/ftbasics
  Create tables for analysis, but also can be used for visualization, including maps and graphs
- NVivo
  http://www.qsrinternational.com/what-is-nvivo
  Analysis of qualitative or unstructured data, requires a license, but many institutions have one
- Open Data Tools
  http://opendata-tools.org/en/
  Collection of tools to help analyze public data sets
- OpenRefine
  http://openrefine.org/
  Open tool for cleaning up spreadsheet data
- Overview
  https://www.overviewdocs.com/
  Search, visualize, and review documents in any format
- Python
  https://www.python.org
  Open source programming language that can be used to automate tasks, analyze data, and so forth, with add-on packages created by others
- qGIS
  http://www.qgis.org/en/site/
  Free, open source GIS software for creation, editing, visualization and analysis
- R
  https://www.r-project.org/
- RStudio https://www.rstudio.com/
  Open source language for data analysis and visualization
- SPSS
  http://www-01.ibm.com/software/analytics/spss/
  Statistical software package, requires a license but common at university and businesses
- Voyant
  http://voyant-tools.org/
  Reading and analysis for digital texts
- Wordle
  http://www.wordle.net/
  Word cloud to visualize word count

To help those learning about data analysis, it is helpful to make note of any books about these tools or about data analysis and statistics that might be available from the library, especially those found online. For example, many libraries have a subscription to Safari books (https://www.safaribooksonline.com/) where those interested can find general books on analysis and books on specific programs.

Visualizing Data

Like analysis, helping one-on-one with visualization of collected or reused data cannot always be offered as a library service, so it is useful to offer suggestions for tools, books, or websites that can help, or possibly some beginner classes should be considered. At minimum, providing a research guide, with some suggestions for open source tools and referrals to any other resources within the institution (e.g., institutionally licensed tools or consulting services outside the library), will help the library to be seen as a place that can help with all phases of the research and data life cycles.

VISUALIZATION TOOLS

- Cytoscape
  http://www.cytoscape.org/
  Open source platform for visualizing complex networks and integrating data. Apps available for specific domains
- *Data Visualization for All*
  http://www.datavizforall.org/
  Online book covering tables, charts, and maps
- Dipity
  http://www.dipity.com/
  Create an interactive timeline.
- Flowing Data
  http://flowingdata.com/
  Not a specific tool, but an excellent resource for exploring types of visualization and how to make sure the chart or graph is appropriate for the data
- Google Charts
  https://developers.google.com/chart/
  Interactive charts for web or browser
- Leaflet
  http://leafletjs.com/
  Open source library to create interactive maps
- MATLAB
  http://www.mathworks.com/products/matlab/
  A licensed product available at many institutions with science and engineering programs. The graphs created are often used in journal articles.
- Pictochart
  http://piktochart.com/
  Easy-to-use infographic maker
- R ggplot library
  http://ggplot2.org/
  Visualization package that can be used in RStudio
- Tableau Public
  https://public.tableau.com/s/
  An easy-to-use tool for interactive charts and graphs

When using free, web-based tools for analysis or visualization, it is important to consider security and privacy if you have any users who will be uploading their own data, even if the site allows for a private account. Read over the terms and conditions of use (this is a good time to find a colleague who likes reading over license agreements), and make sure that data will not be made available to other users, or visualizations made public, unless the researcher agrees. Students doing projects with public data should not find this a problem, but a researcher might have problems with collected data being openly available. Also, some of these tools are also for online, interactive visualizations and will not be helpful if a black-and-white graph for publication is needed.

Citing Data

The last step in the data reuse process is to make sure the data creator is credited. As mentioned in chapter 7, creating a standardized format to cite data, and research products other than articles, is an important step to giving researchers credit for all their work. Many data sources will give a suggested citation format, or the Force11 Joint Declaration of Data Citation Principles (https://www.force11.org/datacitation) could be used (see also chapter 7). The online guide "How to Cite Datasets and Link to Publications" (http://www.dcc.ac.uk/resources/how-guides/cite-datasets) is also a helpful resource. Data reusers should be encouraged to provide as much information as necessary for somebody else to find the data. This is especially important if the data does not have a DOI (digital object identifier).

Key Points

Supporting data reuse is a good way to start offering data services without the need for extensive infrastructure. Many of the databases and tools are publicly available, and there are also free training resources.

- Reusing data is an important way to collaborate and advance research.
- Analyzing existing data can help with decision making.
- Finding data for people to reuse is not a new function for libraries.
- Processing, analyzing, and visualizing data requires skill and it can be time consuming, so libraries need to consider these factors before offering services in these areas of the data life cycle.

The last chapter of this book will consider how librarians can use all the skills and resources covered in this book to support their communities.

References

Butler, D. 2016. "Zika Researchers Release Real-Time Data on Viral Infection Study in Monkeys." *Nature News* (blog). February 23. doi:10.1038/nature.2016.19438.

Chang, Andrew C., and Phillip Li. 2015. *Is Economics Research Replicable? Sixty Published Papers from Thirteen Journals Say "Usually Not."* Washington: Board of Governors of the Federal Reserve System. doi:10.17016/FEDS.2015.083.

Chetty, Raj, John N. Friedman, Nathaniel Hilger, et al. 2011. "How Does Your Kindergarten Classroom Affect Your Earnings? Evidence from Project Star." *Quarterly Journal of Economics* 126, no. 4: 1593–1660. doi:10.1093/qje/qjr041.

Collins, Francis S., and Lawrence A. Tabak. 2014. "Policy: NIH Plans to Enhance Reproducibility." *Nature* 505, no. 7485: 612–13.

Corti, Louise, Veerle Van den Eynden, Libby Bishop, and Matthew Wollard. 2014. *Managing and Sharing Research Data: A Guide to Good Practice.* London: Sage.

DeAngelo, Gregory, and Benjamin Hansen. 2014. "Life and Death in the Fast Lane: Police Enforcement and Traffic Fatalities." *American Economic Journal: Economic Policy* 6, no. 2: 231–57. http://www.aeaweb.org/articles/?doi=10.1257/pol.6.2.231.

Faniel, Ixchel M., Adam Kriesberg, and Elizabeth Yakel. 2016. "Social Scientists' Satisfaction with Data Reuse." *Journal of the Association for Information Science and Technology* 67, no. 6 (June): 1404–16. doi:10.1002/asi.23480.

Goldman, Bruce. 2012. "King of the Mountain: Digging Data for a Healthier World." *Stanford Medicine Magazine* 29, no. 2: 20–25.

Hayden, Erika C. 2015. "The Big Peek." *Nature* 525, no. 7570: 440–42.

Herndon, Thomas, Michael Ash, and Robert Pollin. 2014. "Does High Public Debt Consistently Stifle Economic Growth? A Critique of Reinhart and Rogoff." *Cambridge Journal of Economics* 38, no. 2: 257–79. doi:10.1093/cje/bet075.

Ioannidis, John P. A. 2005. "Why Most Published Research Findings Are False." *PLoS Med* 2, no. 8 (August 30): e124. http://dx.doi.org/10.1371%2Fjournal.pmed.0020124.

Kreibich, Christian. 2015. "How to Ask for Datasets." Medium.com. Last modified April 30. https://medium.com/@ckreibich/how-to-ask-for-datasets-d5ef791cb38c#.z6vjo9yw1.

Kuhlthau, Karen A., Ryan D. Nipp, Amy Shui, et al. 2016. "Health Insurance Coverage, Care Accessibility and Affordability for Adult Survivors of Childhood Cancer: A Cross-Sectional Study of a Nationally Representative Database." *Journal of Cancer Survivorship: Research and Practice.* Published online April 12. doi:10.1007/s11764-016-0542-7.

Leek, Jeffrey T. 2013. "How to Share Data with a Statistician." GitHub. Last updated 2016. https://github.com/jtleek/datasharing.

Leek, Jeffrey T., and Roger D. Peng. 2015. "Opinion: Reproducible Research Can Still Be Wrong: Adopting a Prevention Approach." *Proceedings of the National Academy of Sciences* 112, no. 6: 1645–646. doi:10.1073/pnas.1421412111.

Lowry, Linda D. 2015. "Bridging the Business Data Divide: Insights into Primary and Secondary Data Use by Business Researchers." *IASSIST Quarterly* 39, no. 2: 14–25. http://iassistdata.org/sites/default/files/iqvol_39_2_lowry.pdf.

McKiernan, Erin, Philip E. Bourne, C. Titus Brown, et al. 2016. "The Benefits of Open Research: How Sharing Can Help Researchers Succeed." Figshare preprint. https://dx.doi.org/10.6084/m9.figshare.1619902.v5.

Navar, Ann M., Michael J. Pencina, Jennifer A. Rymer, Darcy M. Louzao, and Eric D. Peterson. 2016. "Use of Open Access Platforms for Clinical Trial Data." *JAMA* 315, no. 12: 1283–84. doi:10.1001/jama.2016.2374.

Obama, Barack. 2016. "Memorandum for the Heads of Executive Departments and Agencies. SUBJECT: White House Cancer Moonshot Task Force." https://www.whitehouse.gov/the-press-office/2016/01/28/memorandum-white-house-cancer-moonshot-task-force.

OSTP (Office of Science and Technology Policy). 2013. "Memorandum for the Heads of Executive Departments and Agencies." Executive Office of the President. Accessed June 9, 2015. https://www.whitehouse.gov/sites/default/files/microsites/ostp/ostp_public_access_memo_2013.pdf.

Partlo, Kristin. 2009. "The Pedagogical Data Reference Interview." *IASSIST Quarterly* 33 (4): 6–10.

Reinhart, Carmen M., and Kenneth S. Rogoff. 2010. "Growth in a Time of Debt." *American Economic Review* 100, no. 2: 573–78. http://www.aeaweb.org/articles/?doi=10.1257/aer.100.2.573.

Schweinsberg, Martin, Nikhil Madan, Michelangelo Vianello, et al. 2016. "The Pipeline Project: Pre-Publication Independent Replications of a Single Laboratory's Research Pipeline." *Journal of Experimental Social Psychology*. In press. doi:10.1016/j.jesp.2015.10.001.

Tennant, Jonathan P., Francois Waldner, Damien C. Jacques, Paola Masuzzo, Lauren B. Collister, and Chris H. J. Hartgerink. 2016. "The Academic, Economic and Societal Impacts of Open Access: An Evidence-Based Review [Version 1; Referees: 2 Approved, 1 Approved with Reservations]." *F1000Research* 5: 632. doi:10.12688/f1000research.8460.1.

Valentino, Maura L. 2013. "Finding Data Sets for Patrons." *Science & Technology Libraries* 32, no. 3: 274–98. doi:10.1080/0194262X.2013.781980.

Vézina, Martin. 2013. "Building jsOrrery, a Javascript / WebGL Solar System." *La Grange* (blog). November 27. http://lab.la-grange.ca/en/building-jsorrery-a-javascript-webgl-solar-system.

The White House, Office of the Press Secretary. 2016. "FACT SHEET: Investing in the National Cancer Moonshot." https://www.whitehouse.gov/the-press-office/2016/02/01/fact-sheet-investing-national-cancer-moonshot.

Wickham, Hadley. 2014. "Tidy Data." *Journal of Statistical Software* 59, no. 10. doi:10.18637/jss.v059.i10.

Womack, Ryan P. 2015. "Research Data in Core Journals in Biology, Chemistry, Mathematics, and Physics." *PLoS One* 10, no. 12: e0143460. doi:10.1371/journal.pone.0143460.

Yozwiak, Nathan L., Stephen F. Schaffner, and Pardis C. Sabeti. 2015. "Data Sharing: Make Outbreak Research Open Access." *Nature* 518, no. 7540: 477–79. doi:10.1038/518477a.

Data Management Roles for Librarians

DATA IS EVERYWHERE. Lots and lots of it. CERN has been releasing data sets from Large Hadron Collider experiments. Data was first released in 2014 and some of it was used in a special high school physics class (Rao, 2014). The second release of data contained three hundred terabytes of data (Liptak, 2016). Data and some tools can be downloaded by anyone from CERN Open Data (http://opendata.cern.ch/). By using predictive analysis on data from its two hundred million customer accounts, a total of one billion gigabytes of data on more than 1.4 million servers, Amazon can provide personalized recommendations and targeted marketing (Ann, 2016). HealthMap (http://www.healthmap.org/) processes data from tens of thousands of sources hourly to provide real-time information on disease outbreaks and their locations around the world. The information is free to everyone, and there is a mobile version of the site as well. eBird (http://ebird.org/content/ebird/) is a citizen science program that collects real-time data on bird sightings through an online checklist. The program has been running since 2002, and more than 150,000 participants have submitted over 140 million bird observations globally (Lagoze, 2014). Mark2Cure (https://mark2cure.org/) is a new citizen science project that identifies concepts and concept relationships in biomedical text and analyzes them to find correlations and mentions, specifically for rare diseases, not easily found with regular indexing methods. This project relies on citizen science to conduct natural language processing tasks (Tsueng et al., 2016). From the largest research projects and companies to the rarest diseases that touch just a few people, data is important, and librarians can help manage that data. To paraphrase Shakespeare, "O brave new world, That has such data in 't!" (*The Tempest*, act 5, scene 1).

⦿ Data Librarianship in Context

Data and Public Libraries

Public libraries are known for promoting information and digital literacy skills and providing lifelong learning opportunities (New York Comprehensive Center, 2012). Public libraries are also equalizing institutions, the place where people can go to get the information they need to be engaged in civic life, and the information is free, whether it be newspapers or magazines or databases provided by the library (Palfrey, 2015). Because of this, public libraries can play an important role in introducing community members to data and other technology issues that could impact their lives, such as open government data to petition for increased services or online privacy concerns. Public libraries are already helping with data literacy by bringing people together in many cities for hackathons (Alvarez, 2015) but they are also providing a venue for Citizen Science Day. The Citizen Science Day Expo at the La Jolla/Riford Library, part of the San Diego Public Library, included more than fifteen groups that work to encourage people to help with data collection or analysis (Tsueng, 2016). The La Jolla/Riford Library also has a biology lab inside the library to allow people to do their own experiments and collect their own data (http://lajollalibrary.org/your-library/bio-lab/).

Data and Business

Data is integral to business. High-performing companies are more likely to use robust data mining and analytics on more data sources, which can be used to deliver better customer engagement and find efficiencies in business practices (Afshar, 2015). Decision making also relies on data. In the music industry, data can be used to inform decisions on when and where to release an album, or whether it should be streamed instead (Haugen, 2015). Business reliance on data impacts librarians who work in business and those who work helping business school students. Librarians with more knowledge of data sources and analytics will be better able to secure jobs in businesses, in knowledge management or the library, and academic business librarians need to be able to teach data information literacy skills to students. Business data has a spatial component as well, so an understanding of geographic information systems (GIS) is also important (Brody, 1999).

Data and Citizen Science

Citizen science projects allow anyone to help as a data collector for a large-scale project, such as the eBird project (http://ebird.org/content/ebird/) from Audubon and the Cornell Lab of Ornithology, or as a data analyst, like the people who help classify galaxies for Galaxy Zoo (https://www.galaxyzoo.org/). Zooniverse (https://www.zooniverse.org/) has gone beyond science to include many projects that include transcription of old letters, diaries, records, and so forth, so citizen science projects are becoming crowdsourced projects. This can have a direct impact on libraries that are trying to digitize collections. The Library of Virginia's Transcribe project (http://www.virginiamemory.com/transcribe/)

has multiple digital collections that are being transcribed by the public. The project is open access and the data will be machine readable, making the letters and other documents a perfect data source for future research.

Data and Patient Care

As mentioned in chapter 13, research reusing biomedical data is very important to the understanding of disease and advances in precision treatments. But there are other indirect ways data can be used. A data specialist was part of the Trafford Innovation and Intelligence Lab (http://www.infotrafford.org.uk/) group that used open data, mortality rates, obesity levels, rates of cardiovascular disease, and levels of physical activity in the area to decide where to place defibrillators around the city. The same group used open and private data from area physicians to try to increase cervical cancer screening, and the result has been a 10 percent increase in screening (Ross, 2015). At a more personal level, precision medicine uses personal genomics data along with amassed data about genomics and treatments to find the best cancer treatments for individuals. Biomedical librarians work with health care practitioners to search for literature and genomic data, and the National Center for Biotechnology Information (NCBI) at the National Library of Medicine (NLM) is responsible for some of the databases that hold the genomic data and tools for sequence analysis. Consumer health librarians help patients find the information they need to understand the data and information coming from their physicians.

Data and Health Care Information

Medical librarians are already involved in many teaching and research activities in hospital and health care education settings, including consumer health education; the privacy issues of patient health records make it a little harder to get involved with patient data, but it is possible. Many hospital systems and academic health care centers are pulling all patient data into an enterprise data warehouse (EDW) to use for integration on multiple sites, management and strategic decision making, and clinical decision support (Evans, Lloyd, and Pierce, 2012). Medical and data librarians have the potential to use their reference and search skills, plus subject and database knowledge, to help health care practitioners search these databases for patient care and research information. The National Library of Medicine (NLM) has been heavily involved in working with genetic databases and tools to study sequences through the National Center for Biotechnology (NCBI), so many librarians started working with data and learning about database construction as a consequence. New York University Health Sciences Library (NYU HSL) worked with the NYU Department of Population Health to create a data catalog that would help researchers locate data sets relevant to their work, including information on licensing and faculty with expertise using the data set (Lamb and Larson, 2016). The data catalog also contains information about data sets NYU researchers have collected, so their data can be shared. NYU HSL is making the code available in GitHub in the hopes that other libraries will set up data catalogs and information can be shared.

Data and Open Science

As mentioned in the previous chapter, making data open, or at least publicly available, should help make science more reproducible. But there are many advocates who think the whole process of science should be done in the open to increase insights and transparency. Two recent papers supporting open research and open access have been posting drafts on two different websites and inviting comments as they edit and rework the paper, to show the value of doing work in the open (McKiernan et al., 2016; Tennant et al., 2016). The 2015 report *Open Data in a Big Data World* (Science International) suggests that open science can help the scientific community have stronger dialogue and better engagement with wider society. The same report suggests that it is the "responsibility" of libraries, archives, and repositories to develop and provide standards for data to ensure data is available and accessible over the long term for those who wish to use it.

Data and Digital Humanities

Data is important to all types of research and scholarly projects, including areas outside of the sciences. Access to more data through computerized databases, 3D scanning, and new imaging technologies is transforming research in archaeology. The Pottery Informatics Query Database (PIQD) archives 2D/3D-scanned ceramics, and it creates mathematical representations of shapes, allowing comparison between times and places and allowing researchers to create a comprehensive ceramic typology for a region (Smith et al., 2014). And archaeologists are doing something libraries have been doing for a while—they are linking their databases of artifacts and other information into larger and larger networks so researchers can search for connections between places and times. The Digital Archaeological Atlas of the Holy Land (https://daahl.ucsd.edu/DAAHL/Home.php) is part of Mediterranean Archaeological Network (MedArchNet; http://medarchnet.org/). People can manipulate maps, organize by time period, search by site or conditions, and review case studies. As with other disciplinary data management, librarians can help with ontologies, subject headings, database construction, and data curation.

While databases of archaeological finds are similar to data collection in the sciences, digital humanities tries to fit data and information together in new ways, to help find new insights. "Hidden Patterns of the Civil War" (http://dsl.richmond.edu/civilwar/) is produced by the Digital Scholarship Lab in the Boatwright Memorial Library at the University of Richmond. The Yale University Library Digital Humanities Lab (http://web.library.yale.edu/dhlab) works on many projects, including Photogrammer (http://photogrammar.yale.edu/), which maps and organizes 170,000 photographs created by the United States Farm Security Administration and Office of War Information (FSA-OWI). Not only are library materials used in these projects, especially special collections materials, but library staff help with the projects as well, and librarians are making sure these projects are cataloged and findable.

Data and Social Good

The Opportunity Project (http://opportunity.census.gov/) was launched by the U.S. government in 2016 to encourage civic leaders, community organizations, and individual citizens to use open government data to increase opportunities for economic and social improvement. The website includes federal and local data, as well as tools to work with the data. Tools include Opportunity Score, that maps neighborhoods by proximity to jobs, and Transit Analyst, that maps transit routes in relation to community assets such as playgrounds, day care, and health care. What Counts for America (http://www.whatcountsforamerica.org/) provides further information and case studies on open data and community improvements. These open resources and tools cover all subject areas, making it important for any librarian to be aware of disciplinary data resources.

Many nonprofit organizations also need data librarians to manage the data gathered by funded research or collect open data to support the organization's mission. The International Food Policy Research Institute (IFPRI) Library (http://library.ifpri.info/) provides the usual library services of access to books, journals, databases, and data sets, but also helps IFPRI researchers with organizing their collected data and sharing that data with other repositories and academic researchers. They also offer training to researchers on data visualizations, tools, and widgets.

Data and Education

Parents and students need to be aware of extensive data collection at all levels of education. Students are tracked throughout their time in a K–12 system, and these systems are now sharing information. Some testing and data collection can only be done with parental permission, but other information is automatically collected if a child is in public schools (Strauss, 2015). Higher education also has many systems compiling information and keeping records about students. Learning analytics is one of the systems used in many places to help students with learning objectives and help teachers create customized education plans. Privacy concerns have slowed the uptake of some learning analytics, and policies are being developed to ensure that privacy, anonymity, and data security concerns are addressed by the systems any school uses (Drachsler and Greller, 2016). Librarians, especially those with teaching roles, need to be aware of these issues when using online learning management systems. And data librarians that support educational research need to carefully screen any databases or data sets they are asked to support.

Data and Privacy

Internet privacy is a big concern for many people. Businesses collect data on what people buy or watch, and many people appreciate the recommendations or deals they get later based on that data. But there are things that people wish to keep private, and at times it can be hard to remain anonymous on the Internet. When does the collection of data about an individual by government or companies become a problem? Even blogs, which on the surface seem to be a public data source, have private aspects that must be considered before mining them for research (Eastham, 2011). Anonymization or deidentification needs to be carefully planned, but at the same time, studies that profess to reidentify people from a given data set need to be scrutinized and proper studies conducted to make sure any problems are resolved (Barth-Jones, 2014). The American Library Association (ALA) has privacy as a core value (http://www.ala.org/advocacy/intfreedom/statementspols/corevalues). As much as librarians want to support open and linked data, it is important to remember the obligation to protect users' privacy and only provide data to others that is consistent with this value (Campbell and Cowan, 2016).

Data and Assessment

Libraries regularly collect data to assess services and user needs. Reference service data has been used to redistribute workload and provide data analysis experience for librarians (Goben and Raszewski, 2015). A database of librarian-mediated literature searches was analyzed by subject and purpose to help with librarian training and to allow for proactive preparation of materials, as well as workload tracking (Lyon et al., 2014). Collecting and analyzing surveys to discover the data needs of researchers is an important step in setting up research data management services (Norton et al., 2016; Whitmire, Boock, and Sutton, 2015; Weller and Monroe-Gulick, 2015).

Librarians also possess the skills to be involved in bibliometric assessment to help researchers understand the various metrics that measure the impact of all types of scholarly research output. While bibliometrics have usually been based on data collected about citation patterns, it is important for librarians to also learn about the theory behind these metrics if they are going to provide impact metrics as a support service (Corrall, Kennan, and Afzal, 2013). Understanding the new citation-independent metrics that are based on usage, both downloads and page visits, and mentions of research in blogs, newspapers, and other venues is also important. Nontraditional scholarly outputs, such as data, software, and blogs, are starting to be considered as part of grant applications and promotion and tenure reviews, and data librarians need to be aware of metrics that can help measure the impact of these types of scholarly products (Khodiyar, Rowlett, and Lawrence, 2014). Thanks to grant funding, Impact Story (https://impactstory.org/) is providing a free service to track all these metrics for researchers with an ORCID (Open Researcher and Contributor ID, http://orcid.org). The skills of a librarian—knowledge of authority control for name disambiguation and subject ontologies—are ideal for helping with academic professional metrics (Lowe, 2013). This is especially true for researchers in arts and humanities, where there is not the same history of metric usage (Priego, 2015).

Data and Scholarly Communication

Data is neither fish nor fowl when discussions of scholarly communications come up. You can't copyright data, but you can license it. Data is not usually owned by the person who collects it and manages it; it is owned by the employer/funder. Data is not really considered a full scholarly product by most people, like an article or book is, and yet, "data are outputs of research, inputs of scholarly publications, and inputs to subsequent research and learning. Thus they are the foundation of scholarship" (Borgman, 2007: 115). As funding agencies start to recognize data as a research product and publishers start to require data to be linked to papers, making sure data is cited properly will help increase the visibility of data and encourage more people to share their data. Data librarians, especially those involved with data curation, can help by making sure data has a DOI (digital object identifier, https://www.doi.org/) whenever possible and helping with the organization of large data sets so specific parts of the data set can be cited separately (Callaghan, 2014). Data librarians should be aware not only of funder and publisher policies, but also policies and recommendations put out by disciplinary organizations (Murphy, 2014), and interdisciplinary groups that represent the data and publishing interests of researchers, such as the Research Data Alliance (https://rd-alliance.org/) or Force11 (https://www.force11.org/).

Data and Public Access Policies

Keeping up with all the various institutional and funder policies and rules may seem to take up a lot of the time of a data librarian, even with the new SPARC (Scholarly Publishing and Academic Resources Coalition) site collecting all the OSTP policies together (http://datasharing.sparcopen.org/). However, it is important to remember that helping researchers comply with applicable policies requiring data management plans and public access to data is not an end in itself. The policies are there to encourage a new open way to conduct research that will benefit everyone. Helping with compliance will only lead to a sustainable data service if data librarians educate as they help. Most publishers will streamline public access for papers and digital data, just as they have for the NIH Public Access Policy. But now, while there is an opportunity, data librarians need to stress the copyrights researchers are giving away and educate them on data ownership so they don't go against institutional policies. It won't be long before authors/researchers go through the process of publication without a thought to copyright, just as they do now, because there will be boxes to check for funders and an upload button for data deposit, so use this transition period to educate. This is especially true with documentation of deposited data. PubPeer (https://pubpeer.com/) has shown that there are many people out there studying papers, looking for discrepancies. If documentation doesn't clearly explain all the data, a retraction could ensue. This is where data librarians can find sustainable work—setting up workflows and data entry forms, helping with data dictionaries, helping capture code for analysis, making sure spreadsheets have a data dictionary to explain every row and column. Facing a retraction is a huge stick, and this kind of data management work is not spelled out in policies.

Finding a Role for Librarians

The examples and suggestions above give some ideas about how data librarians can work with a wide range of researchers in all types of libraries. Data has become a part of every discipline and everyday living, whether people realize it or not. Some of the people who have to deal with data already know how to collect, organize, describe, store, analyze, visualize, and share their data, but most people don't know how to do it all and could use some help. And there are also people who have no idea where to start. Data is information, something librarians have always worked with, and the skills needed to help people with data are the same as those used to help people find a book, website, government agency address, article, video, or children's book they need. But while children learn to read in school, very few students learn about statistics—let alone data information literacy—in high school or college. Data librarians can guide people to the data they need, but they also need to be ready to help people understand the information they have received because it will be in a form most people don't recognize.

Data librarianship is not particularly new. In 2004, Ann S. Gray, data reference librarian at Princeton University Library, was recommending that librarians learn more about data and statistics so they could extend their role beyond acting as intermediaries to statistical resources. But, despite the recognition that data is a hot topic for librarianship (LaGuardia, 2015), and some large research university library directors planning to integrate data management into most university librarians' roles (Marcum, Schonfeld, and Thomas, 2015), the majority of ACRL institutions surveyed are not offering research data services (Tenopir et al., 2015). Interviews with ACRL directors (Tenopir et al., 2015), indicated that many were concerned about the technical capacity of libraries and need for technology training for staff, but it might be more helpful to consider data management as a research service, not a technical service. Sayeed Choudhury, associate dean for research data management at Johns Hopkins University Sheridan Libraries, encourages librarians to promote themselves as providing research support, not just a library service (Choudhury, 2013). Data management should also be considered in the larger context of the institution. A survey of health sciences library directors found that libraries need to align with the institutional mission, and librarians need to "become more involved in the fabric of the institution so that they can anticipate where unique skill sets might be required to foster an evidence-rich environment" (McGowan, 2012: 44).

The National Library of Medicine has been awarding NLM Administrative Supplements for Informationist Services in NIH-funded Research Projects (https://www.nlm.nih.gov/ep/AdminSupp.html) since 2012 to explore the possibility of librarians, especially those who specialize in data, becoming integral to the research process. Several of the librarians from these projects have written about their experiences working with a research team, which include creating a data dictionary that allowed all team members to discuss and request data efficiently (Gore, 2013), recommending tools and workflows to help with the collection of data and specimens (Surkis et al., 2013), and helping with data management and curation (Federer, 2013; Hanson et al., 2013). These librarians show that there is a place for librarians in research, and the focus does not always need to be highly technical. In the initial assessment of the informationist program at the NIH Library (Robison, Ryan, and Cooper, 2009), informationists not only saved time by providing expert information retrieval and training, but they also acted as a portal to collaborators, partners, and contacts. This idea of librarian as facilitator is important when it comes to connecting researchers with the data infrastructure they need within or outside of the institution.

Elaine Martin (2015), director of library services at University of Massachusetts Medical School, is concerned about the hesitancy on the part of librarians and library administration to participate in the data movement. She has proposed a framework for the librarian's role in data management that centers around more than just the technological aspects of data management (see figure 14.1). Librarians already help out in the

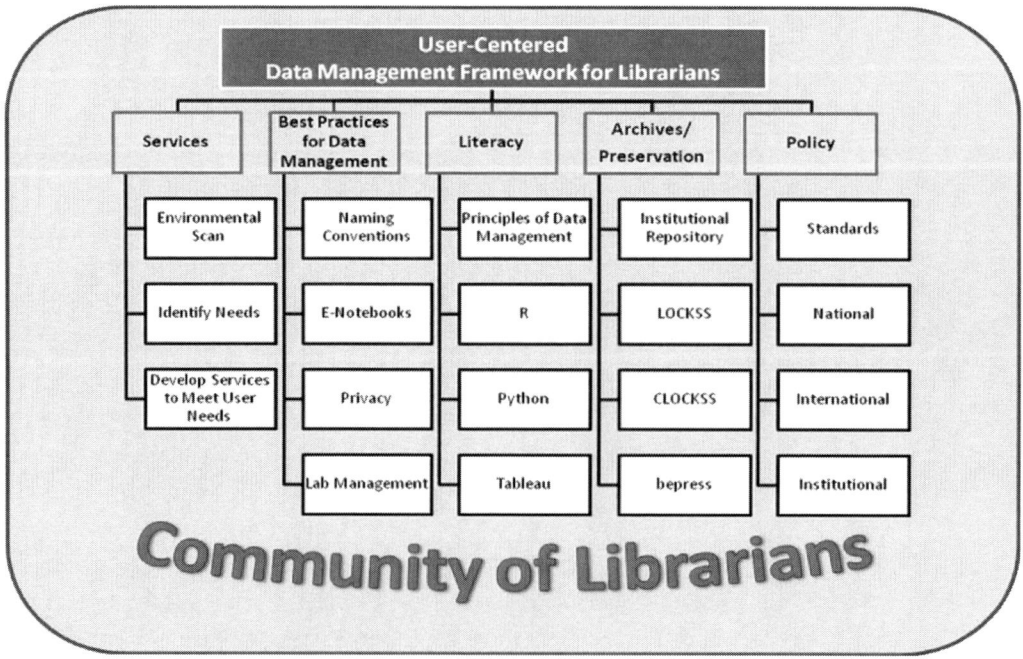

Figure 14.1. User-Centered Data Management Framework for Librarians: Building a Community of Data Science Librarians to Evolve the Data Science Discipline. *Used with permission by Elaine Martin*

areas of services, best practices, literacy, archives and preservation, and policy. Martin also points out that the values library science brings to data—a focus on the user, user needs, and user behavior; an ethical base; collaboration; and equal access to information—are unique among the disciplines that are involved in data science, such as computer science or informatics.

Providing data management help to library users does not need to involve expensive infrastructure. It does require an entrepreneurial outlook—somebody who is willing to sell the service and adapt to community needs if feedback suggest a better way to provide support. There will always be researchers and librarians who do not see a role for the library in data management. However, there will be many more researchers who are happy to have help and guidance on data management, organization, and policies. And there are many librarians and subject specialists working in libraries who see the need for data management support for the researchers and faculty they interact with at their institutions. Data is a big tent and there is room for many different specialties and disciplines, and there is a need for them as well. With careful planning and preparation, including continuing education, librarians can definitely be involved in data management.

Data management is a moving target right now and will be for many years to come as all the stakeholders, researchers, governments, funders, academic institution, companies, and so forth, hash out standardized ways to work with data. There may never be one right way to process a data set, but there are efforts being made to at least bring certain types of data together in a standard way, for example, health records, climate data, or genetic data. From these efforts, it is easy to see various ways for groups to work together to make data usable. In the meantime, librarians and other data professionals will need to include time for continuing education in their schedules to keep up with best practices, new policies and regulations, changes in scholarly communication, and open access and licensing practices.

⊚ Key Points

Technology has made it easy to collect and acquire data about almost anything, but it requires training or help to make sense of it all.

- Collecting and using data is integral to many disciplines.
- Libraries and librarians have the skills needed to help with data management.
- Data can be used to help with social and community concerns, as well as research.
- The field of data management is constantly changing, so lifelong learning is essential for anyone helping with data.

Hopefully this book will inspire librarians to start providing data management services at their institutions.

⊚ References

Afshar, Vala. 2015. "2015 State of Analytics—20 Key Business Findings." *Huffington Post Blog*. http://www.huffingtonpost.com/vala-afshar/2015-state-of-analytics-2_b_8611382.html.
Alvarez, Barbara. 2015. "Hackathons @ the Library." *Public Libraries Online* (blog). http://publiclibrariesonline.org/2015/05/hackathons-the-library/.

Ann. 2016. "How Amazon Uses Its Own Cloud to Process Vast, Multidimensional Datasets." DZone.com. https://dzone.com/articles/big-data-analytics-delivering-business-value-at-am.

Barth-Jones, Daniel. 2014. "The Antidote for 'Anecdata': A Little Science Can Separate Data Privacy Facts from Folklore." *Info/Law* (blog). https://blogs.harvard.edu/infolaw/2014/11/21/the-antidote-for-anecdata-a-little-science-can-separate-data-privacy-facts-from-folklore/.

Borgman, Christine L. 2007. *Scholarship in the Digital Age: Information, Infrastructure, and the Internet.* Cambridge, Mass.: MIT Press.

Brody, Roberta. 1999. "Geographic Information Systems: Business Applications and Data." *Journal of Business & Finance Librarianship* 5, no. 1: 3–18. doi:10.1300/J109v05n01_02.

Callaghan, Sarah. 2014. "Preserving the Integrity of the Scientific Record: Data Citation and Linking." *Learned Publishing* 27: 15–24. doi:10.1087/20140504.

Campbell, D. Grant, and Scott R. Cowan. 2016. "The Paradox of Privacy: Revisiting a Core Library Value in an Age of Big Data and Linked Data." *Library Trends* 64, no. 3: 492–511.

Choudhury, Sayeed. 2013. "Open Access & Data Management Are Do-Able through Partnerships." Talk presented at ASERL Summertime Summit, Atlanta, August 6. https://smartech.gatech.edu/handle/1853/48696.

Corrall, Sheila, Mary Anne Kennan, and Waseem Afzal. 2013. "Bibliometrics and Research Data Management Services: Emerging Trends in Library Support for Research." *Library Trends* 61 (3): 636–74.

Drachsler, Hendrik, and Wolfgang Greller. 2016. "Privacy and Analytics: It's a DELICATE Issue; A Checklist for Trusted Learning Analytics." Proceedings of the Sixth International Conference on Learning Analytics & Knowledge, LAK '16. Edinburgh. ACM Digital Library. doi:10.1145/2883851.2883893.

Eastham, Linda A. 2011. "Research Using Blogs for Data: Public Documents or Private Musings?" *Research in Nursing & Health* 34, no. 4: 353–61. doi:10.1002/nur.20443.

Evans, R. Scott, James F. Lloyd, and Lee A. Pierce. 2012. "Clinical Use of an Enterprise Data Warehouse." *AMIA Annual Symposium Proceedings Archive*, 2012: 189–98.

Federer, Lisa. 2013. "The Librarian as Research Informationist: A Case Study." *Journal of the Medical Library Association* 101, no. 4: 298–302. doi:10.3163/1536-5050.101.4.011.

Goben, Abagail, and Rebecca Raszewski. 2015. "The Data Life Cycle Applied to Our Own Data." *Journal of the Medical Library Association* 103, no. 1: 40–44. doi:10.3163/1536-5050.103.1.008.

Gore, Sally A. 2013. "A Librarian by Any Other Name: The Role of the Informationist on a Clinical Research Team." *Journal of eScience Librarianship* 2, no. 1: article 6. http://dx.doi.org/10.7191/jeslib.2013.104.

Gray, Ann S. 2004. "Data and Statistical Literacy for Librarian." *IASSIST Quarterly* 282, no. 3: 24–29. http://www.iassistdata.org/sites/default/files/iq/iqvol282_3gray.pdf.

Hanson, Karen L., Theodora A. Bakker, Mario A. Svirsky, Arlene C. Neuman, and Neil Rambo. 2013. "Informationist Role: Clinical Data Management in Auditory Research." *Journal of eScience Librarianship* 2, no. 1: article 7. http://dx.doi.org/10.7191/jeslib.2013.1030.

Haugen, Brad. 2015. "Data Will Save Music." Tech Crunch. http://techcrunch.com/2015/02/17/data-will-save-music/.

Khodiyar, Varsha K., Karen A. Rowlett, and Rebecca N. Lawrence. 2014. "Altmetrics as a Means of Assessing Scholarly Output." *Learned Publishing* 27: 25–32. doi:10.1087/20140505.

Lagoze, Carl. 2014. "eBird: Curating Citizen Science Data for Use by Diverse Communities." *International Journal of Digital Curation* 9, no. 1: 71–82.

LaGuardia, Cheryl. 2015. "Where Are We Headed? An Unscientific Survey." *Library Journal* 140, no. 19 (November 15): 14.

Lamb, Ian, and Catherine Larson. 2016. "Shining a Light on Scientific Data: Building a Data Catalog to Foster Data Sharing and Reuse." *Code{4}Lib* 32 (April 25). http://journal.code4lib.org/articles/11421.

Liptak, Andrew. 2016. "CERN Just Dropped 300 Terabytes of Raw Collider Data to the Internet." *Gizmodo* (blog). April 23. http://gizmodo.com/cern-has-released-300-terabytes-of-collider-data-to-the-1772642139.

Lowe, David B. 2013. *A Visible Job to Do: Some Thoughts on Opportunities for Libraries Concerning Academic Professional Metrics*: UConn Libraries Published Works. Paper 46. http://digital-commons.uconn.edu/libr_pubs/46.

Lyon, Jennifer A., Rolando Garcia-Milian, Hannah F. Norton, and Michele R. Tennant. 2014. "The Use of Research Electronic Data Capture (REDCap) Software to Create a Database of Librarian-Mediated Literature Searches." *Medical Reference Services Quarterly* 33, no. 3 (July–September): 241–52. doi:10.1080/02763869.2014.925379.

Marcum, Deanna, Roger Schonfeld, and Sarah Thomas. 2015. *Office of Scholarly Communication: Scope, Organizational Placement, and Planning in Ten Research Libraries*: Ithaka S+R; Harvard Library. http://www.sr.ithaka.org/publications/office-of-scholarly-communication/.

Martin, Elaine R. 2015. "The Role of Librarians in Data Science: A Call to Action." *Journal of eScience Librarianship* 4, no. 2: e1092. http://dx.doi.org/10.7191/jeslib.2015.1092.

McGowan, Julie J. 2012. "Tomorrow's Academic Health Sciences Library Today." *Journal of the Medical Library Association* 100, no. 1: 43–46. doi:10.3163/1536-5050.100.1.008.

McKiernan, Erin, Philip E. Bourne, C. Titus Brown, et al. 2016. "The Benefits of Open Research: How Sharing Can Help Researchers Succeed." Figshare preprint. https://dx.doi.org/10.6084/m9.figshare.1619902.v5.

Murphy, Fiona. 2014. "Data and Scholarly Publishing: The Transforming Landscape." *Learned Publishing* 27: 3–7. doi:10.1087/20140502.

New York Comprehensive Center. 2012. *Public Libraries Informational Brief: Impact of Public Libraries on Students and Lifelong Learners*. New York: New York Comprehensive Center Educational Technology Team. http://www.nysl.nysed.gov/libdev/nyla/nycc_public_library_brief.pdf.

Norton, Hannah F., Michele R. Tennant, Cecilia Botero, and Rolando Garcia-Milian. 2016. "Assessment of and Response to Data Needs of Clinical and Translational Science Researchers and Beyond." *Journal of eScience Librarianship* 5, no. 1: e1090. http://dx.doi.org/10.7191/jeslib.2016.1090.

Palfrey, John. 2015. *BiblioTECH: Why Libraries Matter More Than Ever in the Age of Google*. New York: Basic Books.

Priego, Ernesto. 2015. "#HEFCEMetrics: More on Metrics for the Arts and Humanities." *Ernesto Priego* (blog). https://epriego.wordpress.com/2015/01/16/hefcemetrics-more-on-metrics-for-the-arts-and-humanities/.

Rao, Achintya. 2014. "CMS Releases First Batch of High-Level LHC Open Data." CERN. Last modified November 20, 2014. http://cms.web.cern.ch/news/cms-releases-first-batch-high-level-lhc-open-data.

Robison, Rex R., Mary E. Ryan, and I. Diane Cooper. 2009. "Inquiring Informationists: A Qualitative Exploration of our Role." *Evidence Based Library and Information Practice* 4, no. 1: 4–16.

Ross, Eleanor. 2015. "How Open Data Can Help Save Lives." *Guardian*, Tuesday, August 18. http://www.theguardian.com/media-network/2015/aug/18/open-data-save-lives-emergency-services-disaster-relief.

Science International. 2015. *Open Data in a Big Data World*. Paris: International Council for Science (ICSU), International Social Science Council (ISSC), The World Academy of Sciences (TWAS), InterAcademy Partnership (IAP). http://www.icsu.org/science-international/accord/open-data-in-a-big-data-world-long.

Smith, Neil G., Avshalom Karasik, Tejaswini Narayanan, Eric S. Olson, Uzy Smilansky, and Thomas E. Levy. 2014. "The Pottery Informatics Query Database: A New Method for Mathematic and Quantitative Analyses of Large Regional Ceramic Datasets." *Journal of Archaeological Method and Theory* 21, no. 1: 212–50. doi:10.1007/s10816-012-9148-1.

Strauss, Valerie. 2015. "The Astonishing Amount of Data Being Collected about Your Children." *Washington Post/Answer Sheet*, November 12. https://www.washingtonpost.com/news/answer-sheet/wp/2015/11/12/the-astonishing-amount-of-data-being-collected-about-your-children/.

Surkis, Alisa, Aileen McCrillis, Richard McGowan, et al. 2013. "Informationist Support for a Study of the Role of Proteases and Peptides in Cancer Pain." *Journal of eScience Librarianship* 2, no. 1: article 9. http://dx.doi.org/10.7191/jeslib.2013.1029.

Tennant, Jonathan P., Francois Waldner, Damien C. Jacques, Paola Masuzzo, Lauren B. Collister, and Chris H. J. Hartgerink. 2016. "The Academic, Economic and Societal Impacts of Open Access: An Evidence-Based Review" [Version 1; Referees: 2 Approved, 1 Approved with Reservations]. *F1000Research* 5: 632. doi:10.12688/f1000research.8460.1.

Tenopir, Carol, Elizabeth D. Dalton, Suzie Allard, et al. 2015. "Changes in Data Sharing and Data Reuse Practices and Perceptions among Scientists Worldwide." *PLoS ONE* 10, no. 8: e0134826. http://dx.doi.org/10.1371/journal.pone.0134826.

Tsueng, Ginger. 2016. "Citizen Science Day Expo." *The Su Lab* (blog). March 11 (updated April 8, 2016). http://sulab.org/2016/03/citizen-science-day-expo/.

Tsueng, Ginger, Max Nanis, Jennifer Fouquier, Benjamin Good, and Andrew Su. 2016. "Citizen Science for Mining the Biomedical Literature." bioRxiv preprint, 038083. doi:10.1101/038083.

Weller, Travis, and Amalia Monroe-Gulick. 2015. "Differences in the Data Practices, Challenges, and Future Needs of Graduate Students and Faculty Members." *Journal of eScience Librarianship* 4, no. 1. http://dx.doi.org/10.7191/jeslib.2015.1070.

Whitmire, Amanda Lea, Michael Boock, and Shan C. Sutton. 2015. "Variability in Academic Research Data Management Practices: Implications for Data Services Development from a Faculty Survey." *Program: Electronic Library and Information Systems* 49, no. 4: 382–407. http://dx.doi.org/10.1108/PROG-02-2015-0017.

Glossary

Alternative metrics or "**altmetrics**" is the term used for new measurements of engagement with scholarly output, other than citation-based metrics, such as article citation counts or the h-index. Various tools have been built to aggregate counts such as mention, bookmarking, or downloads across a wide variety of content, including Twitter feeds, blog posts, data sets, software, slide presentations, and mentions in news media, as well as traditional citations in articles, books, or patents. A helpful listing of tools that aggregate content from multiple web locations is collected by Altmetrics (http://altmetrics.org/tools/).

Big data is "high-volume, high-velocity and high-variety information assets that demand cost-effective, innovative forms of information processing for enhanced insight and decision making" (Gartner). Veracity has been suggested as a fourth V for this definition because many think that much of big data is inaccurate. The term is generally applied to data sets so large or complex that traditional methods of processing or analysis are inadequate.

Compiled data—see **Derived data**.

Controlled vocabulary is an organized set of terms that describe a subject area. An example is Library of Congress Subject Headings that are used to describe books, or Medical Subject Headings (MeSH) from the National Library of Medicine that are used to describe biomedical books and articles.

CSV or **comma separated values** files store "tabular data (numbers and text) in plain text. Each line of the file is a data record. Each record consists of one or more fields, separated by commas. The use of the comma as a field separator is the source of the name for this file format" (*Wikipedia*).

Data is "the output from any systematic investigation involving a process of observation, experiment or the testing of a hypothesis, which when assembled in context and interpreted expertly will produce new knowledge" (Pryor, 2012: 3).

Data analysis is the "process of inspecting, cleaning, transforming, and modeling data with the goal of discovering useful information, suggesting conclusions, and supporting decision-making" (*Wikipedia*). Deciding on the statistics to use on a research data set is part of the analysis.

Data citation "provides attribution to research data sources to allow for easier access to research data within journals and on the Internet. Data citations make allowances for increased acceptance and reward for research data to be considered legitimate, citable contributions to the scholarly record. Citing data also supports the reuse of data and ensures that researchers remain accountable for their data. Data citations provide an opportunity for researchers to track back to the individuals responsible for creating the data so that it can be verified and re-purposed for future study" (eScience Thesaurus).

Data curation is the active and ongoing management of data, including appraisal and selection, organization, storage, and preservation. Data curation services require the staff, time, and money to evaluate and choose data, make sure there is adequate metadata, ensure data is usable, and transfer formats if the original formats cannot be sustained.

Data literacy is the ability to collect and evaluate data and use appropriate tools to analyze and represent data to answer a problem and communicate the answer to others (adapted from *Wikipedia*).

Data management generally refers to the organization, storage, access, and preservation of data produced from a given investigation. Data management practices cover the entire life cycle of the data, from planning the investigation to conducting it, and from backing up data as it is created and used to long-term preservation of data after the research project is finished.

Data preservation is often synonymous with data curation but can also be considered only the long-term storage and format transfer aspects of data curation.

Data provenance can be defined as the "origins, custody, and ownership of research data. Because datasets are used and reformulated or reworked to create new data, provenance is important to trace newly designed or repurposed data back to their original datasets. The concept of provenance guarantees that data creators are held accountable for their work, and provides a chain of information where data can be tracked as researchers use other researchers' data and adapt it for their own purposes" (eScience Thesaurus).

Data reuse is "a concept that involves using research data for a research activity or purpose other than that for which it was originally intended. Data reuse can be promoted by submitting data to an appropriate repository (global or institutional) or by ensuring that data is described and comprehensible to any other researcher who may want to use it" (eScience Thesaurus).

Data science uses techniques and theories from mathematics, statistics, and information technology to provide insights from data. Predicting consumer behavior based on past purchases is one area that uses data science (adapted from *Wikipedia*).

Data set (or **dataset**) is a collection of data that generally corresponds to a particular experiment or event. All the answers to a survey would be a data set.

Data visualization is a pictorial representation of data that helps to clarify the characteristics, quantities, and patterns of the data. Visualizations include animations, maps, charts, or graphs.

Database refers to an organized collection of related data and the way it is structured and organized (adapted from *Wikipedia*).

Database management system (DBMS) is a collection of programs allowing users to store, modify, and extract information from a database, such as a library catalog. People who are familiar with DBMS could assume the data management aspects of RDM are similar, but while a researcher may have a collection of research data in a database that is controlled by a DBMS, it is not necessary for most data.

Derived data is raw data that has been enhanced or adjusted to allow new analysis. Text analytics, data mining, a compiled database, or 3D models are examples. Derived data is reproducible, but it can be expensive and time consuming.

Digital curation is used in place of data curation in some instances, but that would leave out data in physical formats, such as lab notebooks.

Digital humanities is an area of humanities research that systematically uses computing and specialist digital technologies, such as data analysis, data capture, data structuring, and text mining, as well as digital information.

Digital migration involves the "transfer of digital objects from one hardware or software configuration to another, or from one generation of computer technology to a subsequent generation. The purpose of migration is to preserve the integrity of digital objects; and to retain the ability for clients to retrieve, display, and use them in the face of constantly changing technology. Migration includes refreshing as a means of digital preservation; however, it is not always possible to make an exact digital copy of a database or other information object and still maintain the compatibility of the object with a new generation of technology" (CDL).

Digital object is "an entity in which one or more content files and their corresponding metadata are united, physically and/or logically, through the use of a digital wrapper" (CDL). An online journal article with the associated formatting information and metadata is a digital object. Data can be a digital object, for example, a series of photographs from an experiment with the associated information and metadata, but not all data is digital.

eResearch and **eScholarship** are used to describe any type of collaborative research that extensively uses networked, high-powered computers and needs data management support.

eScience is "big computational science, team science and networked science. It includes all scientific domains, as well as biomedicine and social sciences that share research approaches with the sciences. eScience is about global collaboration in key areas of science and the next generation of infrastructure that it will enable and support" (eScience Thesaurus); the term "eResearch" is also used.

Experimental data comes from lab equipment such as DNA sequencers, chromatographs, or microscopes. The experiments can be reproduced, but it can be time consuming and expensive.

Field data can be experimental or observed data that is collected in an uncontrolled, in situ environment, such as animal behavior observations or the locations of artifacts on an archaeological dig site.

Informationist is a special liaison librarian or librarian in context who provides personalized information resources for a research team. Informationists generally have some subject expertise as well as information science training. One of the purposes of the National Library of Medicine (NLM)–funded program to provide informationist support to NIH-funded researchers (http://www.nlm.nih.gov/ep/AdminSupp.html) is to help with data management of biomedical research data.

Institutional repository refers to the staff and software that collect together, manage, provide access to, disseminate, and preserve the digital materials produced at an institution.

Knowledge management (KM) is "the process of capturing, developing, sharing, and effectively using organizational knowledge. It refers to a multi-disciplinary approach to achieving organizational objectives by making the best use of knowledge. . . . Knowledge management efforts typically focus on organisational objectives such as improved performance, competitive advantage, innovation, the sharing of lessons learned, integration, and continuous improvement of the organisation" (*Wikipedia*).

Linked data "is about using the Web to connect related data that wasn't previously linked, or using the Web to lower the barriers to linking data currently linked using other methods" (LinkedData.org).

Metadata is "structured information about an object, a collection of objects, or a constituent part of an object such as an individual content file. Digital objects that do not have sufficient metadata or become irrevocably separated from their metadata are at greater risk of being lost or destroyed. Ephemeral, highly transient digital objects will often not require more than descriptive metadata. However, digital objects that are intended to endure for long periods of time require metadata that will support long-term preservation" (CDL). Dublin Core (http://www.dublincore.org/metadata-basics/) is an early, general standard for metadata.

Observational data is captured in real time and can't be replaced, such as sensor readings or images from a one-time event, telemetry, or survey results.

Persistent identifiers are globally unique numeric and/or character strings that reference a digital object. Persistent identifiers can be actionable in that they enable a user to access the digital resource via a persistent link. They are intended to function for the long term. There are several standard persistent identifier systems, including digital object identifiers (DOI) (http://www.doi.org/) and persistent uniform resource locators (PURL) (https://purl.org/docs/index.html).

Primary data is original data collected by a researcher for a specific project, which could be experimental or observational.

Qualitative data is descriptive data.

Quantitative data is numerical data.

Raw data is the data that is initially collected from a source. In general, it has not undergone any processing or analysis. Often the data collected from lab equipment is in a proprietary format and needs to be converted to a usable format that can still be considered raw for most purposes.

Records management is "the planning, controlling, directing, organizing, training, promoting, and other managerial activities related to the creation, maintenance and use, and disposition of records" (NARA).

Research data is "the recorded factual material commonly accepted in the scientific community as necessary to validate research findings, but not any of the following: preliminary analyses, drafts of scientific papers, plans for future research, peer reviews, or communications with colleagues" (OMB Circular 110).

Research data management uses technology to collect, process, and condense information about the research going on at an institution; this can include information about bids, funding, projects, and researchers themselves. The collected information can be used to monitor the research activity and impact of an organization, or to connect researchers with similar projects looking for collaborators.

Research object is a grouping of interconnected resources and metadata bundled together to offer to give context to the contained data, software, images, and so forth (adapted from *Wikipedia*).

Secondary data is generally reuse of data that was collected by somebody else or for some other purpose.

Simulation data is generated from test models, either physical reproductions at smaller scale, or mathematical models. Climate and economic models are large examples. Modeling vehicle shapes in engineering or fluid dynamics in a living system are smaller examples.

ⓖ Sources

CDL (California Digital Library). Glossary. http://www.cdlib.org/gateways/technology/glossary.html.

eScience Thesaurus. http://esciencelibrary.umassmed.edu/professional-educ/escience-thesaurus/.

Gartner. IT Glossary. http://www.gartner.com/it-glossary/big-data/.

LinkedData.org. http://linkeddata.org/.

NARA (National Archives and Records Administration) Records Management Key Terms and Acronyms. http://www.archives.gov/records-mgmt/rm-glossary-of-terms.pdf.

OMB (Office of Management and Budget) Circular A-110, section 36 (d)(2)(i). https://www.whitehouse.gov/omb/circulars_a110#36.

Pryor, Graham. 2012. "Why Manage Research Data?" In *Managing Research Data*, edited by Graham Pryor, 1–16. London: Facet.

Wikipedia, the Free Encyclopedia. http://en.wikipedia.org/.

Index

Alzheimer's Disease Cooperative Study: data ownership case, 80

anonymization of data, 33, 92, 164

assessment: comparison with peers, 108, 109; of data services, 115–16; environmental, 108, 109–10, 123; literature review for background information, 107, 108; of teaching, 150

Bates, Marcia J., 6

Bayh-Dole Act (1980), 80

Bell, Alexander Graham, 65–66

Bermuda Principles, 86

best practices: examples, 31–33

Bracke, Marianne S., 155

Briney, Kristin, 55

Butte, Atul, 160, 161

Cancer Moonshot Task Force, 160

Carlson, Jake R., 4, 44, 72, 150, 155

change management, 107

Choudhury, Sayeed, 179–80

climate data: resources and examples, 162

clinical trials data, 160–61

Collie, Aaron, 138

Creative Commons, 81

data: analysis, 136–37, 167–68; asset, 4; back ups, 55–56; business, 174; citizen science, 174–75; collection, 136; collection best practices, 29; discipline specific services, 138–39; finding, 165–66; health care information, 175; and library public services, 6; and library technical services, 6; licensing, 81; life cycle, 16–19, 28, 123; open science, 175–76; organization, 66; ownership, 80–81; and patient care, 175; privacy, 177; public access to, 91–92; and public libraries, 174; publishing, 84–85, 137; sensitive, 81–84; visualization, 169–70

data citation, 4, 85–86, 170

data committee, 106

data curation, 58–59

Data Curation Profiles (DCP), 7; data curation interview, 46–47; toolkit, 46

data dictionary, 68–69

data documentation, 66–71, 136; best practices, 30; ethics, 67–68

Data Information Literacy (DIL), 147–48; toolkit, 150

data instruction: available curricula, 148–50

data interviews: data consultation, 44; data curation interview, 46–47; data management plan interview, 44–45, 96–97; data reference questions, 42–43; stakeholder interviews, 47; workflow analysis, 45–46

data librarians, 6, 179–81

data management: and reproducibility, 27; benefits for funders, 27; benefits for individuals, 26; benefits for institutions, 26; benefits for repositories, 28; finding partners, 121–22; in libraries, 8

data management plan (DMP): and basic best practices, 28–31; benefits, 95–96; data management plan interview, 44–45; problems, 102–3; templates, 100–102

data preservation, 59–60, 138; best practices, 30–31

About the Author

Margaret E. Henderson has been director, research data management and associate professor, Virginia Commonwealth University Libraries, since September 2013. The position was new to the libraries and the university when she started. Her work ranges from writing data management plans and teaching data management to organizing a university-wide research data committee and helping with data policies. Margaret is a distinguished member of the Academy of Health Information Professionals and has been active in the Medical Library Association, most recently as a member of Continuing Education. Margaret has been an invited speaker at the 2016 eScience Symposium and the 2016 Society for Scholarly Publishing Librarian Focus Group, as well as Beyond the SEA and Library Connect webinars. Margaret was part of the organizing group for the first Midwest Data Librarians Symposium in 2015, and RDAP16 (Research Data Access and Preservation Summit).

Previous to her current position, Margaret was research and education librarian in the Tompkins-McCaw Library and image database manager for the Department of Anatomy and Neurobiology, School of Medicine at VCU. Prior to moving to Virginia, Margaret was the director of libraries and archives at the Cold Spring Harbor Laboratory in New York. She received her MLIS from the University of Western Ontario, School of Library and Information Science, the same library school her grandmother attended.